THE SACRED BAND

OF THEBES

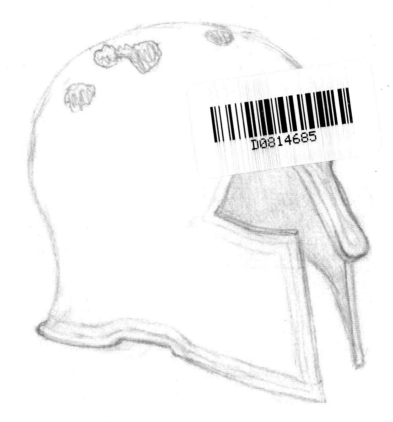

And Other Stuff

Written and illustrated by C. Hilbert

TABLE OF CONTENTS

LIST OF ILLUSTRATION AND MAPS

The Aegean Sea and Boiotia: Courtesy of the University of
Texas Libraries, The University of Texas at Austin 238

All of these are in the Public Domain.

PREFACE

I started out to write a history of the Sacred Band of Thebes, but other stuff kept creeping in, so now it's *The Sacred Band of Thebes and Other Stuff.* It's not a bad place to start for anyone interested in the ancient Greeks; there's a lot of military stuff, and some stuff about Greek sexuality (and other stuff). For the serious student who wants to know more, I have included endnotes and a bibliography. I've written in a fairly un-scholarly style, and I have not avoided the use of contractions, since, to my simple mind, they are the same as elisions. Greeks and Romans elided all the time, and if it's good enough for Plutarch, it's good enough for me.

All translations are my own, and I've attempted to preserve the original syntax as far as possible. In all transliterations, the letter c has been replaced by k (except for the names of the ancient authors, like Plutarch [who should really be Plutarkh] in order to avoid confusion for those checking my sources), simply because the soft c sound did not exist in Greek or Latin. The Greek spelling has been retained as much as it was possible to do so.

The words 'Greek' and 'Greece' will not be used henceforth (except maybe to refer to the language), since the people whom we call Greeks call themselves Hellenes ('Ελληνες) and the place where they live, Hellas ('Ελλας). We only call them Greeks because the first 'Ελληνες whom the Romans encountered were from a tribe called the Graikoi (Γραικοι). From then on the unimaginative Romans called all the 'Ελληνες they met Graeci, and so it has come down to us today, even though we call the time between the death of Alexander the Great and the reign of Kleopatra VII the Hellenistic age. All dates in the text are BCE.

PROLOGOS

Amid the swirling confusion of a headlong cavalry charge, while all around them a great army went down in bloody defeat, a small band of three hundred hoplites stood firm; punching through bronze armor with the butt-spikes of their broken spears, hacking flesh with their cleaver-like kopides, they sold their lives dearly, falling one by one, each in the spot where he stood, until the tide of battle had passed them by, leaving only a heap of mangled bodies to mark the ground where they had fought and died, each man next to the man he had loved, together in death as they had been in life.

It was the year that we call 338 BCE, and war had come to the peaceful fields of Boiotia and the small town of Khaironeia. There, the manpower of Athens and Thebes had gathered together with contingents from the smaller Hellenic states to halt the advance of Phillipos, the Makedonian king, and his impetuous son Alexandros. Historical hindsight illuminates the impossibility of their task, the inevitability of the outcome - such was the disparity between the forces - not in numbers or in bravery, but in the quality of their training and in the genius of the commanders. Phillipos, pupil of the great Epameinondas, turned the Thebans' own tactics against them: refusing his right, he drew out the Athenians and opened a gap between them and their Theban allies through which Alexandros led the Makedonian cavalry to take the Thebans in the rear, while his father now suddenly advanced on the isolated Athenians. Demosthenes, the politician who had roused his countrymen to battle with his fiery rhetoric, threw away his shield and saved himself by ignoble flight while Alexandros rode over the three hundred men of the Theban Sacred Band.

THE LAKEDAIMONIANS

Thirty odd years before the battle of Khaironeia changed the political map of Hellas, the Lakedaimonians (known today by their literary appellation, Spartans), were the most formidable and the most feared warriors in the Hellenic world. The mere sight of a Lakedaimonian red cloak was enough to make their enemies soil their loincloths.[1] They were the most feared soldiers in Hellas because they were the best soldiers in Hellas, and they were the best soldiers because they were the only ones who actually trained at being soldiers.

The armies of most Hellenic states were composed of ordinary people who worked for a living and made enough money to afford the hoplite panoply: shield, breastplate, greaves, helmet, sword, and spear. In times of crisis they would put away the implements of their peacetime occupations and take down from wall-pegs, where they had hung all year long, the more frightening tools of Ares, the war-god.[2] Since they had to work, they didn't have much time to train as soldiers, so some states maintained, at the public expense, small bands of chosen men trained as professional soldiers who would bolster the ranks of militiamen.[3]

As for the Lakedaimonians, they all trained all the time. They had all this time to train because they didn't have to, and in fact weren't allowed to work for a living.[4] They didn't *have* to work for a living because they had serfs, called helots, who did all their work for them. And they weren't *allowed* to work for a living because they were too busy training themselves in military matters because they were afraid that the helots would revolt. One would think that if they hadn't had the helots they wouldn't have been afraid of a helot revolt, and they wouldn't have had to train all the time, but then they would have had to work, and they wouldn't have become the best and most feared warriors in all of Hellas. They had, in fact, become most feared by everybody else because they feared their own servants.

These helots whom the Lakedaimonians both dominated and feared were the original inhabitants of Lakonia, the southeastern part of the Peloponnesos. They were the descendants of those people who had survived the collapse of the Mykenaian palace civilization around the year 1200. When the Lakedaimonians (who were either an invading Dorian tribe or the descendants of the sons of Herakles returning to reclaim their own after years in exile), moved in, they reduced the Mykenaian remnants to serfdom and built four villages on the west bank of the Eurotas River; these villages would one day become the city of Lakedaimon.[5] From there they expanded their territory over a period of centuries, enslaving the non-Dorians as helots and reducing the other Dorian tribes to the status of perioikoi ("dwellers-around," who had no political voice but were liable for military service), eventually conquering Messenia to the west in a series of wars which lasted generations and yielded them more land - and more helots than they knew what to do with. (I know, I just ended a sentence with a preposition. Call it a colloquial use of poetic license, or maybe that's not a preposition; maybe it's an adverb.) It was probably at this time that what we call the Lykourgan system was introduced.

At one time the Lakedaimonians had been much like the other Hellenes, happily writing poetry, sculpting, making pottery, and doing the same things that everybody else did. But then, probably around the time of the final conquest of Messenia, everything changed. The Spartans themselves attributed the change to their legendary or semi-legendary lawgiver, Lykourgos. Lykourgos knew that slaves never willingly serve their masters, and he figured that the helots were no exception and would jump at the chance to rebel and turn the tables on the Spartans, so he essentially put the Spartans on a permanent war-time footing in preparation for a feared revolt of the helots, which incidentally enabled them to become the most efficient warriors in the Hellenic World.

By the fifth century the Lakedaimonians had become, in effect, the rulers of most of southern Hellas, either by direct occupation or by intimidating the other states to join what scholars call the "Peloponnesian League," and what the Lakedaimonians called "The Lakedaimonians and their allies." So they had nothing really to worry about except for the above-mentioned, expected revolt of the helots, for which Lykourgos had long ago prepared them by instituting a regimen of constant training, which compelled them to live as if there were already a war going on. Spartan men ate, drank, and slept together; their food was frugal, their wine cheap, and the barracks no doubt smelly (beans and cabbage both figured prominently on the menu); there were a lot of rules and a lot of punishments for those who broke the rules.[6]

The rigors of the Lykourgan system started at birth. The father of a newborn would bring his child before the elders of his tribe. (This would be like showing your newborn to the senior citizens of your voting district.) If they decided that the baby was healthy, it took its place in the Lakedaimonian scheme of things; if they decided it was not healthy it was sent to the apothetai, which probably means 'the putting away,' but which really means that the baby was thrown off a cliff of Mt. Taygetos or maybe just left in some out-of-the-way ravine. The Lakedaimonians figured that it was best for the baby and best for the state for a sickly child to die quickly rather than linger on as a useless burden.

Barracks life began at age seven. The boys weren't allowed to wear shoes in order to make their feet tougher; they were only allowed one garment, winter and summer, in order to make their bodies tougher. They were fed just enough so that they wouldn't die of starvation and encouraged to steal the rest so that they would become good at foraging. As Plutarch, the famous biographer and essayist (46-120 CE), writes in his

Moralia: "The young men steal whatever of their food they are able, learning to skillfully take advantage of those sleeping or guarding carelessly." If they were caught the penalty was "blows and hunger." If a boy was punished and told his father, the latter was shamed unless he gave his son another beating.[7]

Relationships between older and younger boys were encouraged. The Hellenes believed that the highest form of love was that which existed between equals. Since Hellenic males didn't exactly consider women as their equals, it stood to reason that the highest form of love had to be between men. It was believed that a younger man (eromenos) would be attracted to an older man (erastes), who would be his exemplar, teaching him wisdom and honor, and that conversely the older man would be attracted to a younger man in whom he detected noble qualities.

Most of the other Hellenes seem to have agreed with the following sentiments, expressed in the *Moralia*: " the wedding and sexual intercourse of man and woman…is a necessity for production [of children]…but not anything whatsoever of true love is present in the women's rooms" (women had their own part of the house); the desire for women was a desire for mere physical gratification; it was in the same category as sex with slave boys: an inferior, base thing; "the one true love is love of boys."[8] (The word pais, which means "child," also means "boy," and was used by the Hellenes basically just the same way we use the word "boy." It can mean a small male child, a male slave, or a young male adult. When we call someone a "good old boy" we're usually not referring to a child. It would be wrong to imagine that when Plutarch or some other ancient author refers to "love of boys" that they are thinking of prepubescent males.)

Xenophon (430-360), an Athenian aristocrat who lived with the Spartans, explains the Lykourgan idea of love:

> If someone, himself being such a man as is proper, admiring the soul [the Hellenic word is psyche] of a boy, should try to make him a blameless friend

and to be with him, he [Lykourgos] praised him and considered this to be the most beautiful type of training. But if someone should appear to be desiring the body of a youth, by making this a shameful thing, he [Lykourgos] arranged among the Lakedaimonians that, with respect to sexual pleasures, lovers no less kept their hands off boys than parents kept their hands off their children and brothers kept their hands off brothers.[9]

One may be tempted to think that the reality of the situation might have been quite different - especially in a city where the biggest holiday of the year was called the "Festival of the Naked Boys" (Gymnopaideia). Perhaps the physical relationship that might develop over time was considered a natural adjunct of the more elevated spiritual connection. As it was, the Spartan system worked fine for a long time: older boys formed relationships with their younger counterparts, and each tried his best to be a credit to the other.

Although they were allowed and encouraged to hang out with handsome boys, and notwithstanding the fact that masculine love was considered the highest form of love, the Spartans, like everybody else who didn't want to become extinct, needed to produce babies, so Spartan men were expected to marry and provide strong children for the state. Since they had to live in the barracks until the age of thirty, they had to sneak out at night to visit their wives; if they were caught they were beaten. If they didn't get married and produce children they got no respect, and they weren't allowed to attend the Gymnopaideia.

Spartan women, on the other hand, were allowed a degree of freedom unknown elsewhere in the Hellenic world. While the rest of the Hellenes kept their women isolated and supervised at all times, Spartan women trained almost as hard as their men. The Spartans reasoned that healthy mothers would produce healthy babies. Therefore at Sparta there was no such thing as adultery: if a Spartan woman found a man other than her husband attractive and likely to produce "noble sperm" she could arrange an assignation with him in hopes of begetting offspring who would be useful to the state.[10] On the other hand, if a Spartan man saw a woman who tickled his fancy he could ask the woman's husband for use of his wife, also with a view for the production of healthy children for the state. Whereas sex between women was undoubtedly frowned upon throughout the rest of the Hellenic world, it was common at Sparta for an older, married woman to have a relationship with a younger, unmarried girl.

All this equality seems to have made Spartan women a tough, uncompromising bunch. There are endless stories about mothers who disowned their sons for returning alive when they should have died with honor. Plutarch has recorded some of the "Sayings of Spartan Women" in his *Moralia*:

"Gyrtias, when her daughter's son Akrotatos, having received many blows in some battle of the boys, was carried home as if he were dying, and the family and friends were lamenting, said, 'won't you be quiet; he has shown us what he's made of.' And she said that it's not necessary for the well-born to shout, but to help."

When, years later, Gyrtias learned of Akrotatos' death in battle, she said: "was it not destined that, having come to the enemy, either he at their hands would die or he would kill them? With pleasure I hear that he died worthy of himself, his city, and his ancestors, rather than that he should live for all time as a coward."[11]

Plutarch tells the story of an unnamed woman, who, when her son returned alive from a battle in which everyone else had been killed, picked up a roof-tile, threw it at him and killed him, and then asked sarcastically, "did they send you to bring us the bad news?"[12]

"Another woman, hearing of her son, that he was conducting himself evilly in a foreign country, wrote him: 'an evil rumor of you is spread about; expel this or stop living!'"[13]

It was not only their sons who suffered the biting wit and uncompromising attitude of the Spartan women. Plutarch tells of Gorgous, the wife of King Leonidas (who died in 480, at Thermopylai, fighting against the Persians), "seeing Aristagoras having his shoes put on by one of the slaves, 'father,' she said, 'the foreigner doesn't have hands.'" And when asked by an Athenian woman, "why do you Lakonian women alone rule men?" She answered, "because we alone give birth to men."[14]

This was basically the average Spartan's home-life: training, sneaking around to steal food or to visit one's wife, getting a beating if you were caught, and having to endure the unsympathetic wise-cracking of your own, and no doubt everyone else's mother. With a life like this the only time Spartan men had any fun and the only time the rules were relaxed was when the army was on campaign.

Plutarch, in his *Life of Lykourgos*, tells how on campaign "they gave up the harder things of their training" and how they were "not prevented from beautifying their hair or decorating their weapons and armor...therefore they grew their hair long as soon as they reached the age of eighteen." They took special care when they knew they were about to go into battle. After carefully combing their hair, they oiled it until it was nice and shiny and then separated it into long curls. In other words, they gave themselves a permanent. This custom of growing the hair long was also believed to have been instituted by Lykourgos, who felt that long hair made "beautiful men more handsome and ugly men more fearsome." The harshness of their physical exercises was also softened during campaigns, and "they allowed the young men a way of life not so strict and responsible, so that for these men alone of all people, war was a respite from training for war."[15]

Although the rest of the Hellenes had long ago replaced monarchies with oligarchies or democracies, the Spartans had two kings. They were chosen from two families that claimed descent from Herakles and through him from his father, Zeus, the most powerful of the gods. The kings took care of military matters and were the highest religious officials. The real governing was done by the Gerousia, a council composed of men over sixty, and by the five Ephors. These were five chief magistrates who were elected to office for a year by the assembly of Spartan citizens. In fourth century Hellas to be a citizen one had to be a male who could afford the hoplite panoply. If you fought you voted. In Sparta it was only the Spartans who voted, even though the perioikoi and sometimes the helots had to fight.[16]

Considering how opposite the inhabitants of Lakonia were in all respects to the rest of the Hellenic world it's no wonder that the other Hellenes thought the Spartans were more than just a little strange.[17] Nevertheless, because of their training the Spartans could maneuver on the battlefield while their opponents had their hands full just keeping their lines straight. This gave them the ability to out-flank their enemies who could neither reform to meet an attack from the rear or wheel their line to form a new front. The Spartans had beaten the Persians at the beginning of the fifth century and the Athenians at the end of it. Their king Agesilaos had run rampant throughout Asia Minor and the Peloponnesos during the first quarter of the fourth century, and even though they had to fight constantly to maintain any semblance of hegemony, they were still beating all comers. It took a land-mark military innovation conceived in the mind of the Theban Epameinondas to put a stop to Spartan dreams of domination.[18]

WEAPONS AND TACTICS

Hellenic warfare before circa 1200 BCE had been the province of the nobility. Bronze Age Hellenic warrior-aristocrats rode in chariots driven by noble companions and fought each other with bows and long thrusting spears. Their armor was of bronze, and some wore helmets covered with rows of shinning boars' tusks. On foot they carried huge body-shields and silver-hilted rapiers. The Hellenic Bronze Age was no doubt witness to battles involving hundreds of chariots, a reflection in miniature of the great battles of the Hittites and Egyptians in which thousands of chariot borne warriors took part.[19]

After the collapse of the Mykenaian palace civilization around the year 1200, there were fewer chariots and fewer warrior-aristocrats to ride in them. Nevertheless, what nobility remained still fought from chariots or dismounted to engage in single combat with other noble warrior-aristocrats. There were no organized units; warriors fought in family groups and, like the Japanese Samurai of a later age, formally challenged one another to fight, having first recited the warlike accomplishments of their ancestors and insulted their opponents. These warriors of the Hellenic Dark Ages were armed with javelins, small round shields with a central hand-grip, and long cutting swords, which seem to have been imports from the lands to the north of Hellas. Their armor was of bronze.[20]

Single combats and chariots notwithstanding, the Dark Age Hellenes seem to have ended up fighting, more or less, like the Vikings of a later age. The richest and best armored warriors would form a shield wall, while their light-armed compatriots threw stones or fired arrows from behind or most probably from the flanks, retiring when the engagement reached the stage of a shock encounter. As Tyrtaios put it to the Spartans in the seventh century: "O light-armed, standing near the men in full armor, crouching under a shield...throw great stones and shoot smooth spears."

The introduction of the hoplite panoply led to a refinement of tactics and the abolition of single combat, which must have existed contemporaneously with the shield wall.[21] It seems to have been sometime around the middle of the seventh century BCE when the shield-wall/melee type of combat was replaced by the hoplite style phalanx battle. The aristocracies of most Hellenic states had thrown out their kings and installed themselves as ruling councils; at some point in time someone of them, perhaps Pheidon of Argos, formed up his upper and middle class warriors in line of battle and forbade them to break ranks and engage in single combat.[22]

By this time, due to improved economic conditions, the result of the regrowth of international trade, more of the citizens were able to provide themselves with good quality arms and armor. Bronze breastplates and helmets were augmented with bronze greaves and even thigh-pieces and arm-guards. (These last items were soon discarded, either because they restricted body-movement or because in the context of hoplite warfare they were unnecessary.) The thrusting spear (six to eight feet long, with a bronze butt-spike), was reintroduced and the sword relegated to a secondary role, to be used when the spear was broken or lost. But the most original innovation of the time was the development of the Argive shield (called "το 'οπλον" in many books, but the ancient Hellenes usually used the word "ασπις"). Round, some three feet in diameter and very concave, made of wood, leather, and bronze, it was carried by passing one's arm through a central arm-loop and holding onto a hand-grip inside the leading edge. [23]

At this time the Hellenes had much contact with the Middle Eastern societies whose antecedents had built the first cities in the world two thousand years or so before the ancestors of the Hellenes wandered into their present homeland. There was much trade, and Hellenic art was heavily influenced by, and began to make use of Middle Eastern motifs. Middle Eastern armies had been fighting in close phalanx-like formations for millennia. The Assyrians used large, round, convex shields with central hand-grips. Herodotus says of the Karians, who lived in the southwestern corner of Asia Minor, "it was these men who first put holders on shields; until then all carried shields without holders ... managing them with broad leather straps worn around their necks and left shoulders." Perhaps these "holders" can be equated with the arm loop of the Argive shield. It does not seem unreasonable to assume that the Karians, having adopted the Assyrian design, added the arm-loop, and that the Argive shield was developed by someone, perhaps Pheidon of Argos, hence the appellation "Argive," who had brought back from Asia one of these Karian shields and the know-how to use it, much like the brother of the poet Alkaios, who "came from the ends of the earth," having fought and killed a warrior over eight feet tall while in the service of the Babylonians and brought back with him a sword, its ivory grip bound with gold, possibly a trophy of his "great contest" with a giant barbarian.[24]

The new (at least to the Hellenes), tactic, which was the raison d'etre of the Argive shield, was to get everybody to form into an unbroken line of battle, usually eight ranks deep, lean into the concavity of their shields, and just push the enemy off the battlefield. This othismos aspidon (ωθισμος ασπιδων) – "the push of shields" - was sometimes preceded by a violent charge, the younger men in the front ranks being goaded and encouraged, both physically and verbally, by their older relatives in the following ranks, until both sides met with an audible crash. The shock of such a charge could drive a spear right through a man's shield and breastplate to cause a deep puncture wound, or the shaft might snap off harmlessly. With spears broken and men falling, the stabbing and hacking with butt-spikes and swords would begin a desperate struggle as one side tried to force its opposite number off the field of battle. Finally one phalanx would be pushed into disarray, ranks would be broken, and the cohesiveness of the line would dissolve as each man sought safety in flight.[25]

Since the Argive shield was so large, a good bit of it stuck out to the left of the man who was carrying it and left his right side somewhat exposed. This, as the historian Thucydides tells us, led each man to edge a bit to his right so that he might be protected on that side by the shield of his neighbor. Thus when two hoplite armies faced each other, each one's right wing usually overlapped its enemy's left. So, since all Hellenic states put their best men on the right, each right wing would usually defeat the opposing left wing of the hostile army.[26]

The Spartans especially liked to extend their right so as to outflank their enemy's left. Oftentimes the out-maneuvered opponents would retreat before a blow was struck; if they were foolish enough to stand their ground they would invariably be destroyed by the Spartans' flank attack. With the left out of the way the Spartans would reform and fall upon their enemy's right, which was by now giving their own allies (posted on the left of the Spartan line), a very hard time. Their opponents' inability to maneuver to meet this new attack was usually fatal.

AGESILAOS

Plutarch calls Agesilaos "μικρος" (a small man) and says that his "appearance was negligible." He probably stood about five feet tall in military sandels and had a long curly beard and long curly hair. He walked with a limp.[27] Because his brother Agis was heir to the throne, Agesilaos was brought up as an ordinary Spartan, enduring all the hardships of the severe Spartan system. Even after his accession to the king-ship he still practiced the frugal habits of an ordinary Spartan. In this case his personal inclinations led to good public relations: everybody likes a regular guy, and the Spartan regular guy was a soldier. He was not so much fearless in battle as oblivious of his own personal safety and more often then not was carried off the field bleeding. He had become king at the age of forty-six upon the death of Agis in 398, but it was not an undisputed succession.

Agis' son, Leotykhidas, claimed the throne even though it was common knowledge that he was not the son of Agis but of Alkibiades the Athenian, who had come to Sparta seeking political asylum and had seduced the Spartan King's wife when he was out of town on business. Nevertheless, Leotykhidas had supporters, and it was only after the war-hero Lysander threw his weight in on Agesilaos' side that Agesilaos was chosen king.

Lysander was Agesilaos' former lover and the man who had finally, after twenty-five years of almost constant fighting and continual hardships, defeated the Athenians in 404 in what the historian Thucydides named the "war of the Peloponnesians and Athenians." He had received much monetary assistance from Kyros, a son of the Great King of Persia (who had his own reasons for helping the Spartans), and consequently was able to equip a great fleet, with which he defeated the Athenian fleet (mainly through the carelessness of their admiral, Konon), blockaded Athens and forced her to surrender, then sailed up and down along the coast of Asia Minor, installing aristocrats favorable to himself as ruling oligarchies in the Hellenic cities there. Naturally his influence was very great, even though he had been recalled from Asia because the ephors didn't like the way he was running things.

Not long after Agesilaos' accession a rumor reached Sparta that the Persians were assembling a great fleet off the Phoenikian coast. Lysander, who saw this as an opportunity to regain his influence over the Hellenic cities of Asia Minor, persuaded Agesilaos to undertake an expedition against the Persians.

Agesilaos thought it would be nice if he could sacrifice at Aulis in Boiotia where Agamemnon had sacrificed before he led the Akhaians to Troy (to fight the famous Trojan War, celebrated in song by generations of bards and transmitted to us through the genius of someone called Homer). According to Plutarch, Agesilaos, "crowning a deer with garlands, ordered his mantis (soothsayer) to begin the sacrifice." This was contrary to the usual practice since the Boiotians liked to have their own mantis preside at these functions. When the boiotarkhoi (the magistrates of the Boiotian League, which the Thebans dominated), heard about this they sent officials to Agesilaos forbidding him to make a sacrifice in violation of the laws and ancestral customs of the Boiotians. As they gave him the message they threw the sacrificial thigh bones down from the altar. Agesilaos' army was elsewhere, awaiting his arrival, about to embark on the crossing to Asia, where they happily anticipated a slaughter of the Persians and anyone else who might stand in the way of their gaining large amounts of valuable booty, so, as upset as he was (and he was very upset), Agesilaos could do nothing but leave and sail away, as Plutarch says, "being very angry at the Thebans and despondent because of the omen" (i.e., the interruption of his sacrifice), which, he thought, meant that his mission would be incomplete and come to naught.[28]

Nevertheless, with thirty Spartan advisors, including Lysander, and about eight thousand allies and emancipated helots, he sailed to Asia where he found another ten thousand men waiting for him. Many of these men, including a young Athenian named Xenophon, had been in Asia fighting the Persians for the last six years or so.

Back in 401 Xenophon had joined an army of ten thousand, mostly Peloponnesian, mercenaries, led by a Spartan named Klearkhos, who had been hired by Kyros, the brother of the Persian King, Artaxerxes II. Kyros had always wanted to be king himself. Long before his father, Darius II, died in 404, Kyros had been helping the Spartans in their war against the Athenians, counting on them to return the favor once they had won. So now, along with his own native troops, he led his Hellenic mercenaries into Mesopotamia where he met his brother in battle at a place called Kounaxa. The Hellenes were posted on the right and carried all before them.

Xenophon takes up the story:

> Kyros, seeing the Hellenes victorious in their part of the field and in pursuit, was pleased and already being salaamed to as King by those around him; he was not inclined to pursue, but held his unit of six hundred horse in a tight formation with him, watching to see what the King would do.

Artaxerxes, meanwhile, still had a huge army left and was now in a position to take the Hellenes in flank or rear as they pursued his fleeing left wing.

Xenophon continues:

Then, Kyros, fearing lest his brother might cut to pieces the Hellenic army from behind, rode straight at him. And attacking with his six hundred he defeated the cavalry stationed in front of the king and turned in flight the six thousand and, they say, he killed with his own hands their leader, Artagerses. As the enemy fled in disorder, the six hundred of Kyros rushed headlong to the pursuit, except for a very few left behind close around him, those they call 'homotrapezoi' [men who eat at the same table]. And while he was with these men he saw the King and the troops in close order around him. And he simply could not stop himself, but saying 'I see the man,' he rushed at him and struck him in the chest and wounded him through his breastplate; thus said Ktesias the healer, and he said that he himself healed the king. As Kyros was stabbing his brother, someone threw a javelin and struck him mightily under the eye. And there they fought, the King and Kyros, and those around them in defense of each; as many of those around the King as died Ktesias tells, for he was beside him. Kyros himself was slain and eight nobles of those around him were lying dead near him. They say that Artapates, the most trusted of his scepter-bearing retainers, after he saw that Kyros had fallen, leaped down from his horse to embrace him. And some say that the king ordered someone to slaughter him over Kyros, and some say that drawing a short sword, he killed himself. He had a sword inlaid with gold, and he wore a torque and armlets and other things as the best of the Persians wear, for he had been honored by Kyros because of his good will and honesty. In this way Kyros met his end.[29]

Upon the death of Kyros the rest of his army left the field in a hurry. Only the Hellenes and the victorious Persians remained. Artaxerxes called the Hellenic leaders to a peace conference, and killing some, took the rest prisoner. The Ten Thousand cried and whined for a while and then elected new leaders, one of whom was Xenophon. Xenophon and the other new leaders led the Hellenes to the Black Sea, completely dominating the Persians and the various mountain tribes who tried to stop them. When the Spartans, who had secretly backed The Ten Thousand, heard how easy it was to beat the Persians, they answered the call of the Hellenic cities of Asia Minor who, in 399 requested their help against the Great King. Xenophon and about six thousand of the original ten thousand joined them. When Agesilaos arrived there in 396, he and Xenophon became good friends, and together they terrorized the Persians for about two years.

There, in Asia, Agesilaos fought his toughest battle - with his own conscience and sense of propriety. It seems that the Hellenes in Asia had been used to taking orders from Lysander, who had been posted there before the turn of the century and had pretty much run things until his recall at the end of the Peloponnesian War, and they were still paying him court. This was not at all to Agesilaos' liking, since, as he saw it, he was the king, and Lysander was now his subordinate, so he sent Lysander off to the Hellespont. There Lysander ran into a Persian named Spithridates who had also had a falling out with his boss, Pharnabazos. Lysander induced Spithridates to defect and bring over his army to Agesilaos. With Spithridates was his son Megabates.

Xenophon takes up the story:

Surely is it not worthy to recall his [Agesilaos] mastery over the impulses of Aphrodite, because it's something of a marvel, if not for some other reason? That he kept away from those he did not desire, some would say is just human nature, but he loved Megabates, the son of Spithridates, even as a very passionate nature might love a most handsome man. Now, it was the custom of the time for the Persians to kiss those whom they would honor, but when Megabates tried to kiss Agesilaos he strove vigorously not to be kissed. Is this not now an example of very noble self-control? From then on, since Megabates believed himself to be dishonored and he no longer tried to kiss him, Agesilaos spoke a word to one of his companions to persuade Megabates to honor him again. And when his friend asked, 'if Megabates should be persuaded, will you kiss him,' Agesilaos, having remained silent for a while, answered, 'Not then, by the twin gods, not if I were destined to become the handsomest, and the strongest, and the swiftest of men on the spot. In truth, I swear by all the gods, indeed, to fight that fight again rather than to wish everything, so much as I see, to become golden.' Wherefore some disbelieve these things I do not fail to understand. I truly believe that many more are able to conquer their enemies than are able to control these sorts of impulses.

The exactness of this narration might lead one to believe that the "companion" approached by Agesilaos was none other than Xenophon himself.

Plutarch also records this story:

...love for the boy was instilled in him, although when the boy himself was actually in his presence Agesilaos, suffering in strife, tried vigorously to fight against his desire, and whenever Megabates approached as if to embrace and kiss him, he avoided him. And when Megabates, shamed, stopped, and from then on spoke to him from afar, Agesilaos, grieved in turn and regretting his

28

avoidance of the kiss, pretended to wonder what happened to Megabates that he should not greet him with a kiss. 'You are responsible,' his friends said; you didn't submit, but you fled the kiss of this beautiful man, and you were afraid. And yet even now this one, persuaded, might come within range of your kiss. But don't flinch again!' For some time Agesilaos thought to himself and was silent; 'it's not nesscessary,' he said, 'for you to persuade him. As far as I'm concerned, I would rather fight that battle of the kiss again than that all the gold, as much as I have ever seen, should be mine.'[Or, as Plutarch has him say in the *Moralia*: 'I'd rather be above such things then to take by force the most prosperous city of the enemy.'] He was like this when Megabates was present; when he was gone Agesilaos was truly so excited that it's hard to say if, Megabates having turned around and appeared, he would have remained firm in his conviction not to be kissed.[30]

We'll never know, for, fortunately for the Lykourgan convictions of the Spartan King (and not so fortunately for his Aphroditean* impulses), Spithridates was insulted and cheated out of some booty by one of the other Spartan officers, named Herippidas, and so he took his men and Megabates and left. (It would perhaps be instructive, or at least interesting, to compare the self-disciplined behavior of the Spartan King with the sexual self-indulgence of some of our own recent leaders.)

---

* Aphrodite is the goddess of love.

THE KORINTHIAN WAR

Agesilaos had raided the length and breath of the land, burning and looting as he pleased, and the Persians were powerless to stop him. The Hellenes living in Asia must have laughed to see their former masters, bedecked with silks and jewels, groveling before a short, hairy man who dressed as if he had just stepped out of a bargain basement sale. But the Great King of Persia had not been idle. Realizing that his men were no match for the Spartans militarily, he decided to stir up some trouble for them back in Hellas, hoping that it would lead to the recall of Agesilaos. He sent a Rhodian named Timokrates to bribe the leaders of several Hellenic states to take up arms against the Spartans. At Thebes he gave money to a couple of pro-Athenian politicians, Ismenias and Androklidas, and he greased the palms of politicians at Korinth and Argos, and probably at Athens also (it seems that then, as now, politicians did not hesitate to profit from the machinations and largesse of lobbyists). These states were only too happy to receive money from the Great King. It had been Persian money that had helped the Spartans beat the Athenians in the Peloponnesian War, and the Athenians were dying for a rematch. The Thebans and the rest were also displeased with their former ally, Sparta, for after the Athenian surrender in 404, Lysander had taken all the credit and all the booty. They needed little urging to declare war. They just wanted to make it look like somebody else's idea. So the Thebans induced the Lokrians to attack the Phokaians, who then retaliated against the Lokrians, who then asked the Thebans for help, who then, at the urging of

Androklidas, attacked the Phokaians, who then asked the Spartans for help.

The Spartans thought that it would be a good opportunity to take the Thebans down a peg, and besides that, they were still upset about the Thebans' treatment of Agesilaos at Aulis, so the ephors sent Lysander, who after his falling out with Agesilaos was now back in Sparta, to Phokis to rouse the various peoples there, while Pausanias, the other king, gathered their Peloponnesian allies and marched north. They were supposed to join forces at the city of Haliartos some miles to the west of Thebes. The Thebans asked the Athenians for help, and they consented.

Lysander raised an army in Phokaia and marched to Orkhomenos, the Thebans' chief rival since the Bronze Age. The Orkhomenians didn't need much persuading to join in the attack on Thebes, and so Lysander advanced on Haliartos and reached the city before Pausanias. Once there he decided that he didn't need to wait for the king (and share the glory), so he immediately attacked the city. It was the worst, and the last mistake that he ever made. The Thebans showed up; trapped between the city wall and the Thebans, Lysander was killed and his army routed. This cheered the Thebans, but not for long; the next day Pausanias and the Spartans arrived outside the walls of Haliartos, and the Thebans began to get nervous. The day after that the Athenians marched up, and the Spartans got nervous. The older men were all set for a fight, but Pausanias and his war council, realizing that since the bodies of Lysander and those who had fallen with him were lying right under the city wall and that it would be extremely difficult to retrieve them even if they fought a battle and won, decided to ask the Thebans for a truce so that they could recover the bodies.

It was important to get the bodies back because it was important for them to have a proper burial. It was sacrilegious not to bury them, and besides, the Hellenes believed that if they weren't buried their spirits would wander around forever and never get any rest. As the ghost of Patroklos explains to his dreaming friend (and possibly former eromenos or erastes;

nobody can agree on which), Akhilleus, in book XXIII of Homer's *Iliad*: "honor me with funeral rites, I would pass the gates of Haides as quickly as possible. Shades, the phantoms of the dead, keep me off at a distance, and they don't at all allow me to mingle with them beyond the river. But idly I have wandered throughout the realm of wide-gated Haides."[31]

That's why the Hellenes hated shipwrecks so much: because the bodies wouldn't be found. In fact, after one particular battle in the Peloponnesian War the victorious commanders of the Athenian fleet were executed (except those who were smart enough not to return to Athens), because, as Diodorus the Sicilian, who lived in the first century BCE, writes: "although the Athenians, learning of their success at Arginousai, praised the commanders for the victory, they acted harshly" and condemned them to death because even though they had won, they had failed to recover the bodies of the Athenian dead. The fact that they had also failed to pick up the living sailors whose ships had been wrecked might have had something to do with the harsh verdict.[32]

The Thebans said that they would give back the bodies if Pausanias and his army left Boiotia. Pausanias knew that his Peloponnesian allies weren't exactly eager for a fight, so he agreed to the Thebans' conditions and marched back to Sparta, burying Lysander on the way. The ephors were less than happy about the way things had turned out and charged Pausanias with a variety of crimes. The king was more conscious of his own safety than Lysander had been, and being familiar with the ephors' methods, he wisely went into self-imposed exile. The ephors condemned him to death in absentia, and his son Agesipolis became king.

With Lysander dead, Pausanias in exile, and Agesipolis still a child, the ephors had no choice but to recall Agesilaos. He had been making big plans to invade the Persian heartland in the spring of 394 (and quite possibly would have anticipated Alexander's destruction of the Persian Empire by about sixty years), but upon receiving the bad news he immediately packed up and set off on a march overland back to Hellas, remarking that the Persian King had chased him out of Asia with ten thousand archers. (The Persian gold Daric featured an archer on the obverse.) Most states were happy to let him pass through their territories unmolested; he cut his way through those that weren't, including the Thessalian allies of the Thebans.

While Agesilaos approached Boiotia from the north, the ephors sent Agesipolis' guardian, Aristodemos, with an army from Sparta, marching up from the south. If this was to be a replay of the Lysander/Pausanias campaign, it too failed to achieve its objective.

The Thebans and Athenians, along with the Korinthians and Argives, met the Spartans and their allies near Korinth sometime in July 394. The Spartan right wing extended beyond the Athenians opposed to them, while the Spartan left, composed of allied hoplites, was, in its turn, overlapped by the Theban right. The Spartans flanked the Athenians and rolled up their line. At the same time the Agives, Korinthians, and Thebans drove the Spartan allies off the field. The Spartan line was now facing to the left of their original position, and they just kept going. They met the Argives returning from their pursuit of the Spartan allies and crashed into their unshielded right sides. After brutalizing the Argives, they went on to catch the Korinthians and the Thebans in the same helpless position, unprepared and unable to maneuver, and killed many of them. It seems that they did not press the pursuit, for, as Plutarch says, "they considered it not noble and not like the Hellenes (ουτε 'Ελληνικον), to cut down and murder men who had given up and retreated. And this was not only a noble and big hearted (the Greek is really "big-souled"- μεγαλοψυχος), thing, but also useful: for those who fought against them, knowing that the Spartans killed those who resisted but that they spared those who gave up, considered it more profitable to flee than to fight." The enemy having retreated, the Spartans put up a trophy.[33]

The Hellenes figured that whoever held the ground and the bodies after a battle were the winners. The winners got to put up a trophy, and the losers acknowledged their loss by asking the winners for permission to pick up their dead. The winners would go off and cut down a tree and then chop off most of the branches until the tree assumed a roughly anthropomorphic shape. They'd plant it in the ground right at the spot where the enemy had first given way and turned to flee. This turn-about was called the "trope," which actually means "a turn," so the monument that the victors set up was called a tropaion, to mark the place where the enemy first had turned away from the fight. This, of course, is where we get the word "trophy." The victors would pile rocks or build up a mound of earth around the base of the trophy to help support it. Then they'd dress up the tree like an enemy soldier in arms that they had taken from their dead opponents. The trophy was dedicated to some god, Zeus usually being a good choice, and after it was put up it was never touched again, being allowed to decay, so that the trophy and the enmities responsible for it should both eventually be forgotten.

KORONEIA

Although the Spartans claimed victory, the battle of Korinth was indecisive. The Spartans advanced no further, but the Thebans and their allies had only a short breathing space in which to prepare for the arrival of Agesilaos.

After stomping on any who were stupid enough to try to stop him, Agesilaos entered Hellas through the pass of Thermopylai (the Hellenes called it "the Gates"), where, in 480, Leonidas, the great, great grandfather of Agesipolis, had died with his body-guard, fighting against the Persians under Xerxes, the great, great, great grandfather of Artaxerxes and Kyros. After marching through friendly Phokaia, Agesilaos arrived at the confines of Boiotia. It was August 394, and Xenophon was with him.

Plutarch, in his biography of Agesilaos, says that they were camped near Khaironeia when they saw the sun fade and become crescent-shaped, and news reached Agesilaos that his brother-in-law, Peisander, the commander of the Spartan fleet, (he had been appointed to this office by Agesilaos, who saw nothing wrong in providing a little nepotistic help to his friends and relatives), had been defeated and killed in a naval battle (naumakhia) near the island of Knidos by a larger force commanded by Pharnabazos the Persian and Konon (the man who had lost the Peloponnesian War for Athens).[34]

Since his defeat by Lysander, Konon had been hiding out in Kypros. The Athenians had executed other generals for less, and he wasn't foolish enough to expect any leniency after the way he had lost the fleet and the war. Immediately after his defeat he had sailed straight to Kypros with whatever ships he had left. After a while it became mutually profitable for the Persians to give Konon a fleet to use against the Spartans, and he was now well on the way towards rehabilitating himself in the eyes of his countrymen.

Agesilaos took the news hard: his appointee and relative was dead, and with the destruction of the Spartan fleet Lakedaimonian influence in Asia would soon be reduced to nothing. There was also a more immediate problem. Agesilaos had about a thousand Spartans with him. The rest of his army was made up of allies who had either accompanied him on his march from Asia or who had joined him along the way. He knew that most of these allies would soon develop a new outlook on life if they were to learn the real outcome of the naumakhia, so he told the messengers (αγγελοι - where we get the word angel), who had brought him the news to announce that, though Peisander had been killed, the Spartans had won the battle. He then crowned himself with a wreath, and, after sacrificing an ox to good news (ευαγγελια), as Xenophon says: "to many he sent around some of the meat."[35]

The Hellenes were always looking for an excuse to crown themselves with some king of foliage. They crowned themselves when they were drunk, as Plato writes of Alkibiades joining the συμποσιον (drinking party) of Agathon: "he stood in the doorway, having crowned himself with some thick wreath of ivy and violets." Crowns were also given as prizes for the various pan-Hellenic athletic events, like the Olympics. Roses and myrtle were also popular choices.[36] Agesilaos' idea worked, for, as Xenophon reports, "Agesilaos' men" beat the enemy in a skirmish, probably on the march from Khaironeia towards Koroneia.[37]

36

Agesilaos and his army entered the plain of Koroneia from the north, Xenophon says, "from the Kephisos [river]," and seeing the Thebans and their allies, who seem to have been expecting them and were already drawn up in battle order, having entered the plain from the direction of Mt. Helikon, they immediately formed line of battle in full view of the enemy, with the Orkhomenians on the far left and Agesilaos himself leading the right. Facing Agesilaos were the Argives, and ranged against the Orkhomenians were the Thebans. Both armies were composed of about ten to fifteen thousand hoplites, with additional light-armed troops (peltastai, named after their shield, the half-moon shaped pelta), and cavalry.

The Spartans wore dark red cloaks because, as Plutarch says, "the color seemed to them to be manly and the blood red color to cause more fear for the inexperienced." And since they took great pride in seeing that their shields and weapons were highly polished, in the words of Xenophon, the Spartan army "appeared all bronze and blood-red," and he writes that Agesilaos had "filled their souls full of courage, so that they would be a match for anyone whom it might be necessary to fight against." He goes on to say: "I will describe the battle and how it happened like no other in our time."

In sight of the enemy, Agesilaos sacrificed a female goat, cutting its throat, as was the custom. He then ordered all the men to crown themselves with some kind of wreath and to polish their weapons and armor. They all took time out to do their hair, and then the flute players played the Hymn to Kastor (το Καστορειον), and Agesilaos himself led the singing of the marching song, according to Plutarch, "a sight both noble and terrible," and in rhythm with the flute they marched "into danger."

At first both armies were as silent as armies could be as they slowly advanced against each other (except, I suppose, for the sound of the Spartan flutes). When they were separated by the length of a stadion (600ft., 9in.), the Thebans cried the war-cry (which went something like "ala ala ala ala," etc.), and charged the Orkhomenians on the Spartan left. When they were half a stadion away, the men under Herippidas (including some of the original ten thousand who had fought for Kyros), ran out from the Spartan phalanx, followed by the Ionians, Aioleians, and Hellespontines. Then everybody else joined them. As Plutarch says, "it wasn't much of a contest." The troops opposed to Herippidas gave way at the first impact, and the Argives turned and ran for Mt. Helikon before the Spartans even reached them.

The Spartan phalanx must have gradually slowed and stopped, perhaps allowing the cavalry and peltasts to take up the pursuit to let fly with their javelins at the backs of the fleeing Agives. Some of the foreign hoplites had already ripped up a bit of the local foliage and were busily crowning Agesilaos as victor when he received word that the Thebans had cut their way through the Orkhomenians and were among the baggage animals. Plutarch and Xenophon agree that Agesilaos could have won a "victory without risk" (Plutarch), if he had just waited for the Thebans to march back to Helikon and attacked them from flank or rear. Instead he immediately ordered the phalanx to turn around so as to lead them head-on against the hated Thebans. Plutarch says he was carried away by emotion, but Xenophon calls his decision "indisputably manly."

It's not easy to turn a phalanx around. Everybody just doesn't turn around. In a phalanx the younger men are in the front ranks, and if everybody just did an about-face, that would leave the older men in the front. Naturally it would be preferable to have the younger men in front, so the Spartans performed, and maybe invented, the countermarch.

A phalanx is composed of rank and file. The files in this particular phalanx were twelve men deep, or rather, as the Hellenes referred to them, twelve shields deep. Lined up together they must have presented a front rank of two or three hundred shields and sharp spears, with the weight of the next eleven ranks behind it.

Upon some, no doubt loud, commands the phalanx dresses its ranks, steps right (or left), into open order, and each man turns to his right (or left). The men in the front rank take one step forward, turn to their right (or left), again, each movement in response to commands passed on by enomotarkhoi ("men who lead a band bound by oath"; an enomotia was thirty-two men strong), and march past their files to form a new rank facing in the opposite direction. The next eleven ranks follow them. That's a countermarch. When it's completed the phalanx resumes close order.

Since the place of honor was on the right, and this is traditionally where the Spartan kings stationed themselves, Agesilaos would be, once the countermarch was finished, on the left. Considering his somewhat obstinate nature, the fact that he really disliked, if not outright hated the Thebans, and the testimony of Xenophon who says that sometimes the Spartans considered it advantageous to have the leader on the left, Agesilaos probably stayed put, right where he was, facing the Theban right where their best men would be posted.

The Thebans, who had been rummaging through the Spartans' luggage in search of anything of value, now noticed that their allies were headed in a hurry toward Mt. Helikon, and they must have soon become aware of the movement of the Spartan phalanx, which was now, as the Greek says, "unrolling" (εξελιξας) itself to face in the direction of its own ransacked baggage train and the Thebans who were doing the ransacking. They must have reformed their phalanx as quickly as possible, and then both sides marched straight at each other without hesitation. The Spartans were probably formed up twelve shields deep, the Thebans twenty-five, each fully determined to push the other off the battlefield by main strength.

They had to march slowly, the Spartans keeping time to the sound of flutes, the Thebans perhaps in desperate silence, until they were close enough to charge. Then, as Xenophon says, "they dashed together."

We have his eyewitness account: "striking together their shields, they pushed, they fought, they killed, they died." There was no screaming, no shouting, but no silence either, just the type of sound that "passion and battle might present," the thudding and banging of steel on bronze, the cracking of breaking spears, the involuntary grunts and groans of thousands of men fighting and dying. According to Plutarch the struggle was fiercest where Agesilaos stood amongst fifty volunteers who had come from Sparta to take part in the fighting. He credits these young men "whose love of honor became, in a critical time, the deliverance of the king."

It was and had always been the custom among the Hellenes for the leader of an army, be he king or strategos (usually translated as "general" on land and "admiral" on sea), to fight in the front ranks, and Agesilaos was no exception. He received many blows by sword and spear, was stabbed through his armor and nearly killed before he was removed from the field by some of the volunteers who snatched him up and carried him off "barely alive," while others stood before them, striking men down and falling themselves.

At this point the weight of the Theban phalanx began to tell. The front rank of Spartans had eleven ranks behind them, pushing the living hoplites forward and stepping in to take the places of the dead. Conversely, the Thebans' front rank had twenty four ranks behind them, and this superior pushing power was turning the tide. According to Plutarch:

> as it was a great effort to push the Thebans forward, [the Spartans] were forced to do what from the beginning they had not wanted to do. They retired their phalanx and separated [opened their ranks?] and as the [Thebans] marching very disorderly, passed through, [the Spartans] following and running alongside, struck them from the side. They did not rout them, but the Thebans withdrew toward Helikon, feeling good about the battle, since they themselves were unbeaten.

Xenophon just says that some of the Thebans broke through. Both agree that the Thebans suffered heavy losses in the retreat to Helikon.

It is difficult to understand how a phalanx, once it has engaged the enemy hand to hand, can just separate itself and let the enemy through. Any opening in the ranks of one phalanx is bound to be exploited by its opposite number, and that would mean the destruction of the phalanx that opened its ranks. Perhaps, as Prof. Cliff Rogers of the United States Military Academy has suggested, the two phalanxes were not engaged at the time this maneuver took place. [38]

Plutarch does say that the Spartans διεστησαν; the word διιστεμι means to separate, to stand apart, to open, etc. This is the word I have translated as "retired," since I think that Plutarch meant that the Spartans had "separated" themselves from the Thebans. He then says that they διεσχον; the word διεχω also means to separate; this is where it gets tricky. If the Spartans had already separated (διεστησαν) themselves from the Thebans, what were they separating (διεσχον) now? The only thing left to separate is themselves, i.e., they must have divided their phalanx in two. Plutarch then says that the Thebans διεξεπεσον, and the word διεκπεραω means "to pass through." The only thing around for the Thebans to pass through was the Spartan phalanx.

Polyainos, writing around 160 CE, also seems to be describing this battle, though he doesn't give it a name or a location. In his account, Agesilaos orders the Spartans to separate, which, if Polyainos' source is correct, would mean that the Spartans initiated the "time out" and that the Thebans, for some reason, also took a breather.[39]

What tenuous clues the ancients have left us seem to support Prof. Rogers' suggestion that both sides had backed away from each other to "catch their breaths." This idea in itself is only feasible if the backing away was a mutual thing. One would think that if Agesilaos had passed the word to back off (as Polyainos records), and the phalanx was indeed able to step back a pace or two (a maneuver which itself must have been rather difficult, i.e., several thousand men armed with the large hoplite shield and long thrusting spear trying to walk backward and maintain formation without stumbling over the ground and

41

each other), the Thebans would have interpreted this as a sign of weakness, and, thinking that the Spartans were about to give way, would have moved their own phalanx forward. Therefore, since the ancient sources all agree that the Thebans passed through the Spartan phalanx (even though Xenophon, who was there, doesn't go into detail), it's probably pretty safe to assume that Agesilaos did pass the word to move back and that the Thebans, themselves exhausted by the severity of the fighting, did not immediately press the attack.

Perhaps the Spartans then moved backward step by step, until they had reached a distance that they felt was safe enough for them to divide their phalanx or safe enough for them to turn about face and then retreat to a distance which seemed safe enough for them to divide their phalanx. In any case the now divided Spartan phalanx was still between the Thebans and Thebes. It was now that the Thebans, as Plutarch reports, passed through the Spartans, taking heavy casualties but maintaining good order as they retreated toward Mt. Helikon. This of course raises the question: don't the Thebans know that those of them on the far right are going to be the targets of the Spartans to their right and unshielded sides? Perhaps this was their only way out.

Agesilaos had been wounded "in every way by all sorts of weapons," but he would not go to his tent until he had been carried back to the phalanx and seen that the dead were brought within their lines. While he was about this, some of the cavalry rode up and informed him that about eighty of the enemy had holed up in the nearby temple of Itonian Athena (named after the town of Iton), and were still armed. It would have been a sacrilege to harm them after they had taken sanctuary, so Agesilaos ordered the cavalrymen to "let them go where they wished." [40]

Since this little episode has nothing to do with the battle, other than serve to illustrate the character of Xenophon's friend Agesilaos, and since Xenophon was himself a horse-soldier, it's not unreasonable to suppose that he was among or in command of this unit of horse that apprised the king of the presence of the eighty, still-armed enemy soldiers who had taken refuge in the temple. Xenophon later wrote about horse-soldiers and horsemanship, and his two sons followed in their father's footsteps by becoming cavalrymen themselves.

After the battle Xenophon surveyed the scene:

> When the battle was finally over there were present to be seen, where they had fought hand to hand, the earth mixed with blood; and corpses lying, friends and enemies, together with one another; and shields crushed; spears broken in pieces; short swords bare of their sheaths, some on the ground, and some in bodies, and some still in hands. Then, at the last, since it was already late, having gathered the corpses of the enemy into camp, they prepared dinner and went to sleep.[41]

At dawn the next day, "wishing to put the Thebans on the spot to see if they would fight,"Agesilaos ordered the polemarkhos (war-leader) Gylis to draw the army up in line of battle, to put up a trophy, to have the soldiers crown themselves for Apollo, and to have the flute players all play. The Thebans had clearly had enough and sent out heralds asking for their dead back. Agesilaos agreed to a truce and then had himself carried to Delphi, the most sacred spot in all of Hellas.[42]

DELPHI

Delphi was one of the pan-Hellenic (pan means all), sanctuaries like Olympia (where every four years the Hellenes held the Olympic Games from time immemorial, until the Christians made them stop), and was equally sacred to all Hellenes. It was (and what's left of it still is), located on the southern slopes of Mt. Parnassos, overlooking the Korinthian gulf from the north. For the Hellenes it was the center of the earth. They knew it was the center of the earth because long ago Zeus, the father of gods and men, had let loose an eagle in the far west and sent it flying east; at the same time he let loose another eagle in the far east and sent it flying west. Since the earth was flat at the time, the eagle flying west and the eagle flying east met in the middle, which just happened to be at Delphi. To mark the spot Zeus set down the Omphalos stone. Hesiod, who lived around 700, tells the story of the "great stone" in his poem "Theogony," which deals with the birth of the gods.

Kronos had become king of the gods by castrating his own father, Ouranos (Heaven). He made Rheia (one of the daughters of Heaven and Earth), his wife and

> she bore glorious children: Histia; Demetra; and Here, gold-sandaled; and strong Haides, who under the earth in halls dwells, a pitiless heart holding; and loud-sounding Ennosigaion; and wise Zeus, of gods the father and also of men,

and at the hands of whose thunder the wide earth shakes. And these he swallowed down, Great Kronos, as each one from the womb of the holy mother to her knees came, thinking that not any other of the noble heavenly ones among the deathless might have kingly honor. For he learned from Gaia (Earth) and Starry Ouranos that it had been fated for him at the hands of his child to be conquered, even though he was strong, through the plans of Great Zeus.[43]

Kronos' avant-garde cuisine didn't go over well with Rheia, who wasn't exactly thrilled at the thought of her husband eating her children. She conspired with Kronos' parents, Ouranos and Gaia (who, incidentally, were her parents too), and who also (especially Ouranos), had, so to speak, a bone to pick with their overbearing son, and together they came up with a plan. They sent Rheia to Krete

when the youngest of her children she was about to bear, Great Zeus. Him she received, huge Gaia, in wide Krete to raise and bring up. There she went, bearing him swiftly through the black night, first to Lykton. And she hid him, in her arms carrying him, in a deep cave in the depths of the earth, on Mt. Aigaion, in thickened woods. To him, a great stone swaddled, she handed over, to Ouranosson, the Great King of the gods, the earlier [than Zeus] king. This, seizing with his hands, he put it down into his belly, cruel man. Not did he know in his heart that in the place of the stone his son, unconquered and unharmed, was left behind, who soon was about to, by strength and by the force of his hands having subdued him, drive him out from his honors, and who would rule the deathless.

Swiftly then the strength and shining limbs of this lord grew. With the turning of the years, by the very wise suggestions of Gaia cheated, his offspring back he sent up, great Kronos, crooked of council. He was conquered by the skill and strength of his son. First he vomited forth the stone, which last he had swallowed down. This Zeus set fast in the wide-wayed earth, in most holy Pytho in a cave under Parnessos, a sign to be hereafter a wonder to mortal men.[44]

Delphi was sometimes referred to as Pytho because, as Hesiod also tells us, Apollo, having come down from Olympos, decided to take up residence there. First he had to evict the former tenant, which just happened to be a huge dragon who worked for Here, Zeus' wife. After shooting the dragon full of arrows and watching it writhe all over the place spewing blood until it died, the god said; "entauthoi nun pytheu epi khthoni botiaveire," which means: "here now rot on the manfeeding earth...from this now Pytho it is called, and men call the lord [Apollo] Pythion, after this."[45]

There seems to have been a sanctuary at Delphi back in Mykenaian times, and perhaps the replacement of some Mykenaian Earth-Mother goddess by the masculine gods of the invading Dorians is reflected in the story of Apollo's destruction of Here's dragon.

It's easy to see how the Hellenes, who saw divinities behind every rock and tree and in every stream and river, could come to think of Delphi as a holy place. High in the mountains, far removed from earthly cares, you can look down and see the tiny specks of eagles flying far below and the lands stretching out far and wide. At Delphi, perched between heaven and earth, one was as close as one would ever get to the gods on Olympos.

There stood the temple of Apollo, surrounded by statues and monuments set up by the various Hellenic states to commemorate people and events, along with a stadium for the Pythian Games (the prize was a crown of bay leaves), a theater, and at least sixteen small buildings called treasuries. Each treasury had been build by a particular Hellenic state to house the spoils of war, mostly taken from some other Hellenic state, and many gold and silver offerings to the gods. The Hellenic cities liked to show off, and this is where they did it, at Delphi, where every Hellene from every city could see it.

The Hellenes were constantly competing with one another in athletic, theatrical, and musical events. Some of the winners were honored with statues set up at Delphi by their grateful home-towns. The Hellenes also liked to remind one another of their warlike accomplishments. In the fourth century BCE as you entered the temple enclosure by the main gate you would immediately see off to your right a group of statues dedicated by the Spartans, including one of Lysander being crowned by Poseidon for his victory at Aigospotamoi over Konon and the Athenians. Continuing on up the Sacred Way, past various treasure houses built like small doric temples of different kinds of marble, including those of the Athenians and Thebans, you would go round a bend and eventually pass, on your left, the Athenian colonnade where were hung shields taken from the Spartans in the same war, all the while surrounded by a beautiful view of mountain scenery.

There at Delphi also resided the most famous oracle in the world. Everyone consulted the oracle about everything. People came from all over to ask the god's advice. Nothing important in the history of Hellas happened without someone asking the oracle something. Diodorus the Sicilian tells how the oracle was discovered:

> It is said that long ago goats found the place of the oracle. On account of this the Delphoi still consult the god by means of a goat today. The manner of the discovery was, they say, like this. There was a chasm (khasma) in this very place that is now called the unenterable place (αδυτον) of the temple, and around this goats were in the habit of

going, because this place the Delphians had not yet settled down on.

Whenever a goat got too close to the chasm it would jump up and down and start making sounds unlike the sounds that goats usually make. The man in charge of the goats saw this and went himself to look in the chasm. The same thing that happened to the goats happened to the goat-herd. "The goats did things like those possessed by a god, and this man prophesied the things intended to be."

After the story of the goat-herd's experience got around to the locals, they crowded the place. Everyone who came near the chasm became possessed. Because of this they thought the place was an oracle of Gaia. At first people would prophecy to each other, but then, after a few people had gotten a little too carried away and jumped into the chasm, never to be seen again, the locals decided to appoint a prophetess as the voice of the oracle. Diodorus tells how they built a mekhanen, some sort of device onto which the prophetess would "go up on to" and be possessed safely. He identifies it with the ubiquitous bowl-tripod assembly, which was used for all kinds of stuff from burning incense to cooking dinner, and was also, when made of materials more expensive than iron, a favorite type of temple dedication. How this would stop the prophetess from getting too enthusiastic (enthousiazein is the word the Hellenes used of someone possessed by a god), and jumping overboard is unclear, unless they strapped her in. The word mekhanen could also mean "crane," and since Diodorus also writes later on that the prophetess, who was called the Pythia, denied that the tripod was "the ancestral way," one might think that he's got the tripod thing wrong and that the Pythia was hoisted over the chasm by some type of crane.

Diodorus tells a nice story, but it really doesn't matter whether his mekhanen was a tripod or a crane since no one has ever found a chasm at Delphi big enough for anyone to be suspended over, much less jump into. The khasma of Diodorus is probably a cave that should be identified with the adyton of the temple. Diodorus continues his story:

> It is said that virgins, because of their uncorrupted nature, the same as Artemis [Apollo's sister], sang the prophecies in ancient times. They were suitable to guard the secrets of those receiving an oracular response. But in more recent times they say that Ekhekrates the Thessalian, being near the oracle and seeing the virgin voice of the oracle, desired her because of her beauty, and, having snatched her up and carried her off, forced her.

After this the Delphians enacted a law prohibiting virgins from becoming the voice of the oracle, and they only appointed women over fifty, who were then, as a remembrance of the old days, dressed like virgins.[46]

After some fairly expensive religious requirements had been fulfilled one could ask the oracle a question and receive a usually ambiguous response in the form of some unintelligible sounds emitted by the Pythian Priestess, interpreted by a priest, and written down in dactylic hexameter. (Dactylic hexameter is the meter of epic poetry, e.g. *The Iliad* and *The Odyssey*, which really isn't poetry as we know it, having been sung with guitar-like accompaniment, and goes something like this: THIS is the FORest primEVAL, the MURmuring PINES and the HEMlocks.)

At least that's what historians used to say about the oracle, which just goes to show that modern historians are just as capable of making up a good story as ancient historians, like Diodorus, were. All that we really know about the oracle is that before the Pythia would even think about pronouncing the will of the god, palms had to be greased.

A tax or fee had to be paid (a bribe in the form of a donation could get you to the front of the line; for a really big bribe the Pythia would say anything you wanted her to say, to anyone you wanted her to say it to), and a goat had to be sacrificed. Before the goat could be sacrificed it had to be seen to tremble in all its "parts." Usually the libation of cold water that the priest and his assistants poured over it helped to expedite the procedure. The trembling meant that Apollo was present; no trembling meant no oracular response. After the sacrifice those consulting the god went into the temple of Apollo and sat down. The Pythia was perhaps by now sitting on her tripod in the adyton. One would think that the consultants went into the adyton one by one, or group by group if it was an official consultation on the part of some city or state. The Pythia then heard the question and replied, according to her skills and temperament, in verse or prose. Plutarch tells of some poets who used to hang around the shrine and versify the replies, and this is probably what gave rise to the legend that the Pythia's replies had to be interpreted by the priests and written down in dactylic hexameter. The reason historians used to think that the Pythia's utterances were unintelligible can also be found in Plutarch. He himself was a Pythian priest for many years, and he tells the story of a Pythia who was forced to prophecy against her will. She became incoherent, ran from the temple, and died a few days later. The conception of the Pythia as a raving madwomen was the exception rather than the rule, and errors in the interpretation of certain Greek words perpetuated the myth. The real Pythia gave the best answers she could, and in plain language (unless she had poetic inclinations), and everybody swore by them. It was partly on the advice of this oracle that Xenophon had taken service with Klearkhos and The Ten Thousand. Agesilaos, who had also consulted the oracle before his own expedition, dedicated a tenth of all the spoils from his Asian escapade to the god and went back to Sparta.[47]

SKILLOUS

Xenophon couldn't go back to Athens. Scholars don't really know when, but sometime between 399 and 394 the Athenians had officially banished him. They didn't appreciate the fact that he had worked for Kyros, who had helped the Spartans beat them in the Peloponnesian War, and they certainly were not happy that he had actually fought against his own countrymen at the battle of Koroneia. But his pal Agesilaos didn't let him down. Xenophon "was settled by the Lakedaimonians in Skillous," near Olympia with his wife, Philesia, and his two sons, Gryllos and Diodoros. He was already living there when a certain Megabyzos came to see the Olympic Games (possibly the games of 392). [48]

Megabyzos also had another reason for coming to Olympia. When Xenophon and the eight thousand or so survivors of the original ten thousand mercenaries hired by Kyros had fought their way out of Persian and various other hostile lands and reached the sea, they had divided up the loot, out of which they made thank offerings to the gods. Xenophon had dedicated ten percent of his earnings to Apollo. He tells us in his own words: "Xenophon, having made an offering to Apollo, set it up in the treasure house of the Athenians at Delphi and inscribed upon it his name and the name of Proxenos, who had died with Klearkhos, for he was his friend."

Xenophon was an aristocrat. He had probably served in the Athenian cavalry in the closing years of the Peloponnesian war, cavalry being the aristocratic branch of the armed services. In those days both cavalry and hoplites took servants with them. Xenophon's servants had probably hauled large sums of money, acquired from the sale of booty, all the way back from

Asia. It wouldn't be unreasonable to assume that Xenophon accompanied Agesilaos on his visit to Delphi and while there either bought or had made some kind of offering to Apollo. It was probably at this time that he asked the oracle a question concerning another dedication.

For some reason or another Xenophon felt that he also owed Ephesian Artemis something, but

> that [offering] for Artemis of Ephesias, when he went back with Agesilaos from Asia on the road to Boiotia, he left behind with Megabyzos the custodian of the temple of Artemis because he seemed to be going into danger, and he said that if he survived, to pay it back, and if anything happened to him, to dedicate a thing made to Artemis, whatever he might think to be pleasing to the goddess.

Xenophon, having indeed survived the trek from Asia and the battle of Koroneia, probably spent some time at Sparta before he was finally settled down at Skillous; he then no doubt sent a letter to Megabyzos, who probably decided to kill two birds with one stone, and so made plans to arrive at Olympia just in time for the games. Megabyzos gave Xenophon back his "deposit," and they probably both enjoyed the Olympics.

> Xenophon bought a place for the goddess where the god [the oracle of Apollo] commanded. And there happened to be flowing through the place the river Selinous. And in Ephesos by the temple of Artemis the Selinous River flows. And fish are in both and mussels, and in the place at Skillous hunting of everything, as much as there are wild animals that are hunted. And he built an altar and a temple from the hierou arguriou [the "holy" or "dedicated" silver]. And thereafter, dedicating a tenth of his produce, he made a

sacrifice to the goddess, and all the citizens and neighbors, men and women, shared in the festivities.

Everybody put up tents and camped out. Xenophon says, "the goddess provided barley meal, loaves of wheat bread, and dried fruits for dessert." And there was plenty of barbecue to go around, animals being taken from the "holy pasture" and in the hunt. "For," as Xenophon writes with obvious pleasure, "they made a hunt for the festival, the sons of Xenophon and those of the other citizens and those who wanted to hunt with them."

On this land of meadows and hills, situated about two miles south of the Temple of Zeus at Olympia, Xenophon raised pigs, goats, cattle, and horses, with enough fodder left over to feed the draft animals of those who came for the festival. Xenophon's temple was a smaller version of the great temple of Artemis at Ephesos, and his cypress-wood statue of the goddess was a copy of the gold statue in the great temple. Around Xenophon's temple stood a grove of fruit trees. Outside the temple Xenophon set up a stone stele upon which was inscribed, "Holy place of Artemis. Who holds this and its crops is to sacrifice a tenth each year, and, from the surplus, to repair the temple. And the goddess will take care of whomever doesn't do this."

One can imagine Xenophon being quite pleased with the way things had turned out. He had survived the disastrous expedition of Kyros and the arduous march of The Ten Thousand, and he had found a good friend in Agesilaos, with whom he had campaigned profitably in Asia. Sure, he had been banished from his native land, but he had lived through Koroneia and been rewarded for his services with a nice place at Skillous, and now, with the money received from Megabyzos, he had fulfilled his vow to Artemis and, incidentally, got himself a nice place to go fishing and hunting, which was so productive that he was able to throw a really big cook-out once a year.

THE PEACE OF ANTALKIDAS

When Agesilaos had been in Asia, he had followed Lysander's policy of making damn sure that the cities there were ruled by oligarchies friendly to the Spartans. Now, as he was being carried, bruised and bandaged, back to Sparta, Konon and Pharnabazos were sailing along the coast of Asia Minor uninstalling the oligarchies and promising the cities autonomy.

The next year they raided the Lakonian coast, and Konon stopped off in Athens to help with men and money to rebuild the Long Walls. The Long Walls stretched from Athens to its port Peiraieus. This was to insure that Athens could never be cut off from the sea. When Lysander, financed by the Great King of Persia, had beaten the Athenians in 404, he made them pull down the long walls; now, Konon, the man who had lost the war for Athens, was, ten years later, rebuilding them with money from none other than the Great King of Persia.

With an Athenian fleet on the loose and the Long Walls being rebuilt, the Spartans started to get nervous. They were losing their grip on Asia, and so, to preserve what little they had left, the ephors sent out a Spartan named Antalkidas to talk peace with the Great King. Agesilaos didn't like this at all since he regarded the Persians as enemies of the Hellenes and Antalkidas, who belonged to the party of the other Spartan king, as his political opponent. When the Athenians and their allies got wind of this, they sent their own ambassadors, including Konon, to speak to the king.

Antalkidas told the king's representative, Tiribazos, who happened to be well disposed toward the Spartans, that as far as the Spartans were concerned the Hellenic cities in Asia could just as well be autonomous. The Athenians didn't agree with Antalkidas' plans. They had just managed to get their hands on the islands of Lemnos, Imbros, and Skyros, and they wanted to keep them. The Thebans didn't like the autonomy idea because they feared it might be extended to include the cities of Boiotia, which they wanted to own. The Argives also didn't like it since they had their own plans to annex Korinth. The Great King didn't like it because he was still angry at the Spartans for turning on him after he had helped them win the Peloponnesian War. No peace was signed. Tiribazos was recalled, but not before he managed to have Konon thrown in jail, saying that he was acting contrary to the interests of the Persians. Negotiations broke down completely, and the Spartans sent out a man named Thibron to raid Persian territory. Thibron was careless and soon got himself killed.

Around this time Konon died. The cause of death, some say, was an illness, contracted in Kypros, where he had sought asylum after escaping the dungeons of Tiribazos, but others blame the ill-will of his Persian captors who, they say, murdered him.

Meanwhile the Spartans were habitually raiding Korinthian territory. Korinth's allies, Athens, Thebes, and Argos, weren't particularly upset at this turn of events, but it wasn't exactly what the Korinthians had had in mind when they declared war on Sparta, so the aristocratic party began to talk of peace.

When the democrats got wind of this they weren't exactly thrilled. It was they who had taken the Persian King's money to start the war in the first place, and they weren't about to give up now. So, on a certain holiday, at a prearranged time, with the support of the Agives, they began to kill the aristocrats. (You might want to think of this as if on the fourth of July or some other federal holiday Democrats all of a sudden started going around to Republicans' barbecues and started stabbing to death all the male barbecuers.) Diodorus tells us that about one hundred twenty of the aristocrats met their deaths at the hands of their political opponents, and about five hundred left town in a hurry. Those aristocrats who managed to escape the slaughter returned with the Spartans and seized the port of Korinth, called Lekhaion. The Boiotians, Athenians, and Agives came and joined forces with the Korinthians, but the Spartans and the Korinthian exiles (phugades) killed about a thousand of them, and they retreated to Korinth. In this same year (391), Agesilaos raided the lands of the Argives, burnt whatever crops he found, and then returned to Sparta.

Meanwhile the Athenians were once again getting out of hand. With Persian money they had built up a great fleet, and by 390 they had, quite ungratefully, allied themselves with Euagoras of Kypros and the Pharaoh of Egypt (both in rebellion against the Great King of Persia who had just paid for the Athenian fleet), in hopes of reviving their fifth century overseas empire.

While things were heating up in Asia, back in Hellas Agesilaos set out to give his enemies a hard time. First he stopped off at the isthmus of Korinth, the strip of land which connects the Peloponnesos to the rest of Hellas. He was headed for a place called Peiraion, a mountainous promontory on the west shore of the isthmus, where, he had heard, the Korinthians had hidden all their cattle. He happened to arrive at the isthmus just as the Isthmian Games were about to begin.

The Argives were there, sacrificing at the temple of Poseidon as if they owned the place. They were just about to have breakfast when they heard that Agesilaos was on the way. They stopped what they were doing and went back to Korinth in a hurry. Agesilaos, although he probably could have caught them, let them go and offered his own sacrifice. He hung around for a few days while the Korinthian exiles held the Isthmian Games, and then he marched toward Peiraion. As soon as he left, the Argives held their own games and, as Xenophon says, some competitors won twice and some lost twice, and, one would suppose, though Xenophon doesn't say so, some won and lost.

When Agesilaos arrived at Peiraion he realized that it was too strongly defended to fall to a direct assault, so the Spartans all sat down and had breakfast and then turned around and began to march on Korinth. The Korinthians knew that Agesilaos couldn't take Korinth by storm, but since he was marching straight at them they feared that the city was in danger of being betrayed by someone within the walls. They sent out the Athenian Iphikrates with a large force of peltasts to intercept Agesilaos. Iphikrates managed to march past Agesilaos in the night, and so, the next day, right after breakfast, Agesilaos turned back for Peiraion.

Agesilaos marched along the shore and sent part of his army up on to the heights. That night he camped by the local hot springs. But the mora of Spartans (six hundred men) that had taken the high road had forgotten to bring fire with them. Now it was night, and getting cold on the heights. They had only summer clothing, and the ground was wet and damp from rain showers earlier in the evening. Xenophon says, "they were shivering in the dark, with no heart for dinner." Agesilaos sent ten men carrying fire in clay pots up onto the heights by different routes. The chilled Spartans made huge fires, rubbed oil on themselves, and then had a proper dinner.

Upon learning that the Spartans had occupied the heights the men, women, slaves, and freedmen who had been holed up in Peiraion retreated to the westernmost part of the peninsula, called the Heraion, with most of the cattle. Agesilaos kept coming, marching along the shore while the recipients of the fire-pots descended on the fortress of Oinoe to the north-east, effectively blocking any attempt at retreat or relief and gaining great quantities of booty. Realizing that the situation was now hopeless, the people in the Heraion surrendered unconditionally to Agesilaos. Xenophon writes: "and he decided, as many as were murderers [i.e. those who had taken part in the massacre of the aristocrats], these he would give to the exiles, all the rest he would sell."

While all this was going on, Iphikrates managed to pull off a stunt that made military history: It was the custom of the

Amyklaioi, wherever they were, to go home for the holiday called the Hyakinthia, to sing the paian to Apollo. The Amyklaian contingent of the Spartan army was posted in Lekhaion, and to get back to Amyklai, which was a little south of Sparta, they had to pass by Korinth. So the Spartan polemarkhos in charge of the garrison at Lekhaion ordered the rest of the Spartan allies to guard the walls, while he, with the mora of Spartan hoplites and a mora of cavalry, escorted the Amyklaioi past Korinth. After marching west until they were twenty or thirty stadia outside of Sikyon, the polemarkhos ordered the cavalry to accompany the Amyklaians as far as the Amyklaians wanted and then to catch up with the hoplites. This left the polemarkhos and the hoplites without any cavalry or peltasts. Since hoplites couldn't really run very far in their armor, all good hoplite commanders made it a point to have cavalry and peltasts guarding their flanks in case of attacks by the enemy's cavalry and peltasts. Peltasts didn't carry the heavy Argive shield or wear body armor, so they could move faster than hoplites. Instead of slugging it out with thrusting spears the peltasts could run in, throw their light javelins, and then run away before most hoplites could catch them. The Spartan polemarkhos, perhaps a little over-confident after his countrymen's recent victories, now began to march back to Lekhaion, past the city of Korinth, which just happened to be full of Athenian peltasts under the command of Iphikrates.

Iphikrates and Kallias, the commander of the Athenian hoplites, wasted no time. With the Athenian hoplites drawn up close to the city walls, Iphikrates' peltasts ran up to the Spartans and let fly their javelins, killing and wounding some of the Spartan hoplites. The polemarkhos had the shield-bearers (hypaspistoi, helots who carried the hoplite's equiptment), take the wounded back to Lekhaion. Then he sent out the youngest hoplites in pursuit of the peltasts. It was an impossible task. The peltasts had a javelin's-cast distance head-start, and they ran away as soon as they discharged their weapons. When the pursuing hoplites ran out of steam, the peltasts turned back and threw more javelins. Some ran around to the hoplites' unshielded right sides and let fly from there. About nine or ten hoplites were killed outright. The polemarkhos ordered another pursuit, but this time the peltasts killed even more Spartans, and as the peltasts were encouraged by victory the Spartans were discouraged by defeat. By the time the cavalry caught up with the Spartans they had lost most of the younger, stronger hoplites. The return of the cavalry didn't help. For some reason they stayed close to the hoplites and did not pursue the peltasts far enough. This made the peltasts even bolder. Finally, at a loss, the Spartans made a stand on a small hill about two stadia from the sea and about sixteen or seventeen stadia from Lekhaion.

Those in Lekhaion, seeing the Spartans in trouble, sailed out in small boats until they were opposite the hill. By this time it was all over for the Spartan hoplites. As the Athenian hoplites advanced on them and the unrelenting peltasts struck them down from afar with their sharp javelins, they broke formation, some managing to reach the sea, and some managing to get back to Lekhaion with the horsemen. About two hundred and fifty didn't make it.

All the while this had been going on, Agesilaos, quite pleased with himself, had been sitting in a kukloteuous oikodomematos (some kind of circular building), by a small lake, gazing contentedly at the prisoners being led, and anything of value being carried out of the Heraion. Xenophon, who had probably left Skillous to fight by the side of his friend, and was probably on the scene, mentions the presence of "many ambassadors from abroad," who were watching intently as the Spartans led forth their captives. Among the foreign ambassadors were the Boiotians, who had come to talk of peace. Agesilaos, who never forgave the Boiotians for their treatment of him back at Aulis, "especially arrogantly seemed not to see them, even though Pharakos, who was their proxenos [the person in charge of Boiotian interests at Sparta] was standing near them so that he might introduce them."

To Agesilaos all must have seemed right with the world - he'd just won another profitable victory, and even now, on top of that, he had the immediate pleasure of insulting the hated Boiotians. Xenophon says he was still sitting there, "looking like a man who delights in his accomplishments," when a lone horseman came riding toward him on a mount covered with sweat. To those who questioned him he made no answer, but rode straight up to the king, and leaping down from his horse, ran to him. With a look of sadness on his face he told of the fate of the mora stationed at Lekhaion.

"And when he [Agesilaos] heard this, straight away he leaped up from his seat and grabbed his spear." He called a war-council, ordered the rest of the army to eat breakfast and then to follow him as quickly as possible, and set out with his nine tent companions and his three hundred man bodyguard. When he had passed the hot-springs and come out into the plain of Lekhaion, three horsemen came riding up and told him that the bodies had been recovered. Agesilaos rested and then returned to the Heraion.

Next day Agesilaos held a sale of the prisoners and the booty, and finally summoned the Boiotian ambassadors. They had been there the day before when Agesilaos had made his hasty departure, and they knew of the Spartan defeat and the destruction of the mora from Lekhaion. Now when asked why they had come, they made no mention of peace, but merely said that if Agesilaos didn't mind, they would like to join their own army in the city. Agesilaos laughed and said that he knew that they didn't want to see their army as much as they wanted to see how great was the victory of their friends. "'Wait then, he said, 'I myself will take you, and you'll learn more, being with me, of what sort of thing happened.'" As Xenophon says, "he wasn't lying."

The next day Agesilaos sacrificed and led the army to Korinth. He did not tear down the trophy put up by Iphikrates' men, but any fruit-tree he found standing he cut down and burned as a challenge for those inside to come out and fight. No one did. After this he camped at Lekhaion and, refusing to allow the Boiotian ambassadors passage into Korinth, sent them back to Boiotia by ship across the Korinthian Gulf. As for the Spartans, unaccustomed as they were to a defeat of this kind, Xenophon says that "there was much mourning in the Lakonian camp, except for those whose sons or fathers or brothers died at their posts. These men went around as if they were victorious, smiling and delighting in the disaster to their families." Xenophon never mentions the name of the overconfident polemarkhos who was responsible for this terrible defeat, nor does he record his fate.[49]

Agesilaos led the remains of the mauled mora back to Sparta. Iphikrates capitalized on his recent success by defeating the men of Phliasia and then routing the Sikyonioi. The Argives completed their plan to annex Korinth by installing a garrison.

Next year the Athenians managed to bring Byzantion under their wing. Byzantion controlled the grain-route to the Black Sea, and now the Athenians taxed every ship that sailed through the Bosphoros. The ephors sent out a certain Anaxibios to deal with this matter. The Athenians sent out Iphikrates to deal with Anaxibios.

After some initial success, Anaxibios carelessly led his army into an ambush arraigned by Iphikrates. His force of mercenaries and allies was marching in column down a long slope when Iphikrates and his peltasts, many of whom had been in the action at Korinth, came out of nowhere. Realizing that his army was about to be destroyed, Anaxibios took his shield from his hypaspistes, and, admitting that the present situation was his fault, he advised the soldiers to save themselves as best they could. His only recourse was to die with honor. His boyfriend and the twelve Spartans who were with him stayed and went down fighting.

Back in Hellas the Akhaians asked the Spartans for help against the Akarnanians who were being supported by the Boiotians and the Athenians. So Agesilaos spent the summer of

389 in north-west Hellas raiding the lands of the Akarnanians. A large force of peltasts attacked him as he led his army on a narrow road in the mountains. They weren't led by Iphikrates, and Agesilaos was not Anaxibios; he slaughtered about three hundred of them and returned to Sparta loaded with plunder.

Next year, before Agesilaos could invade them again, the Akarnanians made peace with the Akhaians and allied themselves with the Spartans. At the same time, Agesipolis, who had now come of age, led an army against the Argives. He burned all their crops, right up to the walls of Argos, and marched back to Sparta. The Agives didn't dare march out against him. The Athenians, on the other hand, were running rampant in Asia Minor; by now they practically owned all the lands and cities around the Bosphoros, and their ally Euagoras was slowly taking over the whole island of Kypros. Egypt was still in rebellion against the Great King.

All this made the Persian King nervous, and when Antalkidas turned up as admiral of the Spartan fleet in 388, he sent Tiribazos to the coast to talk peace. Since the Great King knew that the Athenians considered themselves on a roll and wouldn't willingly negotiate, he, along with Dionysios, the tyrant of Syrakousai, gave Antalkidas some ships with which to blockage the Hellespont. It was looking like 404 all over again for the Athenians, and they had to give in. So peace was signed according to the King's terms. The Athenians, Argives, and Thebans didn't like it one bit, but since those who didn't submit would have to face the combined forces of the Persians and Spartans, they signed the treaty (387). The Persian King got the Hellenic cities of Asia, the Athenians got to keep Lemnos, Skyros, and Imbros, but the Thebans had to dissolve the Boiotian League, and the Agives had to leave Korinth. The Spartans promptly appointed themselves keepers of the peace.

Now, with everything going their way, the Spartans decided to punish their Mantineian allies, for, as they said, aiding the Argives and being reluctant to fight on Sparta's behalf. They ordered the Mantineians to tear down their city's walls, and when the Mantineians refused, Agesipolis led an army against them. In the end the Mantineians had to tear down their whole city and live in four smaller villages.

The Thebans, under compulsion, had sent a contingent of hoplites to help the Spartans. Hard pressed, and about to be destroyed by the Mantineians, they were rescued at the last minute by Agesipolis. How could the Spartan King have known that he had just saved the lives of the two men who, fifteen years later at the battle of Leuktra, would kill his brother and destroy the power of Sparta forever?

EPAMEINONDAS AND PELOPIDAS

Epameinondas was born into a famous family. Pausanias, who lived in the first half of the second century CE, wrote that "the deeds of his ancestors were a credit to the race," meaning that they were a credit to Thebes and the Thebans. His father, however, was poorer than most. Even so, Epameinondas managed to get a good Theban education and to study with the famous Pythagorean philosopher Lysis. [50]

The family of Pelopidas was also famous, and his father, Hippoklos, was rich. Pelopidas came into his inheritance while still a young man and immediately began to share the wealth with his friends. Epameinondas would have none of it. He was used to being poor, and as a philosopher he liked living the simple life. Because of his poverty he never married (though he did form relationships with younger men), and devoted his leisure time to the study of philosophy. Pelopidas, on the other hand, got married, had kids, and liked nothing better than physical exercise; Plutarch says he spent his time "in the wrestling schools and hunting." Nevertheless, Pelopidas seems to have admired his friend's stoic ways, and since Epameinondas would not share his wealth, Pelopidas shared his friend's poverty. He ate the simple foods that Epameinondas ate and wore the simple clothes that Epameinondas wore, and he imitated his willingness for hard work and his uprightness as a soldier.

Both men were utterly fearless. And while Pelopidas' bravery bordered on recklessness and would be the death of him, the courage of Epameinondas was based on his sense of duty to his polis and his fellow citizens. In the end his calm determination would kill him just as dead as his impulsive friend.

Plutarch says: "most think their strong friendship began when they served together at Mantineia." They were about eighteen years old and part of a Theban contingent sent to help the Spartans against the Mantineians in 385. According to Plutarch they were fighting the Arkadians, probably with other Spartan allies on the left, when their line gave way. Epameinondas and Pelopidas stood firm; like a two man phalanx they fought off the enemy, no doubt stabbing with their spears at any who got too close. It's easier to kill men whose backs are turned in flight than to kill armored men who are determined to resist to the end. Nevertheless, they were attacked,

> and Pelopidas, seven wounds taking in the front, fell down on many corpses, both friends and enemies, and Epameinondas, although lifeless he considered him, over the body and the weapons he stood; and going forward, he made a desperate attempt, one against many, expecting to die rather than leave behind Pelopidas lying there.

Determined to fight to the death, Epameinondas was speared in the chest, and his arm was laid open by a sword-cut. It was, no doubt, a very bloody scene. Plutarch says it was "a thing evilly happening" and that just when they were out of hope Agesipolis came up with the Spartan right wing and saved them both. [51]

THE SEIZURE OF THE KADMEIA

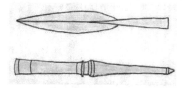

While Epameinondas and Pelopidas were recuperating from their wounds, the Great King of Persia, Artaxerxes II, was busy trying to reconquer Egypt, and things were heating up in the extreme northeastern part of Hellas, at a place called Khalkidike.

The Khalkidian peninsula looks like a hand, lacking a thumb and little finger, with the remaining three fingers widespread, stretching out southeastwardly into the Aegean Sea. Located at the base of the southwesternmost finger, Pellene, was the city of Olynthos. Many of the cities in the area were joined politically as members of the Khalkidian League. Like the Theban-dominated Boiotian League (now defunct in accordance with the terms of the Peace of Antalkidas), and the Spartan dominated Peloponnesian League (now stronger than ever), the cities of the Khalkidian League were dominated by one of their own, namely, Olynthos.

Diodorus says that it was the Makedonian king, Amyntas, driven from his throne by the imperialist Olynthians at the head of the Khalkidian league army, who appealed to Sparta for help to regain his kingdom. Xenophon says that it was the people of Akanthos and Apollonia, cities that were being pressured to join the Khalkidian League, who sent delegates to Sparta, and he records their speech reminding the Spartans how much the Khalkidian League resembled the hated Boiotian League.

According to Xenophon, the Spartans and their allies decided to help the Akanthians and the Appollonians, and they declared war on Olynthos. A certain Eudamidas was put in charge and sent out with a small advance party to establish a Spartan presence in the area and to harm the enemy as best he could. Eudamidas asked the ephors if he could have his brother Phoibidas bring out the rest of the army when it was ready. The ephors consented, and Eudamidas set off for Khalkidike. He immediately won over the city of Poteidaia, on Pellene, not far down the peninsula from Olynthos, and from there conducted the war.

As soon as the rest of the army was collected back in Sparta, Phoibidas marched off. While he was camped outside Thebes, on the way to Olynthos, he was approached by a Theban politician named Leontiades. In return for Spartan help in repressing the party of his opponents (led by Ismenias, who hated the Spartans and had been among those who had taken the Persian King's money to start the Korinthian war), he offered to let Phoibidas and his men into the Akropolis of Thebes, called the Kadmeia. From this position they would command the city; in the words of Leontiades (put into his mouth by Xenophon): "the Thebans will be altogether under the power of the Lakedaimonians and of us your friends... and we will send with you many hoplites and many horsemen so that with a great force you will help your brother." Phoibidas couldn't resist the thought of the glory that would be his if he could pull off this coup, and he agreed to help Leontiades.[52]

It just so happened that it was the Festival of the Thesmophoria, when only women were allowed in the Kadmeia. It was summer 382, it was noon, and the streets were quiet when Leontiades betrayed his city to the Spartans. The women in the Kadmeia probably did not put up much of a fight. Ismenias was arrested, and about three hundred of his followers fled to Athens. Xenophon doesn't really approve of Phoibidas' actions; he calls him "not indeed, logistikos," which really means "he didn't use his brain," and says of Phoibidas, "not at all sensible he seemed to be." [53]

Phoibidas' occupation of the Kadmeia was indeed an aggressive and illegal act; the ephors condemned it, and, recalling Phoibidas back to Sparta, "relieved him of his command and fined him one hundred thousand drakhmai; nevertheless, they held the Kadmeia with a garrison." And Agesilaos said that it was okay for a commander to act without orders if the act turned out to be beneficial to the Spartans. Ismenias was accused of barbarizing, of taking the Persian King's money, and of being the cause of all the troubles in Hellas. He was convicted and executed by the Lakedaimonians and their allies.[54]

Diodorus has a different view of the proceedings. He says that the Spartans gave their commanders orders "in secret, that, if they ever had the opportunity, they should seize the Kadmeia." According to Diodorus, Phoibidas was sent out first, but on his way to Olynthos stopped off at Thebes and occupied the Kadmeia, was then recalled by the ephors and replaced by his brother Eudamidas, who was then sent out to Olynthos. [38]

Plutarch also blames the Spartans, who, he says, "especially hated the party of Ismenias and Androkleidas, to which Pelopidas belonged." It was too "freedom-loving and democratic." And he goes on to say that "the deed was Phoibidas', but the plan was Agesilaos'." It was, in fact, a sound move as far as Spartan foreign policy went. There were Theban ambassadors at Olynthos at that very moment, and an alliance between Thebes and Olynthos would undoubtedly have been bad news for the Spartans.[39]

Now Xenophon was there when all this happened, and Plutarch and Diodorus hadn't even been born yet. So you might want to believe Xenophon because he was practically an eyewitness. You might not want to believe Diodorus because he doesn't seem to be very critical of his sources. Remember the story about the chasm at Delphi? But even though Diodorus lived hundreds of years after the fact, he used as his source the historian Ephorus (c.405-330), a pupil of the great orator Isocrates (436-338), who was a contemporary of Xenophon (c.430-355), and Ephorus probably used as his source his own contemporary, the historian Kallisthenes (?-327, Aristotle's nephew). And we have to take into account the fact that Ephorus favored the Athenians and wrote his history accordingly (which is reflected in the pages of Diodorus), and Xenophon favored the Spartans and, while not actually changing history, omitted things which were distasteful to him and which he couldn't bring himself to include.

But you might want to believe Plutarch (keeping in mind that he also used Ephorus), especially when you consider that an unofficial take-over of the Kadmeia was beneficial to the Spartans, who, as stated above, refuted the act but did not reverse it, and when you consider the fact that Agesilaos had never forgiven the Thebans for their treatment of him at Aulis, fourteen years before. In any case, Thebes was in Spartan hands, and the Olynthians were next on the list.

All the while this had been going on Eudamidas had been fighting the Olynthians, or, according to which ancient account you believe, he was sent out shortly after the ephors recalled Phoibidas, and then engaged the Olynthians. Everybody seems to agree on what happened next.

Agesilaos' brother Teleutias, whose daring naval victories in the Korinthian war (which unfortunately lie outside the scope of this book), had made him a famous warrior among a nation of warriors, was sent out at the head of ten thousand men to defeat the Olynthians and demolish the Khalkidian league (382). He enjoyed some initial successes, but in the spring of the following year (381) he became annoyed at the sight of some Olynthian cavalry that had fearlessly come up close to his army while he was busy destroying the Olynthians' crops. He ordered his peltasts to chase them away, and when they turned on the peltasts and killed their leader, Tlemonidas, and more then a hundred of his men, Teleutias lost his temper, armed himself, led out the whole army, cavalry, peltasts, and hoplites, and pursued the Olynthians too close to their city wall. Xenophon takes up the story: "And many others, beyond measure, very near the walls pursuing, evilly retreated, and these men, when from the towers they were being struck, were forced to retreat confusedly and to ward off the missiles." Teleutias' pursuit came to an abrupt halt as a shower of arrows, javelins, and sling-stones struck his men. The Olynthian peltasts and cavalry rallied and charged out at them, and the

Olynthian hoplites followed. Softened up by the arrows of the archers and the sharp javelins of the cavalry and peltasts, the Spartan line gave way before the attack of the Olynthian hoplites. "And Teleutias, there fighting, was killed." At his death the rest of his army scattered and fled.

In reference to this Xenophon has a lesson for us all:

> Surely, from these sort of experiences, I say, men learn especially that one must not, indeed, punish a household slave in anger. For often masters, being angry, have suffered greater evils then they have inflicted. Still more, for those fighting, to attack in anger but not with reasoning is a complete mistake. For anger is unforeseeing, but reason considers no less that it might not suffer anything than how it might somehow hurt the enemy.[57]

In other words an angry man does not foresee the consequences of his actions, but a man following a reasoned course of action provides as much for his own safety as for the destruction of his enemy.

The Spartans calmly received the news of Teleutias' defeat and death. In council they decided that the Olynthians' high spirits needed to be lowered and that a small force wouldn't be enough, so they sent out another royal personage and another army.

Agesipolis, gathering allies as he went, arrived outside Olynthos in the spring of 380 with such a huge force that the Olynthians didn't dare march out against him. He destroyed whatever bits of the surrounding countryside that Teleutias had missed and then went on to ravage the lands around the cities allied with Olynthos. He took by force the town of Torone on the peninsula of Sithonia to the north. While all this was going on Agesipolis got sick. It was the height of summer, and he was running a high fever. "As before he had seen in Aphytis the temple of Dionysos, a desire for its shady precincts and shining, cool waters seized him. He was brought there, still living; nevertheless, indeed on the seventh day from when he got sick, outside the temple, he died." The average Spartan was usually buried not far from where he expired, but not so the Spartan kings. The body of Agesipolis was preserved in honey and brought back to Sparta for a kingly burial. [58]

Agesilaos cried when he heard the news of his fellow king's death. Politically speaking they hadn't always seen eye to eye, but the Spartan kings ate together and may have even lived together when they were at home, and Agesipolis and Agesilaos had gotten to be pretty chummy. The younger king always treated Agesilaos with respect, and they also had quite a bit in common. They were both fond of hunting, horses, and young men. Plutarch seems to think they even partied together. Agesilaos truly missed his young friend.

The Spartans had now lost a king and king's brother in the war against Olynthos, and Diodorus tells us what happened after Agesipolis died. "Having received the sovereignty, Kleombrotos, his brother, was king nine years. And the Lakedaimonioi, appointing Polybiadas strategos, sent him away to the Olynthian war. This man, receiving his command and actively and commandingly managing the war, had many victories." [59]

The Spartans sent out Polybiades because Agesilaos was busy trying to restore the Spartan-friendly oligarchs to the town of Phlios from whence they had been exiled by the democrats. He eventually succeeded after a long siege. Meanwhile, Polybiadas defeated the Olynthians in the field and laid siege to Olynthos. Blockaded by land and sea, the Olynthians could only starve or surrender. They sent ambassadors to Sparta and in the end became subjects and allies of the Spartans.

Diodorus says:

> And with the Olynthians registered in the alliance of the Spartans, many of the other cities sought eagerly to serve under the hegemony of

the Lakedaimonians. Wherefore in these critical times the Lakedaimonioi held the greatest strength and the hegemony of Hellas both on land and on the sea. For the Thebaioi were garrisoned, the Korinthioi and the Argeioi, because of the recent war, were humbled, and the Athenaioi were getting a [bad] reputation among the Hellenes because of their kleroukhias [imposed on] those whom [they had] defeated.[60]

A kleroukhia was a bunch of Athenians who were settled by Athens on the land of some state that had been unfortunate enough to come under their sway, one way or another, and most of the places that had kleroukhiai didn't really want them. The Spartans were now sought as allies by Dionysios, the powerful Tyrannos of Syrakousai. (Yeah, that's where we get the word 'tyrant' from; only for the Hellenes it just meant a man who had seized power unconstitutionally. In those days there were good and bad Tyrannoi.) As Xenophon says, "Things having gone well for the Lakedaimonioi...now beautifully and firmly the sovereignty seemed to them to be built."[61] But things were about to take a turn for the worse.

THE LIBERATION OF THEBES

Xenophon gives a moral explanation for the events that followed the occupation of Thebes:

Many other things someone might be able to mention, both Hellenika and barbarika, [in reference to] how the gods don't overlook those who are impious and who do unholy things. Now, indeed, I will speak of the matter lying before us. For the Lakedaimonioi [after] swearing oaths to allow the cities autonomy, holding onto the akropolis in Thebes, at the hands of the very men alone [i.e. the Thebans] who were treated unjustly, were punished, and [with respect to] those of the [Theban] citizens who led the Lakedaimonioi into the akropolis and planned to surrender the polis to the Lakedaimonioi so that they themselves could rule as tyrannoi, only seven of the exiles were strong enough to bring down their administration.[62]

As with the seizure of the Kadmeia, there are conflicting accounts of its recapture and the subsequent liberation of Thebes. Plutarch and Xenophon are our principle sources, and they disagree in detail and about certain key events. Plutarch has the liberators of Thebes split into two groups, to deal with their enemies simultaneously; Xenophon's liberators, all in one group, kill their enemies sequentially. Pelopidas is a leader in Plutarch, but Xenophon doesn't even mention him.

Plutarch includes the story of the liberation of Thebes in his *Life of Pelopidas*. Did he make up the story of the two bands of liberators in order to give Pelopidas a leading role? Plutarch didn't write history as we nowadays expect it to be written. He was a bit less interested in the facts and more interested in the moral of the story. His *Life of Pelopidas* is the story of a patriotic man who helped to raise his country to the heights of power and glory and then threw away his life foolishly and in so doing deprived his fatherland of his further services. It was coupled with the story of the Roman Consul Marcellus, who also died needlessly (doing the job of a cavalry scout when he should have been doing the job of a general), just when his country needed him most. Did Plutarch stretch the facts to increase the stature of his protagonist?

On the other hand (which is a good old Hellenic expression which looks like δε in the ancient tongue), Xenophon undoubtedly hated the very name of Pelopidas because he had led the Theban charge at Leuktra (371), which destroyed Sparta's ambitions forever, and may have failed to mention him on that account. He also conveniently forgot the name of the Spartan harmost who lost the Kadmeia and was fined a ruinous sum. But he also lived while these things were happening, and Plutarch didn't. What follows is a combination of the two accounts.

Pelopidas, Androkleidas, and the rest of the Theban exiles had fled to Athens and were officially banished by Leontiades and his fellow revolutionaries Arkias and Philippos who now held power in Thebes. They had probably each assumed the title of Polemarkhos, which means war-leader, no doubt attempting to legitimize their tyrannical rule. The polemarkhs were normally out-ranked by the boiotarkhs, but I suppose that a polemarkhos with a Spartan garrison in his hand is worth more than a Boiotarkh with an Athenian army in the bush. Epameinondas was allowed to remain in Thebes unmolested since Leontiades and his fellow tyrannoi considered him nothing more than a poor philosopher.

The Spartans sent letters to the Athenians urging them not to receive and not to encourage the Theban exiles but to drive them out since they had been proclaimed common enemies by the allies. I suppose that the allies in this case were all the poleis that had signed the treaty of Antalkidas and were now really dominated by the Spartans, including the new rulers of Thebes. The Athenians ignored the Spartan injunction; Plutarch says it was not only because of their "ancestral and inborn philanthropy," but also because the Thebans had helped them overthrow the oligarchy installed by Sparta as a consequence of the Peloponnesian War.[63] In fact, the liberators of Athens had hidden out in Thebes just as now the would-be liberators of Thebes were hiding out in Athens.

But the Spartans and the new rulers of Thebes didn't stop at letter writing. Leontiades sent assassins, "men unknown," who killed Androkleidas "by treachery" but failed to kill any of the others.[64] This may have been the wake-up call for the rest of the fugitives, who had been wined and dined by the best of Athenian high society since their arrival. In Plutarch's account it is Pelopidas, "although he was among the youngest," who, privately and collectively, urged his fellow phugades forward for the liberation of their homeland.[65] In any case, secret letters were sent to their friends in Thebes, and a plan was worked out. A man named Phillidas "managed to become scribe to the polemarkhs Arkhias and Philippos."[66] This Phillidas also shows up in Xenophon's story where he meets one of the exiles named Melon while on a business trip to Athens. It is not unreasonable to suppose that Phillidas' real business was the liberation of Thebes.

A date was set for the deed. At the end of their term of office the Polemarkhs always celebrated a festival of Aphrodite, and for this year's festival Phillidas was making all the arraignments. For months he had been promising Arkhias and his boys the most beautiful women in Thebes as their dates for the festival, and they were eagerly looking forward to it.

Leontiades, Arkhias, and their fellow oligarchs must have been quite distracted by their anticipation of the forthcoming Aphrodisia (Xenophon says that "they were this sort of men"[67]), for they failed even to suspect in the least the machinations of Phillidas, and they seemed to have been equally unaware of the activities of Epameinondas, who hung about the gymnasia urging the young men to wrestle with their Spartan guests in order to show them that the Spartans weren't that tough. He told them that they should be ashamed of themselves, to allow men whom they had beaten in wrestling to hold their city in thrall. For two and a half years they had been subject to the oligarchs and the Spartans, but now it was the winter of 379 and things were about to change.

A few days before the big party, as Plutarch tells it, Pelopidas, Melon, and ten others set out for Thebes disguised as hunters, with dogs and nets so that anyone whom they should meet on the road would not suspect their real purpose. Xenophon just mentions Melon and six others. He says they got to "the place at night. Then they spent the day in a deserted place."[68] They sent a messenger on ahead to inform a man named Kharon that they were on their way. Kharon had offered to hide them in his house until it was time to act.

Plutarch tells what happened next:

> Kharon, did not, at the approaching danger, turn away from the plan, for he was a noble man and he prepared his house, but a certain Hipposthenidas, not a worthless man, but a patriot and a man well-disposed towards the Phugades but deficient in the sort of courage, as much as, this being a desperate opportunity, the matters to be undertaken demanded, as if he had become dizzy before the greatness of the contest being in his hands [liable to happen] quite at any

time, by a reckoning, having considered that in a manner they were shaking the hegemony of the Lakedaimonians and that they were attempting to dislodge an armed force from that place [Thebes] trusting in the hopes of men without means and in exile, going home in silence, he sent one of his friends to Melos and Pelopidas advising them to postpone [things] for the present and, going back to Athens, to wait for a better opportunity. Khlidon was the name of the man sent, and with haste toward his home he turned his steps, and leading out his horse he asked for the bit and bridle. His wife was at a loss, since she did not have [it] to give, saying she had lent it to one of the neighbors; abuse first there was, then words of ill omen, his wife cursing him and those who sent him with evil roads, and so Khlidon, using up much of the day upon these things through anger, and at the same time from [this] chance event taking omens, gave up the journey altogether and did something else. So close they came, the greatest and most beautiful of deeds, right at the beginning, to missing the opportunity.[69]

While Khlidon and his wife were arguing, Pelopidas and the other exiles were entering the city at different points, now dressed as farmers and mingling with the real farmers who were coming in late from the fields. It was still daylight, but as it was snowing and windy nobody noticed them except those who were expecting them. They spent the night and the next day at Kharon's house. On the second night after their arrival the party began.

This kind of party was called a symposion, which translated literally comes out as "together drinking." If you were a guest at a symposion, you'd be in the men's room (to andron, though in this case Xenophon says the party was at the Polemarkheion, which might mean a public building or just the house of the present Polemarkh), reclining on a couch, with some kind of festive wreath on your head, drinking wine served by good-looking slaves (male or female), in a rather large, shallow cup called a kylix, which would probably be painted with erotic scenes. When you got to the bottom of the cup you might find a depiction of two men, or a man and a woman, or a group of people engaged in some kind of amorous activity. There were always entertainments at symposia. Flute girls might play while a juggler performed, or there might be a slightly drunken philosophical discussion. Since this particular symposion was supposed to be an Aphrodisia, a festival of Aphrodite, the entertainment was going to be ta Aphrodisia, or "the things of Aphrodite," which meant sex.

For a long time now, probably some months at least, Phillidas had been promising to bring the best looking hetairai in Thebes to the party. Hetairai were high-priced call-girls. They were not street-walkers and were probably prized as much for their ability with regard to intellectual stimulation as for their talents respecting any other type of stimulation. Since hetairai moved in the highest circles of Hellenic society they probably had a lot to talk about, as opposed to the average wife, whose life mainly consisted of marrying a man older than herself, bearing him children (especially male children), and then running the household. (The Hellenic word for "running the household" is "oikonomia"; that's where we get the word "economics.") In any case Arkhias and his buddies were about to have a rude and, in fact fatal awakening, for Phillidas' call girls were in reality the Theban exiles who expected to make short, bloody work of their drunken enemies.

However, the party had just started, and nobody was drunk yet, when someone showed up and said that the exiles had returned and were hiding somewhere in the city. Phillidas did his best to distract Arkhias and change the subject, but Arkhias nevertheless sent one of his servants to Kharon's house asking him to come right over. Now Xenophon doesn't mention this, and one wonders why, of all people, Kharon was summoned. Is this just a dramatic fiction of Plutarch's, or was

Kharon suspect, possibly because he was known as a friend of Melon or one of the other exiles? Whatever the reason, Plutarch tells us that it was evening and that the exiles had already put on breastplates and were strapping on their swords, when the messenger arrived at Kharon's house. "Suddenly a knocking at the door, someone running forward and learning from the servant saying [that] he had come for Kharon from the Polemarkhs, he went inside confused and gave the message."[70]

Most of the exiles believed themselves betrayed and the plot exposed, but they decided that "it was necessary" for Kharon to obey the summons and present himself to the polemarkhs without hesitation as if all were normal; after all they had no real idea why the Polemarkhs had sent for Kharon; it could be anything, and if they panicked now, the whole enterprise could fail. So they decided to play it cool and send Kharon over to see what Arkias wanted.[71]

Kharon, "taking from the women's quarters his son, still a boy, but in beauty and in strength of body being first of those of his age, put him in the hands of those around Pelopidas, saying that if any deceit and treachery of him [Kharon] was discovered, to treat this one [his son] as an enemy and not to spare him." At this, moved by the "pathos" of the scene and by the spirit of Kharon, many of the exiles started to cry. And Plutarch says "they were all irritated" that Kharon should think any of them "cowardly and broken by the present circumstances so that they would suspect him," and they begged him not to get his son mixed up in the plot, but to send him out of the way so he could grow up to be the avenger of his city and his dear ones. This Kharon refused to do, asking what sort of life could be more beautiful for his son than death with his father in such fine company. "So, praying to the gods and hugging and encouraging all of them, he went away, self consciously arraigning the form of his face and the pitch of his voice to appear very unlike what he was doing."[72]

When Kharon arrived at the symposion, he was met outside by Arkhias and Phillidas. They informed him of the rumor that the exiles had returned and were hiding somewhere in the city and that some of the citizens were helping them. According to Plutarch "Kharon was thrown into confusion at first," but, quickly recovering his composure, asked who were the exiles and who were their accomplices among the citizens. When he saw that Arkhias knew nothing for certain, Kharon realized that "from no one of those in the know had been the information; 'look at this now,' he said, 'some empty word should not trouble you. Nevertheless, I'll look into it.'" Phillidas agreed, and leading Arkhias back inside, "much unmixed [wine] he threw down." (The ancients mixed their wine with water in a big mixing bowl called a krater, and I suppose that Plutarch either means that Phillidas threw much unmixed wine down Arkhias' gullet, or that Arkhias himself threw the wine down his own gullet; in any case Arkhias ended up drunk, as we shall soon see). Kharon returned to his own home to find everyone resigned to their supposed betrayal and ready to die gloriously "with much slaughter of their enemies."[73]

Meanwhile, back at the symposion, another messenger arrived. This man came from Athens with a letter for Arkhias from a hierophantes (a priest who teaches ritual), who was a guest-friend of Arkhias and who also happened to be named Arkhias. This letter actually contained detailed information of the plot. The messenger was brought to Arkhias, and handing him the letter said, "He who sent this urges [you] to read [it] immediately, for about something serious it is written." But Arkhias was now quite drunk. He smiled and said, "Oukoun eis aurion ta spoudaia," which means "in that case, for tomorrow the serious stuff." He stuffed the letter under a cushion and forgot about it, resuming his conversation with Phillidas, who, come to think of it, may have been sharing his couch, as was common for men at a symposion, and so therefore would have been in a perfect position to help Arkhias get drunk. Sort of like a mob hit in the movies. It's always somebody whom the victim considers beyond suspicion who betrays him. Plutarch says of Arkhias' reply, "These words, preserved as a proverb, are used even today among the Hellenes."[74]

After this the party got a little rowdier, with Arkhias and his guests calling for the hetairai. Phillidas went out to get them. He returned with Melon and his men, dressed as women and wearing thick crowns of silver fir and pine, which in the low light of oil lamps hid their young, beardless faces in shadow. To the drunken guests they were merely the realization of their expectations. Xenophon says that three of them were dressed as housewives and the rest as maids. They stood in the foyer ignoring the drunken applause that greeted them and refusing to enter until the servants were dismissed. Phillidas gave the servants wine and sent them away. Xenophon says that each one of the hetaira/assassins sat down next to his victim, while Plutarch says that they stood in the door and surveyed the room; then drawing their swords and revealing themselves they rushed "through the tables for Arkhias and Philippos."[75] Whichever way it happened it must have been a bloody scene: Everybody's lying around on couches, drunk and expecting to have a good time, when suddenly a bunch of call-girls whip out swords and start stabbing Arkhias and Philippos, while Phillidas tries to keep the rest of the party-goers on their couches and quiet. Unarmed and inebriated, Arkhias and Philippos were no doubt cut and stabbed until they were dead. All who resisted were also quickly cut down. The andron must have been awash with blood, the couches soaked, the floor wet with spilled wine, water, and blood.

Xenophon says that Phillidas and some of the others went next to Leontiades' house, but Plutarch says that it was Pelopidas who led the attack on Leontiades. He writes, "A more difficult task presented itself to those with Pelopidas: for they were going after a sober and clever man, Leontiades, and they found his house shut." In Plutarch's version of the story Leontiades is already asleep when the exiles reach his house. They knock on the door for a long time, until one of Leontiades' servants opens it. As he raises the wooden bar and opens the door the exiles push their way in, thrust the servant aside, and rush toward the bedroom. Leontiades, awakened by the commotion and hearing the sound of running, realizes what is happening, gets out of bed, and pulls out a dagger. "But," Plutarch says, "he forgot to throw down the lamps," which would have plunged the room into darkness and confused his attackers. With lights blazing, Leontiades, "rushing violently, met them before the doors of his bedroom, and striking the first one coming in, Kephisodoros, he threw him down." Kephisodoros is dead from one blow, and Pelopidas is right behind him. Pelopidas and Leontiades fight in the narrow doorway, stumbling over the corpse of Kephisodoros. One can only imagine the desperate grappling and stabbing in that confined space. After a hard fight Pelopidas kills Leontiades.[40]

The exiles next went after Leontiades' neighbor, Hypates. They broke into his house in the same way as they had gained entry to Leontiades' house, and in the same way Hypates heard them and, being somewhat less resolute than the late Leontiades, he went out the back door while they were coming in the front. But Pelopidas and his boys were young and fast. They caught Hypates before he got too far and killed him, no doubt quite bloodily.

Xenophon tells a slightly different story: Phillidas, taking three men, went to the house of Leontiades. Knocking on the door he said that he had a message from the Polemarkhs. Leontiades was reclining after having had dinner, and his wife was sitting next to him, knitting. Suspecting nothing, since he trusted Phillidas, he asked him to come in. Phillidas and his men came in and killed him. They told his wife to be quiet or they would kill every one in the house.

The exiles now went to the Anakeion, the temple of Kastor and Pollux, where the late tyrannoi had imprisoned some of the citizens whom they had felt needed to be imprisoned. They killed the guard and released the prisoners. Then they went around town taking down the weapons that were hanging in public places, stoai (colonnades) and such, as trophies. Plutarch says they also broke into the workshops of those who made swords and spears. Epameinondas and Gorgidas joined them, "having assembled not a few of the young men and the best of the old men."[77] They gathered at the shrine of Amphion and sent messages to the rest of the exiles who were waiting outside the city and to a force of Athenians, perhaps volunteers, who were just beyond the border. They also made loud proclamation of what they had done, calling on all the citizens to come out and fight for freedom. Since it was night, and nobody could really tell what was going on, most people stayed indoors and waited to see what would happen.

Plutarch blames the Spartan harmostes (governor) for not mobilizing his fifteen hundred men and counter-attacking when he had the chance, but the Spartans just sent messengers to Sparta apprising them of the situation and to Plataia, asking for support, and waited for daylight.

As dawn broke over the ancient city of Thebes, priests led Epameinondas, Pelopidas, Gorgidas, and their men into the assembly and "urged the citizens to help the fatherland and the gods."[78] They got a standing ovation, and Pelopidas, Melon, and Kharon were elected boiotarkhs. Kharon led the Theban cavalry, which met the Plataians who were coming up to support the Spartans, and killing more than twenty, sent them back to Plataia in a hurry.

Xenophon says that when the cavalry returned and the Athenians arrived, the Thebans laid siege to the Kadmeia, and the garrison, seeing the enthusiasm of the attackers, sued for peace.

Plutarch doesn't go into detail, merely recording that the Akropolis was surrounded and assaulted as quickly as possible so that it could be taken before the Spartan relief force could arrive, and that the garrison was "sent forth under a treaty."[79]

Diodorus, on the other hand, has a grander story to tell. The Lakedaimonians and their allies, numbering fifteen hundred, fought back and "those besiegers, many they killed, and not a few they wounded." The Thebans sent ambassadors to Athens, and the Athenians "voted on the spot to send off as powerful a force as they could for the freedom of the Thebans."

And "likewise from the other cities throughout Boiotia many soldiers came running, and quickly a great force was gathered for the Thebans, for hoplites came together not less than ten thousand and two thousand and horse more than two thousand." They assaulted the Kadmeia "day and night."

And those in the Kadmeia, garrisoning, called upon by their leaders, strongly warded off the enemy, hoping [that] shortly the Lakedaimonians would come with a great force. So while they had food sufficient they held out against the dangers, and many of the besiegers they killed and wounded, having as a helper the strength of the akropolis. But as the lack of necessities increased... [and as there was still no sign of the relief force] ...they quarreled with one another. The Lakedaimonians thought it necessary to hold out as far as death, but those of the allied cities fighting with them, being many more, declared[that they were for] handing over the Kadmeia. And those from Sparta itself, being few, were compelled to retire from the Kadmeia. Therefore, these men, making a treaty, and under terms, gave up and went back to the Peloponnesos."[80]

Xenophon says that, "as they went out, as many as they [the Thebans] recognized as being of [their] enemies [i.e., those who, like Leontiades, had aided the Spartans - in this case the aristocratic party of Thebes] seizing, they killed." Some managed to get away and were saved by the Athenians, but, "they, indeed, the Thebans, even the children of those being dead, as many as there were, seizing, they cut their throats."[81]

By this time the Spartans had received the messengers from the besieged garrison and had called out the army. Agesilaos was now about sixty-three years old and, according to Spartan law, was no longer subject to military service outside

84

the boundaries of Spartan territory. Using his age as an excuse, for some reason or another, he declined to lead the army, so Kleombrotos was given his first command.

The retreating Spartans and their allies met Kleombrotos and the relief force at Megara, about twenty-five miles from Thebes. Plutarch says that two of the Spartan harmostes were executed and a third "fined so much money, himself from the Peloponnesos he removed."[41] Diodorus agrees with Plutarch (they probably both got their information from Ephorus), but Xenophon just mentions that the Spartans killed the harmost and called out the army against Thebes. Kleombrotos went on into Theban territory.

It was the middle of winter, and the Athenian Khabrias just happened to be guarding the road to Eleutherai with a body of peltasts, so Kleombrotos took the road to Plataia, which also led into Theban territory. At the top of the pass over Mt. Kithairon Kleombrotos' peltasts ran into the men who had been imprisoned by Leontiades and his followers and who had been released by Pelopidas and his followers. They had probably been better off in prison, for the Spartan peltasts killed just about all one hundred and fifty of them.

Kleombrotos marched to Plataia, then to Thespiai, then to a place called Kynoskephalai, or "the heads of the dog," deep in Theban territory, and camped there for about two weeks. He probably spent most of this time just trying to feed his army. And, since it was the dead of winter, his army must have spent much of its time trying to stay warm. Kleombrotos does not seem to have been too eager to engage the Thebans. He may have been waiting for the Thebans to send out someone to talk to him so that he could resolve the situation diplomatically and thus gain some political influence at Sparta. Xenophon doesn't report any negotiations, but that doesn't mean they didn't happen. If they did, nothing came of it.

After camping at Kynoskephalai for sixteen days, Kleombrotos went back to Thespiai. There he left a Spartan named Sphodrias as harmostes. He gave him some of the allied troops and all the money he had brought from Sparta with which to hire a force of mercenaries. Then Kleombrotos marched back to Sparta.

While this was going on the Athenians had second thoughts about helping the Thebans. There was, after all, a huge army of Spartans and their allies, led by one of the Spartan kings, sitting within striking distance of Attika, and they were sure that the Spartans were not happy over the loss of the Kadmeia, and they, the Athenians themselves, were partially responsible for it. So they quickly brought to trial the two strategoi who had led the Athenian forces at Thebes. One strategos wisely decided to leave town, and he was officially banished. The other went to trial, was condemned and executed.

In those days execution in Athens meant one of three things: if you were lucky you got to pinein koneion, that is, to drink poison, like Sokrates did in 399; if you weren't that lucky you were thrown into an abyss. There was also the tympanon, which usually means "drum," but could mean wheel, or stick, or drum-stick. No one really knows how the tympanon was used to kill a person, but when one remembers that the Hellenic idea of punishment and revenge was exactly the opposite of the Christian ethic of turning one's cheek, one can only speculate that it was harsher than both the poisoning and the precipitating methods.

Things must have looked bad for the Thebans now, considering the Athenian about-face and the recent unopposed invasion of their homeland, but Pelopidas and Gorgidas, the latter now also, according to Plutarch, a boiotarkhes, had a clever plan.

SPHODRIAS

Plutarch's Sphodrias is a brilliant soldier but possessed of a rather shallow intellect. When approached by a certain businessman, who is also a friend of Pelopidas and Gorgidas, who offers him money and fame and a guarantee of Theban neutrality if he should march on the Peiraieus, he takes the bait, as the saying goes, hook, line, and sinker.

Expecting fame and fortune if he should seize the port of Athens, Sphodrias left Thespiai at night and marched towards the Peiraieus. At dawn he was still ten miles away from his objective and now had lost the element of surprise. No doubt the emissary of Pelopidas and Gorgidas had neglected to mention that the trip from Thespiai to the Peiraieus would take more than the space of one night. After burning a few houses and stealing a few cows, Sphodrias turned back towards Thespiai.

Diodorus says that it was Kleombrotos who "persuaded Sphodriades to seize ton Peiraia."[83] Perhaps Agesilaos' fellow king was attempting to rehabilitate himself in the eyes of his countrymen after his rather non-productive foray into Boiotia. A successful seizure of the port of Athens would have made up for the loss of the Kadmeia and perhaps would have boosted Kleombrotos' popularity. (Remember, the political systems of the Hellenic states resembled and influenced our own two-party system. Most Hellenic states had an aristocratic party and a democratic party [unofficial – nobody signed up like you do today], but the Hellenic states were divided along class lines, more or less like the USA today, always at odds with one another, and you might want to think of this factionalism as Republicans vs. Democrats, although the Hellenes often went from words to weapons in their political contests. The Spartan double kingship was also a type of two-party system, but rather more like Republicans vs. Republicans.)

The Athenians, getting wind of Sphodrias' expedition, stood to arms and also arrested the Spartan ambassadors, who happened to be in Athens, no doubt denouncing the present government of Thebes for killing the former government of Thebes, and who were, predictably enough, staying at the house of their proxenos, Kallias.

In the Hellas of those days states did not maintain embassies in other countries as we do today. There was no Spartan embassy in Athens and vice versa. Diplomatic ties were maintained privately by certain families and were passed down from generation to generation. Thus Kallias and his family were the proxenoi of the Spartans at Athens, and at Sparta some Spartan and his family would be the proxenoi of the Athenians. And somebody else would be the proxenos of the Thebans, and somebody else would be the proxenos of the Korinthians and so on and so forth.

The Spartan ambassadors were just as surprised as the Athenians when they heard what Sphodrias had done. They told the Athenians that if they had known about the attempt on the Peiraieus they would not have been so stupid as to be hanging around waiting to be arrested, and they certainly wouldn't have been at the house of their proxenos, which was the first place anyone would look for them. They said that it would soon become clear that the polis of the Lakedaimonians had not known of this, and that they would soon hear of the death of Sphodrias at the hands of the state. The Athenians believed them and let them go. The ephors recalled Sphodrias and indicted him on a capital charge. He was smart enough not to show up in court. Things now looked very bad for Sphodrias, but love was to be his savior.

Sphodrias had a son named Kleonymos who was just at that age that the ancients found most attractive in a male, "being just out of childhood," and he was known both for his beauty and for his noble character.[84] Now Agesilaos had a son too, named Arkhidamos, and Arkhidamos was in love with

Kleonymos. The Spartan kings were political rivals and each had their respective supporters, and since Sphodrias belonged to the party of Kleombrotos everybody expected that Agesilaos and his party would demand blood, and, being the stronger party, no one wanted to deny them what they wanted. But Sphodrias asked Kleonymos to ask Arkhidamos to ask Agesilaos to go easy on him. Kleonymos and Arkhidamos were having dinner in the Philition, or public dinning room, when Kleonymos, in tears, begged Arkhidamos to save his father. Arkhidamos started crying too, and confessed to his friend, "I am not able to look my father in the face..." (Agesilaos was no doubt a stern parent. He had been raised as a common Spartan and so had endured all the sufferings and wounds of the average Spartan warrior. He was a frugal, well disciplined soldier whose lifestyle was beyond reproach, and he probably expected everyone else, especially his relatives, to be just like him. And he was the King. He must have been hell to live with. No wonder his son was afraid to approach him, even more so when everybody knew that Sphodrias had done a really stupid and criminal thing.) Nevertheless, Arkhidamos could not say no, and he told Kleonymos: "believe that I shall willingly do everything I can to do this for you!"[85]

It took a while for Arkhidamos to get up the nerve to approach his father on this subject. He'd get up early in the morning and wait for Agesilaos to leave the house, but before he could get to him, someone else would approach the king, and Arkhidamos would lose his nerve. Just as he'd regain his resolve someone else would come up to Agesilaos, and Arkhidamos would have to wait all over again. This went on for a couple of days, and since he had no good news to bring Kleonymos, Arkhidamos stayed away.

Kleonymos and his father, seeing that Arkhidamos, who before had been hanging around Kleonymos constantly, was now nowhere to be found, thought that Arkhidamos had already approached his father and been punished for it. Agesilaos, on the other hand, suspected what it was that kept his son at his heels, but said nothing of it.

Finally Arkhidamos got a chance to speak to his father. He told him that Kleonymos had asked him to ask him to pardon his father. Agesilaos didn't blame him for asking, but, he said, he couldn't see how he could pardon a man who, as everybody knew, had done wrong. Arkhidamos couldn't argue with the logic of that and went away. But he didn't give up. Later on he tried again, saying that if Sphodrias had done nothing wrong, he knew that Agesilaos would pardon him, but now, even though he had committed a crime, couldn't Agesilaos pardon him for the sake of his son? Agesilaos answered rather cryptically, "Then, if it is likely to be a good thing for us, thus it will be."[86]

Arkhidamos didn't consider this good news and went away hardly hoping for the best, but somehow word reached the friends of Sphodrias that Agesilaos was going around saying to anybody who asked him his opinion of the matter that although it was impossible that Sphodrias was not guilty, it was a hard thing to kill a man who, as a boy, young man, and adult had continuously served the best interests of the Spartan state. "Sparta has need of such soldiers." Since Agesilaos practically ran the state, ephors and gerousia notwithstanding, and Kleombrotos was in Sphodrias' corner, Sphodrias was acquitted. Kleonymos rushed to see Arkhidamos and told him, "you'll never be ashamed of our friendship." Indeed, both Sphodrias and Kleonymos would repay their benefactors in blood.[87]

THE FORMATION OF THE SACRED BAND OF THEBES

Meanwhile, back in Thebes, Gorgidas "first organized" the Sacred Band of Thebes, turning a popular military theory of the day into physical fact.[88]   This theory, as expounded by Xenophon, states that, "the strongest army would be composed of παιδικων [there's no way to literally translate this word without making it sound bad; "favorite boys" would be an accurate translation. But these guys weren't children. See the note for the original text.] and lovers."[89]   And the Sacred Band of Thebes was formed of one hundred and fifty male couples; it was, as Plato would say, "an army of lovers."[90] But the idea of a picked force of three hundred chosen men was not a new one in Thebes. Diodorus, writing about the battle of Delion (424), says of the Boiotian army, "fighting in front of all [were] those called the charioteers (heniokhoi) and warriors (parabatai, literally "men who stand beside"), three hundred chosen men."[9] The Sacred Band was maintained and trained at the state's expense and quartered on the Kadmeia, possibly as a precaution against any repetition of the Phoibidas affair.

   The words that historians translate as Sacred Band are Hieros Lokhos.   Hieros is usually translated as "holy" or "sacred," but it could also mean "dedicated." Lokhos is used of a military unit. "Hieros Lokhos" is always translated as "Sacred Band," but the real meaning of the phrase might be more correctly rendered as "The Dedicated Company," because the three hundred men in the Hieros Lokhos were dedicated to each other. They had taken what basically amounted to marriage vows at the tomb of Iolaos, the supposed beloved of Herakles.

Whether this was true of Diodorus' heniokhoi kai parabatai is not known.

While this sort of marriage (today we might call it a gay marriage), didn't turn heads in Thebes, where according to Xenophon "man and boy being paired together, marry," it certainly was not considered proper in Sparta, although, if we believe the ancient historians, though the rules according to Lykourgos regarding physical contact between male lovers were pretty strict, they don't seem to have always been observed. [92] Nor was it condoned at Athens where the older lover of a younger man was supposed to be satisfied with intercrural intercourse, and for a younger man to allow his lover to go any further was not at all acceptable. But, as anyone can see just by looking around today, what society considers acceptable and what people actually do in the privacy of their own homes is not always the same, be it legal or illegal. And, while an Athenian suitor might give the young man he admired a horse or a dog, at Thebes the older man would give the object of his affections a suit of armor, which would be like giving someone a suit of armor today, the price of armor having remained the same over the last two thousand years. (For more about this stuff see Dover, K. J. *Greek Homosexuality*. Cambridge: Harvard University Press, 1989.)

Xenophon's idea that, "the strongest army would be composed of "παιδικων τε και εραστων" is infallibly logical in the context of hoplite warfare where an unbroken line meant victory, and to leave one's post was not only the greatest disgrace but also the greatest treachery as it could lead to the dissolution of the formation and bloody defeat. Who better to post side by side but lovers; what man would run off and leave his beloved to die; what man alive does not want to appear strong and confidant in the eyes of the person he loves? As Plutarch writes, "For while tribesmen take little thought of tribesmen and clansmen take little thought of clansmen in time of danger, a body of men in close array, joined together by the friendships of love, is indestructible and unbreakable. Since each man is obligated by love, in times of danger they will stand fast in defense of one another" (literally, "they will stand over one another").[93] Under the leadership of Pelopidas the Sacred Band would demonstrate the truth of these arguments.

INVASION 378

Back in Athens the Sphodrias affair was having exactly the effect that Pelopidas and Gorgidas had hoped for. The Athenians were busy allying themselves with as many states as possible, starting with Khios, Byzantion, Mytilene, and Rhodes. This was the beginning of what scholars call The Second Athenian Confederacy, the first one, which we call the Delian League (after the island where the league was founded), having been dissolved at the end of the Peloponnesian War. At the same time, the Athenians were also building ships, and there was also another kind of treaty made with the Thebans, all in preparation for another war with Sparta.

The ephors got nervous and called out the army. They had not been impressed by Kleombrotos' ineffectual invasion of Boiotia, so they asked Agesilaos if he would lead the army. This time he did not refuse, saying that he could refuse nothing that seemed good to the state (and to Agesilaos). He borrowed mercenaries from the Orkhomenians (there were at least two places named Orkhomenos at this time; Xenophon, who tells the story, probably means the Orkhomenos in the Peloponnesos at this point), who were at war with the people of Klitor, and he forbade them and anybody else to fight while he was off fighting.

Agesilaos sent his new mercenaries off to seize Mt. Kithairon, and so when summer 378 arrived in Boiotia so did Agesilaos, with eighteen thousand hoplites and fifteen hundred horse. He probably brought his army quickly to Thespiai by a forced march in order to surprise the Thebans. After a few days R and R at Thespiai, he led his army against the Thebans.

His enemies had not been idle. They had encircled the plain and the most valuable lands about their city with a ditch and a palisade. But Agesilaos simply moved his camp from place to place and, right after breakfast each day, ravaged the lands on his side of the new rampart. The Thebans kept pace with him on their side of the fortification, denying him the opportunity to enter unawares and devastate the undamaged lands inside.

After one of his plundering/ravaging expeditions, just as he had returned to camp, the Theban horse, unseen up to this point, suddenly charged out of exits made in the rampart. They caught the Spartan peltasts getting ready for dinner and the Spartan cavalry dismounting. The Thebans must have been watching and waiting for just such an opportunity. Xenophon writes as if he were there, and since he was a good friend of Agesilaos, he may have been, or then again, he may have heard the story first-hand from someone who was there, perhaps from his friend Agesilaos himself. "Of the peltasts, many they cut down, and of the cavalry, Kleas and Epikydidas, Spartiatai, and of the perioikoi, one, Eudikos, and some of the Theban exiles not yet having mounted their horses."[94]

Spartan camps were circular, and the king's tent was in the center. Around it were the tents of the polemarkhs. Each mora had its assigned space of ground. Given the fact that Agesilaos had about twenty thousand men, the camp must have been quite large, and, since Xenophon tells us that Agesilaos "turned back with the hoplites to help," it seems that the light-armed troops and the cavalry were billeted farthest from the center and that the hoplites were still under arms and still headed toward their own tents when the Thebans struck.[95]

There may have been some Spartan cavalry still in the saddle, or perhaps some units had hurriedly remounted, for Xenophon goes on to say, "and the [Spartan] horse charged against the [Theban] horse, and the ten [age groups] from eighteen, of the hoplites, ran with them." He says that the Thebans "seemed like they had drunk a little at noon. They stood their ground against those charging at [them] so as to throw their spears, but they reached [them] not." The Theban horse turned in retreat, but the Spartans managed to kill twelve of them.[96]

One can imaging Agesilaos counting the bodies. Did he watch as some of the Spartans, having first put off their own panoply, pulled the weapons and armor from the bloody dead, while some others dug a hole, and still others went off to find a suitable frame for the trophy? Was sunset burning in the west when they came back, maybe with a young tree stripped of its branches or the poles of a ruined fence, which they fashioned into what we might recognize as a crucifix? Was he standing by while the Spartans, having dropped the cross into the hole and propped it up, built a mound or a pile of rocks around it, and, after testing its stability with a few good shoves, hung upon it, first a blood-stained breast plate, fastening it over the wood as if it were a man's chest, and next draped over that a baldric from which depended a sword in its sheath, then covered the stump with a helmet, perhaps the best and most expensive one they had found, and nailed to the tree a pair of greaves, and leaned against its base a shield, and thrust into the ground close by a spear? Did he then go off and have a frugal dinner with his tent-companions? To imagine such a scene is not unreasonable.

Agesilaos seems to have been inspired by the Thebans' surprise attack. Putting two and two together, he realized that the Thebans always showed up on their side of the rampart in order to keep pace with him right after breakfast because he always led the Spartans out at the same time every day, which happened to be right after breakfast. So one day he sacrificed at dawn and led the army out as quickly as possible. The Thebans were nowhere to be found, so he entered the circle of the rampart and cut down and burned his way right up to the walls of Thebes. No one came out to stop him.

After this, with the campaigning season coming to an end, he marched back to Thespiai and fortified the place. Leaving Phoibidas there as harmost, he headed back toward Sparta. At Megara, at the southeastern end of the isthmus of Korinth, he dismissed the allies, and then "he led back the citizen army towards home."[97]

Naturally Diodorus has a different story to tell concerning the events of summer 378. He doesn't mention the Theban stockade, but Xenophon doesn't mention what Diodorus mentions. We might be correct in thinking that Xenophon left out what Diodorus records because, according to Diodorus, Agesilaos' plan to defeat the Thebans in a pitched battle was foiled by the Athenian Khabrias. And this made Agesilaos look bad. I'm inclined to believe that Diodorus and Xenophon were both being selective and that if you put both stories together you get an idea of what happened in summer 378. If you believe that, then Diodorus' account probably follows Xenophon's account.

Diodorus says that as soon as the Athenians heard of the Spartan invasion of Boiotia they sent five thousand hoplites and two hundred horse to reinforce the Thebans. He doesn't mention the Theban fortifications. He does mention that "terrified by the reputation of Agesilaos, they [the Thebans] were hesitant to await the contest in the plains on level ground."[98] So they occupied the crest of an oblong hill about two miles or so from Thebes. This must have happened after Agesilaos had penetrated the stockade and was probably on his way to Thebes, looking for a fight. Perhaps the position had been chosen by Khabrias.

This man, whom Diodorus calls, "Khabrias, the Athenian, leader of the mercenaries," had spent the last nine years fighting the Persians, first in Kypros, for King Euagoras, who was in revolt against the Persians, and then for the Egyptians, who were also in revolt against their Persian masters. He had been recalled just in time to guard the passes of Kithairon during Kleombrotos' winter invasion of Boiotia. And he had probably brought with him one or two thousand of his veteran mercenaries. Now he and they were part of the Athenian contingent sent to help the Thebans in the summer of 378. He may have even been the architect of the Theban stockade, since he probably had helped to fortify the approaches to Egypt against Persian invasion just a few years before and most recently had in all probability put up a stone wall and a system of watchtowers designed to prevent access to Attika by way of the Elusinian plain, the usual invasion route followed by the Spartans, and most lately by Sphodrias.[99]

Agesilaos, observing the Theban position, led his men forward in battle order and sent the light armed troops ahead "testing their [the Theban's] disposition regarding battle." The Thebans, having the advantage of being on higher ground, beat them back easily. Diodorus says that Agesilaos then "led the whole army at them, drawn up together terrifyingly."[100]

It was now that Khabrias put into operation a plan that he had no doubt pre-arraigned with his Theban allies, most notably Gorgidas, who was now leading the Hieros Lokhos. Khabrias and the Athenians held the left of the line, directly opposite Agesilaos and the Spartans. Marching forward on Agesilaos' left were the Spartan allies, directly opposed to the Thebans, whose Sacred Band formed the front rank of the right of the Theban line. The Spartans must have come on slowly to preserve order in such a large army. They no doubt marched in silence but for the sound of the flutes that kept them in step and perhaps other rustling and trampling noises that great armies on the move are accustomed to make. Diodorus is quite correct in his estimation of the terrifying effect of the sight of the relentless Spartans advancing behind eighteen thousand sharp spears: more than one opposing army had had second thoughts at this point.

Just when the armies were at that distance when either one could have charged the other, the Theban army moved as if in response to a single word of command. They took off their shields, rested them against their knees, and stood with their spears at the upright, probably what we would call "at ease." In the words of Diodorus, "Agesilaos was amazed." This was something Agesilaos, and indeed no Spartan at all, had ever seen. The Athenians and the Thebans were, in effect, ignoring the most fearsome army in the world as it came straight at them with murderous intent.[101]

The Roman biographer Cornelius Nepos (c. 100 – 24 BCE) says that Agesilaos halted the advance with a trumpet call. He may well have been amazed, but he wasn't stupid. To continue uphill against such a determined and obviously well-disciplined and well-trained force would have been senseless slaughter. Had the enemy shown signs of wavering or indecision, the advance would surely have continued. But with the enemy holding the high ground, the issue hung in the balance, and even a Spartan victory would have perhaps been too costly in terms of Spartan dead.

Agesilaos looked up at his enemies and "called them forth into the plain."[102] (Do Diodorus' words mean that the Spartans actually yelled at the Thebans and the Athenians to come down and fight? Did they call them names when they didn't? See Appendix One.) Perhaps he was hoping for a replay of the battle of Mantineia, forty years before, when the Agives, Arkadians, and Athenians left their position on high ground and met his half-brother Agis on level ground. Agis crushed their left wing and then wheeled to defeat their right. Forty years later the Thebans and Athenians stayed where they were. Khabrias had no desire to risk his men in defense of Thebes if he didn't absolutely have to, and the Theban leaders knew that when the summer campaigning season was over Agesilaos would leave, and then it would be their turn to begin the revival of the Boiotian league.

"Since the Thebans did not come down, the phalanx of foot he led away; the horse and light infantry, having been sent away, ravaged the land fearlessly, and of much spoil he became master." Xenophon doesn't mention any spoil, merely recording that Agesilaos "cut and burned as far as the city," fortified Thespiai, and left Phoibidas in charge while he lead the Spartans home.[103]

Khabrias' defiance of the Spartans went down in history as his most famous exploit. And Khabrias was no slouch. He went and fought victoriously wherever the Athenian people sent him, on land and on the sea. He finally died fighting for his country a few years after Agesilaos died fighting for his. And although he had fought Athens' many enemies in many far off places, it was his psychological victory over the Spartans that was admired the most. (But it seems to me that the fact that he did not defeat the Spartans in a pitched battle but merely managed to avoid being defeated by them just goes to show how feared the Spartans actually were.)

To commemorate Khabrias' stratagem the Athenians set up a statue to him at public expense. It portrayed him as a hoplite with shield against his knees and spear upright. Nepos says, "on account of this [exploit] even today throughout all Greece [his] fame is celebrated." And he adds that "afterwards athletes and other artists" had their own statues posed in the attitude in which they had won their victories.[104]

We know that Gorgidas was leading the Hieros Lokhos, and was standing on the hill with Khabrias when he backed down Agesilaos, but where were Pelopidas and Epameinondas while all this was going on? Well, Plutarch says that Pelopidas was among the youngest of the exiles. Now the youngest men of the hoplite class served in the front line of the phalanx, so you might expect to find Pelopidas there. But Plutarch says he was now a boiotarkhes, kind of like a senator in the Boiotian league, which is confusing because the Boiotian league had been dissolved by the peace of Antalkidas. But even boiotarkhoi were expected to fight in the Phalanx, and since Pelopidas was one of the youngest hoplites, he would probably have taken his place in the front rank anyway. Plutarch also says that Gorgidas stationed the Hieros Lokhos in the front ranks of the hoplite phalanx; that might put Pelopidas in the Sacred Band. But we know that he had a wife; that would seem to argue against him being in the S.B. But maybe he wasn't married yet. Then again, since he was a boiotarch he might have taken his place in the front rank anyway and not have been a member of the SB. Someone else was no doubt strategos in command of the army as a whole, since what we know of Pelopidas' character would seem to argue against him pursuing a policy of defense behind a ditch and a palisade.

Perhaps Epameinondas, who, as a contemporary of Pelopidas was also a young man, and who, according to Plutarch, was not elected Boiotarkhes, was chosen as strategos to lead the army against Agesilaos. Perhaps it was he who ordered the cavalry attack on the retiring Spartans. Was Epameinondas observing the Spartans and studying their military technique? Was the cavalry attack a reconnaissance in force? Was he cautiously, by waiting and watching, trying to discover their weaknesses? Was it the lessons learned in this year's and in the next year's campaign that would suggest to him the tactic that he would use at Leuktra, which would put an end forever to Spartan domination on the battle-field ?

Were Kharon and Melon, also Boiotarkhoi, back at Thebes taking care of things at home while Epameinondas, Gorgidas, and Pelopidas led the army? We don't know. None of the ancient historians mention what Epameinondas and Pelopidas were up to in the summer of 378.

Plutarch says that sometime during that summer's fighting Agesilaos was again wounded. Antalkidas, the king's political rival, in true Spartan fashion, said to him: "surely, beautiful lessons you are receiving as pay from the Thebans; unwilling and inexperienced - you taught them to fight." Plutarch doesn't mention Agesilaos' reply, and Xenophon doesn't mention the incident at all.[10]

PHOIBIDAS

Agesilaos had left Phoibidas as harmost in Thespiai. Phoibidas may not have been the most intellectual of men, but he wasn't lazy. He wasted no time sending out "bands of robbers" who raided Theban territory, rounding up any Thebans they happened to come upon and stealing whatever wasn't nailed down. He also "ravaged the land."[106]

To the Thebans he must have been quite a dangerous annoyance, but he wasn't Agesilaos and the entire Spartan and Peloponnesian army, so the Thebans, with their whole army, invaded Thespian territory. Xenophon says that as soon as the Thebans entered Thespian territory, "Phoibidas, with the peltasts pressing [them], not at all allowed them to disperse from the phalanx." He goes on to tell how the Theban retreat was quicker than their advance and how the mule-drivers began to throw away the crops that they had taken. One wonders how they had been able to take anything if they had not had the opportunity to leave the phalanx.[107]

According to Xenophon, "a terrible fear fell on the army," and Phoibidas pressed them even harder, hoping to turn retreat into a rout. "He led vigorously and called on the rest of his men to attack, and he ordered the Thespian hoplites to follow." Perhaps in his mind's eye he could already see himself putting up a trophy.[108]

And as they retreated, the Theban horse, to a wooded valley not to be passed they came; first they gathered together, and then they turned back because of doubt in how to cross. On their side, the peltasts being few, the first ones fearing them [i.e., the Theban horse], fled.

102

It didn't take long for the Theban cavalry to realize that the tide of battle had turned in their favor. They had nowhere else to go, so they attacked the peltasts who were in no particular order, having been scattered in pursuit, and who had outdistanced their own hoplites, and who now were hesitating in front of, and actually fleeing from the very men who had just been fleeing from them. "Phoibidas and two or three with him died fighting."[109] Diodorus adds that "fighting brilliantly, and receiving many wounds ("traumasi," that's right, it's the modern word "trauma"), in front, heroically he laid down his life."[110]

It's painful to imagine Phoibidas and those with him suddenly engulfed by the enemy cavalry, fighting back desperately as the horsemen, stabbing downward with their long sharp spears, surrounded them. Phoibidas must have received many wounds indeed, both in front and in the back. Stabbed through and through, he must have fallen covered with blood. The Thebans would have taken his armor; they may have used it for the trophy that they no doubt set up at the point where the peltasts turned in flight. The Thespians, probably on the day after their defeat, would have sent a herald to ask for a truce in order to recover the bodies of Phoibidas and the rest. It would not have been a pretty sight. The blood would have dried a dark brown, and the ugly wounds would have been clearly visible. Washed and shrouded in his red Spartan cloak, Phoibidas' body would have been buried in Thespian territory.

With Phoibidas dead, his peltasts, who were mercenaries, fled towards Thespiai. When the fleeing peltasts reached the Thespian hoplites, the Thespian hoplites fled also, even though, as Xenophon mentions, they had been especially confident that they would "not give way to the Thebans," and, in fact, "weren't being pursued at all, for it was already late. Not many were killed; nevertheless, the Thespians didn't stop until they were inside the walls [of Thespiai]." One might wonder how any were killed since they weren't being pursued "at all."[111] Xenophon doesn't say.

Polyainos (who wrote a book of military stratagems around 150 CE), says that Gorgidas lured Phoibidas into a trap:

> Gorgidas, leading the Theban horse, drew them up in battle order against Phoibidas and his peltasts. Narrow was the place. Gorgidas, pretending to flee from them, retreated from the peltasts foot by foot. As the enemy pressed him, he slowly led them to a wide place. There, Gorgidas, raising his helmet on a spear, gave the signal to about face.

Polyainos' story has the same ending as Xenophon's. The peltasts flee as the cavalry turns and pursues them to the walls of Thespiai.[112]

After this, the fortunes of the Thebans were on the rise. They continued the campaign against Thespiai, and they also campaigned against the other Boiotian cities. The democrats from these cities, escaping their Spartan inspired oligarchies, went over to the Thebans, possibly in a movement coordinated with the Theban campaigns against their respective Poleis. As Xenophon says, "in these cities the friends of the Lakedaimonians needed help." It seems that the only help they got was a new polemarkh and a mora shipped across the Korinthian gulf to Thespiai.[113]

INVASION 377

When spring came 'round again the ephors called out the army and asked Agesilaos to lead it against the Thebans. He willingly complied and sent a message to the polemarkh in Thespiai to secure the passes of Kithairon. Then he made the diabateria, the "crossing sacrifice," and marched to Plataia. Once there he used a favorite old stratagem to put the Thebans off their guard.[114]

When he had first gone to Asia, back in 396, he had leaked to the press, so to speak, the news that he would attack Karia first. The Persians had then promptly transferred the bulk of their forces to Karia. Agesilaos had then attacked and ravaged Phrygia with impunity. The next year he again announced that he was going to attack Karia. The Persians, not believing him, fortified Phrygia, and Agesilaos invaded Karia.

Now, in summer 377, as he arrived in Plataia, he sent messengers to Thespiai ordering a market to be prepared for the army and for any foreign ambassadors who wished for an audience to await him there. The Thebans, getting wind of this, sent a strong force to guard the road to Thespiai. Agesilaos got up early the day after he arrived at Plataia, sacrificed at dawn, and took the road to Erythrai. He made a two-day march in one day and passed the Theban stockade at a place called Skolos before the Thebans knew what was happening. He devastated the Theban fields as far as the walls of Tanagra, which was held by "friends of the Lakedaimonians." The Thebans, finally, Xenophon says "slowly," Diodorus says "little by little," advanced against him and occupied a hill called the "breast of the old woman," which lay between Agesilaos and Thebes.[115]

Agesilaos once again chose wisely not to advance uphill in the face of a determined enemy who refused to meet him on level ground. It seems that Khabrias was there repeating his successful tactic of the year before. No ancient historian records the name of the commander of the Thebans, but considering their records and their characters it could have been Epameinondas or Pelopidas or Gorgidas. Perhaps all three were there in some capacity or another. Gorgidas was probably still in command of the Sacred Band, or perhaps he had already died. We know that by 375 Pelopidas had taken over as leader of the Band, but we don't know whether Gorgidas died in battle or because of some illness.

Agesilaos led the Spartans around the hill straight towards Thebes itself, no doubt in an attempt to put his army in between the Thebans and their city. The Thebans on the hill hurriedly left their position and headed, at a run, back to Thebes. Some of the Spartans ran after them. But the Thebans held the high ground and threw their spears down at the attacking Spartans.[116]   One of the polemarkhs, Alypetos, was struck and killed.

The Skiritai and some of the Spartan cavalry charged up the high ground and attacked the Theban rear guard, but as they got near the walls of Thebes the Thebans turned around and stood their ground. The Skiritai stopped their pursuit and retreated from the high ground "more quickly then walking." The Thebans put up a trophy because the Spartans had retreated. Agesilaos led his men back to the Thebans' original position and camped for the night. On the next day he led the army back toward Thespiai.[117]

On the march he was harassed by the Thebans' mercenary peltasts, who kept calling on Khabrias to join them. Khabrias wisely decided not to. And the Olynthian horse, who, in accordance with the terms of their treaty with Sparta, were serving with Agesilaos, turned back and charged uphill at the peltasts. As Xenophon points out, a man on a horse can go uphill faster than a man on foot, and the Olynthians caught up with and killed "very many" peltasts.[118]

Back in Thespiai Agesilaos found the Thespians at each other's throats. Those who favored the Spartans wanted to kill those who didn't, especially a man named Menon. Agesilaos did not permit the executions, and he made the Thespians swear oaths to one another. Then he led the army to Megara and dismissed the allies.

Diodorus has a slightly different version of the campaign of 377. He says that the Thebans prevented the Spartans from ravaging their land. He may, in fact, be half right, for Xenophon himself only mentions that Agesilaos ravaged the land to the east of Thebes. The Sicilian chronicler also says that the Spartans and Thebans fought a battle and that Agesilaos recalled his men by a trumpet. Perhaps there was more fighting than Xenophon wished to admit, and perhaps the Skiritai and the cavalry were recalled by a trumpet. Diodorus also mentions the Theban trophy.

The campaign of summer 377 seems to have been one of maneuver and counter maneuver. First, Agesilaos shows up at Skolos when he's supposed to be going to Thespiai. Then, Khabrias and the Thebans occupy the hill between Agesilaos and Thebes. Then, Agesilaos goes around the hill and heads for Thebes, probably in an attempt to put his army between the Thebans and their city, but the Thebans get there first and Agesilaos is forced to withdraw and return to Sparta having failed, for the second time, to achieve his objective of drawing out the Thebans and annihilating them in a pitched battle.

Having dismissed the allies, Agesilaos visited the temple of Aphrodite in Megara. Xenophon tells what happened next:

> going up from the Aphrodision to the town hall, some sort of vein broke, and blood from his body poured into his good leg. The calf became swollen and the pain intolerable. A certain Syrakusan healer opened the vein at his ankle. But once it began, the blood flowed both night and day, and

107

doing everything, they were not able to stop it before he fainted. Then, indeed, it stopped. And so he was carried back to Lakedaimon, and he limped the rest of the summer and through the winter.[119]

Which must have been pretty bad since he already limped with his other leg. One is tempted to conjecture that since he already limped with one leg, this new limp would have evened things out. In reality I'm sure it made things much worse, and poor old Agesilaos, who was now in his late sixties, probably had a very hard time getting around.

Xenophon also tells the story of the Spartan Alketas:

Especially suffering, the Thebans, from lack of food, because for two years they took not fruit from the land, they sent, in two triremes, men to Pagasai for food, giving them ten talents. And Alketas, the Lakedaimonian guarding Oreos [a town on the northern tip of the big island of Euboia], while these men were buying food, manned three triremes, taking care that it should not be reported. And when the convoy was on its way back, Alketas seized the food and captured the men, being not less than three hundred. These he shut up in the akropolis, the very place [where] he was quartered. Attending him [was] a certain one of the Orietoi, a young man, as they say, beautiful and noble; [Alketas] going down from the akropolis, was with him. The captured men, noticing this negligence, seized the akropolis, and the city revolted. So, easily then the Thebans conveyed food.[120]

NO INVASION 376

So the Thebans ate well, and Agesilaos felt bad. When spring 376 arrived he was bed-ridden, so the ephors asked Kleombrotos to lead the army against the Thebans.

One can imagine the muster of the army of the Lakedaimonians at Sparta. The ephors decided which year-groups were going to go out and fight. They sent heralds to proclaim their choices in public, probably at the Spartan assembly.

Now the ephors would probably call up at least two mora of Spartan citizens for the hoplite phalanx and a mora of cavalry. That's about fifteen hundred men, give or take a hundred or two. And each man has a helot to carry his shield, and, I suppose, whatever else his master wants him to carry. So at least three thousand men are due to arrive at the muster, not to mention the wagons and baggage animals and their drivers, and a small herd of animals for sacrifice. Perhaps the Perioikoi, at least those who came from places south of Sparta, like Amyklai, would also present themselves at the muster. The Peroikoi north of Sparta could be picked up on the way to Thebes. It would not be unreasonable to imagine a total force of fighting men three to six thousand strong, with an equal number of servants, mustering at Sparta for Kleombrotos' campaign against Thebes. (Xenophon says that there were six thousand Lakedaimonian hoplites at the battle of Nemea in 394.[121])

Before this force could go anywhere, a sacrifice would have to be made to Zeus the Leader. And it was best made as early as possible. Xenophon says when it was "still dark."[122] The Hellenes figured that the early bird catches the worm - or the attention of Zeus. The Spartans wanted to be the first case of the day, so to speak, so they sacrificed before everyone else, while it was still dark. This might lead one to suppose that the troops had either arrived the night before or that they had to get up really early to be there on time, or maybe some had come in the night before, and those who lived closer to the place of muster got up and out of their own beds, and with their helot servants in tow, made their way to wherever it was that the army was assembling.

With the king at the sacrifice are two ephors, all the officers, and the guy in charge of the baggage. If the sacrifice turns out well, somebody called the "fire-bearer, taking the fire from the altar, leads the army to the boundary of the land."[123] There the king sacrifices to Zeus and Athena, and if the sacrifices are good, the fire-bearer takes up the fire and leads the way to wherever they're going. In this case the sacrifices were good, and Kleombrotos set out for Thebes. No doubt the allied contingents met him on the way.

Back in 379, Kleombrotos had not been especially eager to fight the Thebans. And his attitude hadn't changed since then. Perhaps he felt that the war against Thebes was Agesilaos' problem, since he had not only accepted Phoibidas' seizure of the Kadmeia as being something beneficial to Sparta, but had also helped in the aquital of Sphrodrias - two illegal acts which had roused, respectively, the Thebans and the Athenians against the Spartans. Kleombrotos wasn't about to help further the designs of his political rival. He didn't bother to have the Spartans stationed in Thespiai, or anyone else for that matter, secure the passes of Kithairon as Agesilaos had done before the two previous invasions. He just sent some peltasts on ahead of the main force to seize the heights. Not surprisingly, the Athenians and Thebans had gotten there first. They hid in ambush (a favorite Hellenic tactic since the Bronze Age), only revealing themselves when the peltasts were "on them." About forty peltasts got the surprise of their lives. With the peltasts repulsed, Kleombrotos figured it would be impossible to force the passes of Kithairon, and so "he led back and dismissed the army."[125]

Back at Sparta there was a big conference of the allies at which they blamed the Spartans for prosecuting the war in a lackadaisical manner. Between them they had enough ships, they said, to blockade the Athenians and starve them into submission, just like they had a quarter century ago. And they could use ships to transport an army to Boiotia or anywhere else they chose.

The Spartans thought this was a good idea, so they sent out a fleet under the command of a Spartan named Pollis, which patrolled the waters around Attika. His blockade was effective, and the Athenians were forced to send out Khabrias with a fleet to deal with Pollis. With eighty-three triremes he met Pollis with sixty-five ships near the island of Naxos in September 376. Both commanders stationed themselves on their respective right wings. At first Pollis had the upper hand, ramming his way through the Athenian left, destroying the trireme of the left-wing commander, Kedon, and killing Kedon himself. But Khabrias used his superior numbers to good effect, reinforcing his left and defeating the ships in front of him, sinking more than twenty and capturing eight, for a loss of eighteen of his own. Diodorus reports that, if Khabrias had not stopped to pick up the Athenians whose ships had sunk and the bodies of those who had been killed, he would have destroyed the entire Spartan fleet. But Khabrias, remembering the battle of Arginousai back in 404, when the victorious Athenian commanders were condemned to death for failing to pick up survivors and bodies, even though a fierce storm was raging, took care not to make the same mistake. But Pollis was defeated, and the Athenians didn't starve.

In Athens, the population was ecstatic at the return of Khabrias. The battle of Naxos was their first real naval victory in almost thirty years (Konon's defeat of the Spartans at Knidos in 394 doesn't count, since Pharnabazos and the Persian fleet did all the dirty work). It happened to fall on the Festival of the Great Mysteries, and so every year henceforth, on that day, Khabrias, whose fondness for parties was well known, would, in effect, buy everyone a drink, by distributing wine to the celebrants.

At the same time, Konon's son Timotheos was sent to sail around the Peloponnesos to keep the Spartans occupied, while the Thebans, as Xenophon says, "boldly marched against the neighboring cities and took them back again."[125] And Timotheos kept the Spartans busy. He took the island of Korkyra and defeated a Spartan fleet. Source material for this period is rather scarce, but it seems that the Thebans had little trouble recovering the Boiotian cities, for in the same summer they began to raid Phokis. The Phokaians asked the Spartans for help, and they shipped Kleombrotos and an army across the Korinthian gulf to Phokis. Kleombrotos sent two Spartan mora to garrison Orkhomenos.

TEGYRA

Pelopidas had been elected boiotarkh three years before, immediately after the liberation of Thebes, in which he played no small part. Sometime between 378 and 375, Gorgidas, the founder of the Hieros Lokhos, had died (there is no record of the cause of death), and Pelopidas had taken his place as commander of the Sacred Band of Thebes. He was itching for a fight.

Plutarch records several actions fought in those years: a Spartan defeat at Plataia, the deaths of Phoibidas at Thespiai and of the Spartan harmost Panthoidas at Tanagra. But he says that they were not "ek parataxeos," i.e. the combatants were not drawn up in line of battle, and that they were not stand-up fights in the open according to custom. [126] The Thebans used hit and run tactics; they feigned retreat and then turned on their pursuers. That's what happened to Phoibidas at Thespiai, and perhaps Panthoidas also fell victim to this stratagem. But the next time the Thebans met the Spartans there would be no time for guerrilla tactics or clever maneuvers.

Pelopidas was keeping a close watch on Orkhomenos, waiting for an opportunity, and when it was reported to him that the Spartan garrison had left on a foray into Lokris he decided to attack the now undefended city. With this object in mind, he led out the Sacred Band and "not many of the horsemen." Diodorus says there were five hundred Thebans, so Plutarch's "not many" would be two hundred cavalry.[42] Upon reaching the outskirts of the city he learned that it had been re-garrisoned by the Spartans. Since his force was too small to attack a well defended position he turned back, intending to return to Thebes by way of the mountainous territory of Tegyra. There, as Plutarch tells us in an heroic account:

> in [the territory of] Tegyra the Thebans, returning from Orkhomenos, and the Lakedaimonians, marching out of Lokris from the opposite direction at the same time, ran into one another. As soon as they were seen coming out of the pass, some one, running up to Pelopidas, said 'We have fallen into the hands of our enemies.' 'Why not rather,' he said, 'these men into ours?' And he immediately ordered all the horse to ride by from the rear so as to strike first, and he himself formed the three hundred hoplites in close order.

The Spartans must have been in marching order when Pelopidas ordered the cavalry to attack, as they would have been most ineffective against hoplites in line of battle. It is to Pelopidas' credit that he grasped the situation so quickly and without a second thought sent in the cavalry to keep his enemies occupied while he formed his hoplites into a close and deep formation, intending to break the enemy phalanx by applying the irresistible pressure of his deepened formation against a small area of the Spartan line.

Plutarch continues: "There were two mora of Lakedaimonians. Ephoros says a mora is five hundred men, and Kallisthenes, seven hundred; some others, including Polybios, say nine hundred. The Spartan polemarkhs, Gorgoleon and Theopompos, confidently set their phalanx in motion against the Thebans." Plutarch doesn't mention the cavalry again. One might suppose that, having distracted the Spartans long enough for Pelopidas to get the Hieros Lokhos into their particular formation, the Theban horse were now guarding the flanks of the small phalanx of Theban hoplites.

The Spartans advanced; they were used to winning, and by all accounts they outnumbered their opponents. Pelopidas led his small phalanx straight at the Spartan commanders stationed on the right of the Spartan line, and in attacking them he may have advanced obliquely, foreshadowing the use of this tactic at the battle of Leuktra four years later. Plutarch says that both sides fought with

> heart and strength; first the polemarkhs of the Lakedaimonians engaging Pelopidas fell. Then with those around them [the polemarkhs] being struck and killed, panic seized the whole army and it stood apart both ways for the Thebans wishing to pass through to go back the way they had come, and when this opportunity was given, Pelopidas led towards those who were united and passed through, killing, so all fled headlong.

Plutarch's Greek is a little obscure, but he seems to be saying that the Spartan Phalanx separated itself so that the Thebans could pass through and continue on their way to Thebes. But Plutarch uses the same language in describing the battle of Koroneia (394), where he also has the Spartan line disengage and separate to let the Thebans pass through. It is more than likely that the Thebans simply broke the Spartan line and that what Plutarch calls "two mora of Lakedaimonians" really consisted of a few true Spartans around the polemarkhs, his "those around them," and a larger contingent of Spartan allies, some from the Peloponnese and some raised locally from anti-Theban Boiotians. And, if Pelopidas did attack the Spartan commanders, then he would have had to attack the right of the Spartan line. If this is what happened, then it is most probable that his small but heavy column crushed the Spartan right, which then caused their left to withdraw in some confusion. This is exactly what would happen four years later at Leuktra.

Once the Spartan right wing was out of action, Pelopidas' cavalry could ride around and attack their enemies from the rear. Judging from Plutarch's account it seems that some of the Lakedaimonian hoplites ran and some, "those who were united," tried to fight it out. Any who maintained formation would have been crushed between the Theban hoplites in front and the cavalry behind. Pelopidas would use this very tactic nine years later in his last battle on the ridge at Kynoskephalai. If the polemarkhs had not been killed, they might have been able to reform their phalanx. However, unlike the Spartans, who would rather die than turn their backs, their allies probably had no problem throwing away their shields and spears and running for their lives. With their leaders dead they had little incentive to stand and fight.

The Thebans did not pursue them very far. They didn't want to run into the Orkhomenians or the Spartan relief garrison. But they had just beaten twice their number of, if not actual Spartans, Spartan-led troops in a pitched battle, and had forced their way through the defeated army. Plutarch says, "Standing up a trophy and stripping the dead of their weapons, they went back home feeling great."[127]

The power of Pelopidas' tactical dispositions was clear: the deepened Theban formation had broken the thinner Spartan line. The Spartans had more men, but Pelopidas' tactic was to concentrate his forces and attack the Spartan leaders. By concentrating his force he was actually able to out number the Spartans at the point on their line where he attacked. The rest of the Spartans could not attack his flanks because the Theban cavalry were guarding them. It was no doubt also part of Pelopidas' plan to take out the Spartan command and control center, in this case the polemarkhs, Gorgoleon and Theopompos. The concentration in depth of the Theban formation overwhelmed the Spartans by its irresistible weight. In essence this was a battle of column against line. The Theban column, its flanks guarded by cavalry, broke the Spartan line. Pelopidas then used his cavalry to surround the Lakedaimonian units that did not flee; caught between his phalanx and his horse, they were destroyed.

Gorgidas had originally stationed the men of the Sacred Band at intervals along the front rank of the entire Theban army. He must have reasoned that the presence of these professional soldiers spread out along the front line would have encouraged the untrained militia-men who were fighting beside and behind them. Regardless of this, after their victory at Tegyra demonstrated their potency as a cohesive unit, they were always used as such.

In this same year Polydamas of Pharsalos in Thessaly arrived in Sparta. Xenophon tells a nice story about him:

This man even in the rest of Thessaly was very popular, and in his own city he was thought to be a good and noble man, so that the Pharsalioi, being involved in factional strife, entrusted to his keeping the akropolis, and the business of taking the public revenue they committed [to him] as much as was written in the laws, to spend on sacrifices and on other [matters of] administration. And from that moment indeed, he used this money to guard and maintain the citadel for them, and he managed the rest [of the administration of the state] and he gave an account [of expenses] for the year. And whenever there was a public deficit, from his own [resources] he put forth [i.e., balanced the budget] and whenever he might have a surplus of the public revenue he paid himself back.[129]

Polydamas was the hereditary Spartan proxenos of Pharsalos and had come to Sparta seeking military aid against Jason of Pherai. Pherai was another city in Thessaly, and Jason had by this time made himself master of most of Thessaly and some of the surrounding areas. Pharsalos was his next target.

Xenophon records Polydamas' speech to the Spartans detailing the strength of Jason's forces and his appeal for help.

The Spartans had to refuse. They weren't happy about this because they knew that Polydamas would have no choice but to join Jason, who was in fact an ally of their enemies the Thebans, but since they had already sent an army into Phokis and they needed the rest of their forces to keep watch on the Peloponnesos, around which Timotheos was sailing with the Athenian fleet, they had no one else to send to help Polydamas. He went back and submitted to Jason who now became the ruler of all Thessaly.

PEACE AGAIN

Xenophon continues:

The Lakedaimonians and their allies were assembling in Phokis; the Thebans withdrew to guard the passes into their land. The Athenians, seeing the Thebans increasing in power because of them [Xenophon must be referring to the Athenian naval activity directed against the Spartans and the coasts of the Peloponnesos], and not contributing money for the fleet, and they themselves being worn out from war-taxes and piracy from Aigina and from the guard on the lands, desired to stop the war, and, sending ambassadors to Lakedaimon, made peace.[130]

Diodorus adds some information that Xenophon omits:

Artaxerxes, King of the Persians, intending to make war on the Egyptians and hurrying to put together a mercenary army worthy of mention, decided to help end the wars of the Hellenes. So, he hoped, the Hellenes, freed from the war at home, would be most ready for enlistment as mercenaries. On which account he sent ambassadors to Hellas calling on the cities to put together a common peace (koinen eirenen).

The Hellenes, gladly receiving this proposition, because they were worn out by the unrelenting wars, all made peace, so that all the cities would be autonomous and without garrisons.

The Thebans alone were not inclined to accept the terms of the treaty. They wanted, as Diodorus reports, "all Boiotia to be subject to the Thebans ordering." The Athenians spoke out against this, probably in the assembly of the Athenian Confederation, and Kallistratos gets the credit for composing the best speech. But in answer, Epameinondas "composed a wonderful speech in the common council." This didn't stop the rest of the Hellenes from willingly ratifying the treaty. "The Thebans alone chose to be outside of the treaty, and Epameinondas, through his own arete, raised the spirits of the Theban citizens and encouraged them all to go against the public decree."[131]

Xenophon doesn't mention the Persian King. No doubt it bothered him to see the Persians take the initiative in Hellenic affairs. But both Xenophon and Diodorus agree that the Hellenes were tired of the constant fighting and that the Athenians were not pleased to see a resurgence of Theban power.

It was now probably near the end of the year that we would call 375. The Thebans were happy and proud that they had the power to resist the rest of the Hellenes and the will of the Persian King and because their dream of a reconstituted Boiotian League was slowly but inexorably becoming a reality. Back in Lakedaimon they were not happy. The Spartans had lost the battle at sea and now, under the terms of the treaty, had to withdraw their garrisons from Boiotia and the army under Kleombrotos from Phokis. Agesilaos must have been pissed.

The Athenians had mixed feelings. On the one hand, there was a defiant and powerful Thebes. On the other hand, there was peace and a chance for profit from Artaxerxes' war with Egypt. It was at this time that the Athenians put up Khabrias' statue and others, including one to Timotheos, who was turning out to be a better naval commander then his father. They also sent Iphikrates to help the Persians.

IPHIKRATES

Without the Spartan garrisons to back them up, the Spartan-backed oligarchies in the Peloponnesos were in big trouble. The democrats exiled them and confiscated their property. There were revolts and attempted revolts of both democrats and aristocrats, and people were executed and exiled all over the Peloponnesos. Diodorus is our only authority for the political aftermath of the treaty of 375.[132]

When spring 374 came around the Great King of Persia set in motion his plan to recapture Egypt. It must have been in spring or early summer that Iphikrates arrived in Ake (Acre) where the muster was held. Pharnabazos, who had fought Agesilaos during the Spartan king's Asian campaign some twenty years before, and who was now in his seventies, was appointed to command the Egyptian expedition. According to Diodorus, the preparations took more than a year to complete and included the muster of two hundred thousand barbarians, twenty thousand Hellenic mercenaries under the command of Iphikrates, and five hundred ships. There was also a huge crowd of camp followers to provide a market and other necessities for the soldiers.

Iphikrates was impatient of the delay and complained to Pharnabazos, saying that Pharnabazos was quick to speak but slow to act. Pharnabazos answered that he was master of his own words but that the Great King of Persia was master of his deeds. Finally, at the beginning of the next summer, probably in the year 373, the expedition set out to reconquer Egypt. As the huge army marched southward the fleet kept pace with it, sailing along the coast.

As they arrived near the Nile delta they could see that the Egyptians had put to good use the time afforded them by the

Persians' lengthy preparations. "The king of Egypt, Nektanebos, learning of the greatness of the Persian force, took heart, especially in the strength of the lands, Egypt being completely difficult of access, and also in the fact that the approaches by land and from the sea were well fortified."[133]

Each of the seven mouths of the Nile was protected by a fortified city or town, with towers commanding the harbor entrances. The Pelousian mouth was especially fortified because it was the first to be encountered by those coming from Syria, and this would be the logical approach for the Persian army. According to Diodorus, "this he fenced off with a ditch, and walled off the harbors at the most opportune places, and of the approaches, those passes on the land he made to be marshy, and those navigable he blocked up with earthen embankments. Wherefore it was not easy for the ships to sail in, nor for the horses to approach, nor for the infantry to go forward."[134]

The Persian generals took one look at the fortifications around Pelousion and decided to try a landing somewhere else. It seems that the army, or at least part of it, was now traveling with the fleet, though Diodorus does not come right out and say so. Perhaps they had marched as far as Pelousion, and finding it too well protected for a frontal assault, decided to attempt an amphibious landing elsewhere. The fleet put far out to sea, sailing out of sight of land so that their movements and direction would not be seen by the enemy.

At the Nile mouth called Mendision they found a beach large enough for a landing, and Pharnabazos and Iphikrates disembarked with three thousand men and made for the walled town at the river mouth. The Egyptians met them with an equal number of horse and foot, and a fierce battle raged. Diodorus says that "the Persians were reinforced by men from their ships, and the Egyptians were encircled." Perhaps once battle was joined the Persians landed more men behind the Egyptians so as to take them in the rear. Diodorus continues, "many [Egyptians] were killed and not a few captured, and those left behind [I guess he means those who were not killed or captured and somehow escaped the encirclement], were pursued to the town. Those around Iphikrates rushed together with the garrison inside the walls, and taking the fort, they razed it and those living there they enslaved."[135]

At this point things began to go sour for the Persians. Iphikrates, learning from captives that Memphis was undefended, advised an immediate attack on the city. "Those around Pharnabazos thought it was necessary to await the whole force of the Persians to more safely bring the expedition to Memphis."[136] The Persian main force may have still been on the boundary of Egypt on the wrong side of the Pelousic mouth. Diodorus doesn't say.

Iphikrates asked to be allowed to go ahead with the mercenaries, promising to take Memphis with this force alone. The Persians didn't like this idea, suspecting that he meant to take Egypt for himself. When Pharnabazos refused his request, Iphikrates said that "if they should reject the immediate opportunity they would make the whole campaign unsuccessful." The Persian generals "were jealous of him and slandered him unjustly."[137]

The Egyptians, on the other hand, wasted no time in sending a "suitable guard" to Memphis and "all their forces" against the beach-head at Mendision.[138] There they mounted an unrelenting attack against the invaders. The Persian assault on Egypt was halted. The fighting around Mendision went on until the Etesian winds began to blow and the Nile began to flood. Rather than spend the winter on hostile soil, the Persians decided to give up their attempt on Egypt.

Sometime during the voyage back to Asia the tension between Pharnabazos and Iphikrates came to a head (possibly as a result of the aforementioned slanders, which, combined with their several disagreements, did nothing to mollify the situation between the two), and the latter, remembering the fate of his countryman Konon at the hands of Pharnabazos' countrymen, made secret preparations, seized a ship, and departing at night, sailed back to Athens.

Pharnabazos sent ambassadors to Athens who denounced Iphikrates as being responsible for the failure of the Egyptian expedition. The Athenians answered that if they found that Iphikrates had "acted unjustly, they would punish him according to his responsibility; and they themselves, after a little while, appointed Iphikrates strategos of the fleet."[139]

Diodorus also reports that Iphikrates made several modifications to the hoplite panoply, possibly based on theories he had conceived or things he had seen during his service in Egypt. "For the Hellenes used large shields, and because of this they were hard to move; he did away with the ασπις and made the πελτα symmetrical, aiming at two things: one, to provide enough shelter for the body, and two, to enable the pelta to be, because of its lightness, easily moved."[140] He increased the spear by half its length and nearly doubled the size of the sword. He also invented boots that were "easy to untie and light," and which ever afterwards were called "Ιφικρατιδας."[141] Nepos adds: "instead of linked and bronze [breastplates] he gave linen."[142]

Diodorus writes that these innovations were tested and their efficacy confirmed by use, but where and when he does not say. Perhaps, as General Sir John Hackett suggests in his book "Warfare in the Ancient World," Iphikrates had armed his men with the smaller round shield during the Egyptian expedition.[143] Herodotus mentions various contingents of the Persian army who carried ασπιδας μικρας, small round shields, and it is possible that Iphikrates saw some of them and decided that it would be an improvement over the large Argive shield.[144] It must have been Iphikrates himself who came up with the idea of a longer spear, no doubt to offset the reduced protection of the smaller shield. If Iphikrates did implement these changes during the Egyptian campaign, that would account for Diodorus' tests.

Iphikrates continued to serve his country for another twenty years and, according to Nepos: "lived to old age, admired by his fellow citizens."[145] Since none of the ancient sources mention his death in battle, it is probably safe to assume that Iphikrates, in contrast to most of his contemporaries, died in bed.

ZAKYNTHOS AND KORKYRA

Timotheos had taken the island of Korkyra in 375, and by the terms of the treaty of that year had evacuated it. He had managed to leave it in the hands of the democratic party in keeping with the general Athenian policy. And on his way back to Athens he also managed to stop off in Zakynthos and return the Zakynthian democrats who had been exiled by the Spartan-backed oligarchs. It wasn't long before old enmities broke out anew, and the Zakynthian democrats, probably with the clandestine backing of Timotheos, who seems to have been lingering in the neighborhood, drove out the oligarchs. But the oligarchs returned and drove out the democrats again. They took refuge with Timotheos, who then backed their return invasion of Zakynthos.

The Zakynthian oligarchs asked the Spartans for help, and the Spartans promptly sent ambassadors to Athens to complain about Timotheos' obvious violation of the treaty. Finding no satisfaction there, they dispatched a fleet of twenty-five triremes under the command of Aristokrates, and by 373 what had essentially been, for the last two years, a cold war (with the Spartans helping the various oligarchies that they had set up over the years, and the Athenians aiding the democrats of the now, by the terms of the treaty of 375, autonomous cities), once again turned hot.

In addition to the triremes under Aristokrates bound for Zakynthos, the Spartans, urged by certain aristocratic elements in Korkyra, sent another twenty-two warships, commanded by Alkidas, to bring about yet another oligarchic revolution in that strategically important (the Korkyrans had a big fleet, and were in a good position to intercept anyone sailing to Italy or Sicily), island. The Athenians prepared a fleet of their own for the defense of Korkyra and sent Ktesikles to help the Zakynthians.

So the summer of 373 was a busy time for all the major powers. The Persians and Iphikrates were in Egypt, and Sparta and Athens were busy sending out fleets and preparing for war again. This gave the Thebans a free hand.

PLATAIA

For the Plataians, before the battle that the Athenians fought at Marathon, no reputation existed. They took part in the battle of Marathon, and later, when Xerxes came down [to the sea], they dared to go on board ships with the Athenians. And Mardonios the son of Gobryos, campaigning for Xerxes, they fought off in their own land. Twice it befell [them] to be driven from their homes and brought back again to Boiotia. In the war of the Peloponnesians against the Athenians the Lakedaimonians seized Plataia by a siege, and in the peace which Antalkidas the Spartan made for the Hellenes with the King of the Persians, the Plataians, coming back from Athens, were resettled. But again a second evil would overtake them.[146]

So Pausanias, writing in the second century of the Common Era (some five hundred and twenty five years after the events he records), begins his story of the destruction of Plataia by the Thebans.

No one of the ancient historians tells us what the Sacred Band was up to after the battle of Tegyra. There is no precise record of Theban activities for the year that we call 374. But by the terms of the treaty of 375 the Spartans had withdrawn their garrisons from the Boiotian cities, and it is no stretch of the imagination to suggest that the Thebans were implementing their plans for a new Boiotian League, either by the same sort of guerrilla tactics they had used against the Spartans or by attempting to sow internal dissension among the populace of the various Boiotian cities that they intended to dominate. Whatever their activities, by 373 the Plataians were sufficiently alarmed to send to Athens for help. Diodorus says, "In Boiotia the Plataians, holding to their alliance with the Athenians, sent for soldiers, choosing to give over the city to the Athenians."[147]

Pausanias doesn't mention anything about an alliance with the Athenians. He says that there was no open war between Thebes and Plataia and that the Plataians blamed the Spartans for starting the war by their occupation of the Kadmeia. Now, they said, they were at peace. The Thebans replied that the Lakedaimonians had made the peace and the Lakedaimonians had broken it, and as far as they were concerned all treaties had been dissolved. The Thebans' reply was no surprise to the Plataians, and they set a strong guard over their city.

According to Pausanias, the Plataians knew that when the Thebans held an assembly of the people for the purpose of administration of government they were accustomed to call all the citizens (males of the hoplite class), together at once, and they were apt to go on for a long time. So they kept a close watch on the Thebans, and while their enemies deliberated, they went out to take care of their crops.

A certain Neokles was boiotarkh at the time, and he wasn't fooled by the Plataians' stratagem. He called an assembly and ordered each man to come with his arms. Then he quickly led them by a roundabout route to Plataia, taking at first the road to Athens, which the Plataians had foolishly left unwatched. He arrived at Plataia around noon, probably as Diodorus reports, with the cavalry. That would account for the surprise and swiftness of his advance. Most of the Plataians were captured out in their fields; some made it back to their city. With most of their men captives of the Thebans, the people of Plataia had to surrender. Pausanias says that the men were allowed to leave with one garment, the women with two. Diodorus says that they made a deal to be allowed to take their movable property and never to enter Boiotia again. Both agree that Plataia itself was razed to the ground (Pausanias adds, "except for the temples"), and that the Plataians sought refuge in Athens.[148]

> After this the Thebans razed Plataia to the ground, and Thespiai, unfavorably disposed towards them, they pillaged. And the Plataians to Athens with [their] children and women fleeing, obtained equal citizenship by the kindness of the people. And those were the things concerning Boiotia at that time.[149]

Where was the Sacred Band? Perhaps they were part of an infantry group sent to support the cavalry of Neokles. Perhaps after the capture of Plataia the whole force went on, as Diodorus says, and pillaged Thespiai, burning crops and cutting down fruit trees. There is no certain record of their actions between the victory at Tegyra in 375 and the battle of Leuktra in 371, but they were no doubt in the forefront of some, most, or all of the fighting in which the Thebans were involved in those years.

MEANWHILE, BACK IN KORYRA

Timotheos had been sent out in the spring of 373 to take care of Athenian interests in Korkyra. He first needed to raise money and manpower for his fleet, so, while Iphikrates was in Egypt and the Thebans were dealing with the Plataians, Timotheos was sailing around the islands and off the coast of Thrake, equipping his fleet.

By the end of the summer the Spartans had sent Mnasippos with sixty-five triremes to help the Korkyran aristocrats bring their city into the Spartan camp. The Athenians sent Ktesikles to stop him. After some initial success, Mnassippos became overconfident and careless and was defeated and killed by Ktesicles and the Korkyran democrats. The rest of the Spartans abandoned Korkyra. While all that was going on, Timotheos was deprived of his command at the instigation of his political enemies because he was taking too long to get things done. Iphikrates, who had returned to Athens after the ill-conceived Persian expedition to recover Egypt had failed, was appointed in his place. By the time he got to Korkyra, Mnasippos was dead, and the Spartans were gone. He did, however, manage to capture some triremes that Dionysios, the tyrant of Syrakousai, had sent to help the Spartans. His crews spent the winter working as freelance laborers for the Korkyrans while he took the peltasts and hoplites to Akarnania and supported them by raiding his country's enemies there.

OMENS AND PORTENTS

"Around this time the Lakedaimonians had held the hegemony of Hellas for nearly five hundred years. A divine portent foretold the loss of their leadership."[150] Diodorus' divine portent was none other than Halley's Comet. For eighty-seven days throughout the summer and fall of 373 Halley's Comet burned like a "torch" in the night sky of Hellas. The philosopher Aristotle, who was eight or nine years old at the time, recorded its appearance in his writings.[151]

Though he reports it as a theion, a "divine thing," Diodorus adds a disclaimer:

> some of the natural philosophers attribute the genesis of the torch to natural causes; they declare that these sort of phenomena of necessity happen at ordained times, and the Khaldians in Babylon and other astrologers are successful in making distinct predictions concerning these sort of things; they don't wonder whenever this sort of thing happens, but if it doesn't happen, [because] each one accomplishes its own peculiar cycle with eternal movements and predictable motion.[152]

Perhaps Diodorus' theion not only presaged disaster for the Spartans but also for certain others, for sometime in this same year the Peloponnesos suffered a major earthquake. As Diodorus tells it:

> the hour increased the magnitude of the event, for the earthquake did not happen during the day, when it would have been possible for those in

danger to help themselves, but, the calamity happening at night, the buildings, because of the magnitude of the earthquake, fell in on themselves, and the people, because of the darkness and the unexpected and incredible nature of the circumstances, were unable to reach safety.

Most of those left behind inside disappeared among the falling houses. As day broke some escaped from the buildings, and, thinking that they had fled the danger, met with a greater and more incredible disaster. For the sea, raising up, lifting high a great wave, all with their fatherland were overwhelmed and disappeared. This disaster happened to two cities of Akhaia: Helike and Boura, of which Helike held the rank of greatest of the cities of Akhaia before the earthquake.[153]

Also in this period, Thespiai was destroyed by the Thebans, perhaps as Diodorus mentioned, just after the ruin of Plataia.

ANOTHER PEACE TREATY

Let's recap a bit. Back in 404 the Spartans and their allies, including the Thebans, and with help from the Great King of Persia, Artaxerxes II, defeated the Athenians and their allies in the Peloponnesian War. By 395 the Athenians, this time with the Thebans and the Persians on their side, were again at war with the Spartans. This conflict ended in the Persian-sponsored Peace of Antalkidas (387) and ushered in a nine-year period of Spartan hegemony. Peace ended in 378 with the liberation of Thebes by Pelopidas and his fellow exiles. This war ended in 375 as the result of another Persian peace initiative. But by 373 hostilities had broken out again. Now, two years later, as Plutarch says, "it seemed a good idea to everyone to make peace with everyone."[154]

Diodorus once again attributes the peace initiative to Artaxerxes, "at this time Artaxerxes, the king, seeing Hellas again in disorder, sent out ambassadors, calling for [the Hellenes] to end the civil wars and conclude a common peace, making it according to the agreements that were made before."[155]

Xenophon, as usual, doesn't see things the same way as Diodorus. The Persian king is only mentioned obliquely in one of the speeches Xenophon attributes to the Athenian ambassador, Kallistratos. Here are some highlights of Xenophon's account:

> The Athenians, seeing their friends the
> Plataians driven out of Boiotia and taking refuge

with them and [seeing] the Thespians begging them not to allow them to be cityless, no longer approved of the Thebans, but, on the one hand, they were ashamed to make war on them [they were still allies], and on the other hand, they considered it to be purposeless [i.e., they could see no immediate profit for themselves]. However, they no longer wished to work in common with them, especially when they saw them campaigning against their old friends in the city of the Phokaians, and [when they saw] cities [that had been] loyal in the war against the barbarians, [the Persian invasion of Hellas, back in 480], and their own friends, being destroyed.

On account of this the people, voting to make peace, first sent ambassadors to Thebes calling on them to follow, if they wished, to Lakedaimon, for peace. Then they themselves sent ambassadors.[156]

Among the Athenian ambassadors, "Kallistratos, the demagogue, was present." He had been out with Iphikrates, but he had promised

Iphikrates, if he should send him off, he would either send money for the fleet or work for peace. Therefore, he was at Athens working for peace. When they [the Athenian ambassadors] stood facing the committee of the Lakedaimonians and their allies, first of them spoke Kallias the torchbearer, [an officer at the mysteries of Eleusinian Demeter]. He was the sort of man who no less enjoyed being praised by himself than by others.[157]

The beginning of his speech is interesting for the light it shows on the hereditary nature of proxenia, the practice of

136

having a private citizen represent a foreign state's interest in his own state. If Kallias had been in Athens he would have been entertaining Spartan ambassadors, just as he had back in 378 during the Sphodrias affair. He was no doubt now being entertained in his turn by the Athenian proxenos at Sparta.

Kallias begins:

> Oh Lakedaimonian people, not only have I been your proxenos, but my father received it from his father, passed down by his father to his family. And I wish to make this clear - how the city [Athens] feels about us. There, whenever there might be war they make us generals, and whenever they desire peace, they send us out to make peace. And twice before now I came to end war, and in both missions I worked out a peace for you and for us. Now I am here a third time, and I think that now is, by far, the right time for a truce because I see that things do not seem one way to you and another way to us, but both you and we are angry at the destruction of Plataia and Thespiai. How, therefore, can it not seem right for those who are thinking the same things to be friends rather than enemies? And certainly it is wiser not to fight if the difference might be small. And if we are in agreement, is it not something to wonder at if we don't make peace?[158]

Kallias goes on to explain how, because of the ancient connection between the Athenian Triptolemos and the Spartan kings' ancestor Herakles, they should have never started fighting at all. He ends his speech with a sensible injunction which probably expressed the general feeling of the Hellenes with regard to war, "if indeed it is ordained by the gods that wars be among men, it is necessary for us to start them as slowly as possible, and whenever they happen, to end them as quickly as possible."[159]

Xenophon continues his narrative:

After this Autokles, considered to be an impassioned orator, began. 'Lakedaimonian people! I am not ignorant of the fact that what I'm about to say will not be a source of enjoyment to you. But it seems to me that whoever wishes the friendship they will make to last as long as possible must make clear to one another the reasons for the war. You always say that it is necessary for the cities to be autonomous, but you yourselves are the biggest obstacle to autonomy. You put in your treaties with your allies this first: that they should follow wherever you lead. Indeed, what has this got to do with autonomy? You make enemies without consulting your allies, and you lead them [the Spartan allies] against them, so that often they, who are said to be autonomous, are forced to campaign against those who wish them well. Yet this is of all things the most opposite to autonomy; here you set up dekarkhias [councils of ten], and there you set up triakontarkhias [councils of thirty], and you manage these leaders not so that they might rule lawfully, but so that they are able to hold down the cities by strength, so that you seem to enjoy tyranny rather than constitutional government. And, when the King [of Persia] proposed that the cities be autonomous, you especially appeared to believe that, if the Thebans did not allow each city to govern itself and to live according to which laws it wished, they [the Thebans] would not be complying with the dictates of the King. And then you seized the Kadmeia and did not allow the Thebans to be autonomous. It is necessary that those intending to be friends do not require possession of the rights of others and thereby show themselves to be as greedy as is possible.'

Saying these things he made all silent, and those hating the Lakedaimonians he made happy.[160]

Kallistratos then spoke in a more conciliatory tone:

O Lakedaimonian people, it seems to me that I am not able to say that mistakes were not made by both us and you. And I don't think that one should never again be friends with those who have made mistakes, for I don't see anyone going through life without making mistakes. And it seems to me that people who make mistakes are sometimes easier to get along with, especially if they are punished by their mistakes, like us.

Kalllistratos goes on to point out that, since the Spartans' "thoughtless" seizure of the Kadmeia, the very cities in Boiotia which the Spartans worked hard to make autonomous (Kallistratos is being very conciliatory now, considering that the Spartan idea of autonomy for the Boiotian cities was to install Spartan harmostes and garrisons), were now joining the Theban camp. Like all lawyers, Kallistratos is not exactly being accurate. The Spartan reverses didn't actually start until 378, about four years after Phoibidas' seizure of the Kadmeia. I suppose one could consider that if the Spartans hadn't taken the Kadmeia the Thebans would not have had to liberate their city and might not have embarked on a course which would lead to the eventual reformation of their Boiotian league, but it's hard to believe that an autonomous Thebes would not have tried its best to revive the Boiotian league anyway. Either way, given the political climate, the Spartans and Thebans would have, sooner or later, been at each others' throats.

Kallistratos then expresses his wishes for a renewed friendship between Athens and Sparta, and then goes on to explain how there are some who wish to prevent a treaty by slandering the Athenians. They say,

> that we haven't come because we want to be friends but because we're afraid that Antalkidas will come with money from the king. Be assured that they are talking nonsense. Of course the King has written that all the cities in Hellas [should] be autonomous. Why should we be afraid of the King when we're saying and doing the very same things as the King?
>
> Why have we come? Not because we're without resources. You can learn if you wish, looking at the situation on the sea, on the land, how things stand at present. It's clear that some of our allies are doing things not pleasing to us and not pleasing to you.

Xenophon's Kallistratos here echoes Xenophon's own opening remarks about the Athenian displeasure with the Thebans' destruction of Plataia and Thespiai.

Kallistratos continues:

> At this point let us examine the situation from a practical viewpoint. It is clear that of all the cities some support us, and some support you, and in each city some Lakonize and some Attikize. If we should be friends, from what quarter could we, in all likelihood, expect any difficulty? For if you were our friends, who would be able to distress us on land, and on the sea who could hinder you if we were your friends? But we all know that wars are always happening and ending and that if we don't want peace now, we'll want peace later.

Why should we wait until we are worn out by a multitude of evils? Shouldn't we rather make peace as quickly as possible before something terminal happens?

Kallistratos goes on a bit more, condemning athletes who continue past their prime and gamblers who stake all on a lucky throw, and saying how it's nescessary for the Hellenes to make sure that they don't get into a winner-take-all situation where one side is totally destroyed, and how they should all be friends "while we are strong and successful, and with you on our side and we on yours, we might become greater among the Hellenes than we were in the past."[161]

This speech went over well, and as Xenophon writes, "the Lakedaimonians voted to receive the peace." According to the terms of the peace, the governors would be removed from the cities, the armies would be disbanded, both naval and land forces, and the cities would be autonomous. If anyone should break the treaty, anyone who wished could help those who had been wronged, but no one was under oath to do so.

To these terms the Lakedaimonians swore on behalf of themselves and their allies, and the Athenians and their allies swore city by city. The Thebans, being registered among the cities taking the oath, their ambassadors, having come forward again on the next day [or "coming back the next day"] demanded to change what had been written [to read] instead of the Thebans, the Boiotians having sworn. But Agesilaos answered that he would change none of those who swore the first time and registered [their names]. If indeed, they didn't wish to be included in the treaty, he would erase [their names] he said, if they should command [it]. So all the rest made peace; with the Thebans alone was there a disagreement. The Athenians therefore held the opinion that now the

Thebans, as the saying goes, would have to pay the piper, and the Thebans themselves departed feeling altogether depressed.[162]

Such is Xenophon's account of the Peace of Kallias. Plutarch's is a little different:

It seemed a good idea, therefore, to everybody, to make peace with everybody. And the ambassadors of the Hellenes came together at Lakedaimon to make a peace treaty. One of whom was Epameinondas, a man renowned for his erudition and philosophy, a test of his strategic skills not yet having been given. This man, seeing all the rest yielding to Agesilaos, alone had the courage to speak his mind, and he made a speech, not on behalf of the Thebans, but on behalf of Hellas altogether, pointing out that war made the Spartans stronger, on account of which all the rest suffered, and calling for peace to be made with equality and justice. This way it would last, with everyone being equal.

Thereupon Agesilaos, seeing the Hellenes paying close attention to, and admiring greatly this man, asked him if he thought it just and equal for Boiotia to be autonomous. And Epameinondas quickly and boldly asking him in turn if he thought it just for Lakonika to be autonomous, Agesilaos leaped up and angrily asked him to state clearly if they would leave Boiotia autonomous. And Epameinondas asking the same thing in return, if they would leave Lakonika autonomous, therefore Agesilaos became harsh, and was well pleased at the excuse [i.e., that the Thebans would not leave Boiotia autonomous and would thus be violating the terms of the treaty], so that immediately he erased the name of the Thebans from the peace and declared war on them. The rest of the Hellenes having been reconciled, he ordered them to depart, having left reconcilable differences to peace and irreconcilable differences to war. For it was a job to clear up all the disputed points and make a treaty.[163]

The two accounts are similar in their treatment of the Persian King. Plutarch omits him entirely while Xenophon mentions him only indirectly and in a general sort of way, which is open to interpretation. But the ancient authors differ widely in their treatment of Epameinondas. Xenophon doesn't mention him, and Plutarch makes him the star of the show. But Plutarch also neglects to mention just about everything that happened between the battle of Tegyra in 375 and the peace talks which are the present subject. Diodorus mentions the Persian King but doesn't mention Epameinondas in his brief account:

Artaxerxes, the King, seeing the Hellenes again in disorder, sent ambassadors, calling on them together to end the civil wars and conclude a common peace, making it according to the agreements that were made before. All the Hellenes gladly receiving his words, all the cities except the Thebans made a common peace. For the Thebans alone, ruling Boiotia under one administration, were not admitted by the Hellenes because the resolution of all was that city by city the oaths and treaties were to be ratified. Therefore, being outside of the treaty just as before, they held Boiotia for themselves under one government.[164]

Pausanias does mention the exchange between Epameinondas and Agesilaos, but he thinks it happened "when the Lakedaimonians made with the Hellenes the peace that they say is called [the peace] of Antalkidas; at that time, Agesilaos

asked Epameinondas if they [the Thebans] would allow the Boiotians to take the oath of peace city by city; 'not before' he answered, 'O Spartans, not before we see your perioikoi taking the oath city by city.'"[165] This is perhaps the sentence that justified Agesilaos' erasure of the name of the Thebans from the register of oath-taking cities. But how do we fit these accounts together? Xenophon mentions a second day, when the Thebans came back to alter the register of cities that had taken the oath. Is this when the famous exchange took place between Epameinondas and Agesilaos? Was the whole assembly and were all the other ambassadors present?

Plutarch's account has Epameinondas make his speech after the treaty has been signed. It is after Epameinondas' speech that Agesilaos asks him if the Thebans are going to allow the cities of Boiotia to be autonomous, and it is after Epameinondas' counter question that Agesilaos erases the name of Thebes from the treaty. This clearly puts the treaty-signing before the speech of Epameinondas, at least as Plutarch saw it. But why would Epameinondas bother to make a speech against the Spartans and for peace if the treaty was already signed? Did he call for a second meeting just so the Thebans could change their entry in the register to "The Boiotians" and then make a speech calculated to gain support for his position, and was he then questioned by Agesilaos (Plutarch), admitting in the end that he would not let the Boiotians swear for themselves until the Spartans let the cities of Lakonia swear independently (Pausanias), with the result that Agesilaos not only refused to change what was written, but also, after offering to delete the Thebans from the register (Xenophon), interpreted Epameinondas' statement as being tantamount to the Thebans asking to have their name removed, and then removed it (Plutarch)?

And why didn't the Thebans just take the oath for the Boiotians on the first day? Perhaps, as some scholars suggest (see The Ancient Greeks, by John V. A. Fine), and as Plutarch implies, they were afraid of Agesilaos and were only roused by Epameinondas after they had already signed as Thebans.

Maybe it was Epameinondas' speech that gave them the courage to demand the revision to read "Boiotians" instead of "Thebans." Whatever the details were, the result was that, as Diodorus puts it, "the Lakedaimonians and the Thebans started a war."[166]

LEUKTRA

"After this," says Xenophon, "The Athenians led their garrisons out of the cities and recalled Iphikrates and the fleet."[167] They also ordered Iphikrates to give back whatever he had seized since the treaty had been signed. The Spartans also withdrew their garrisons and harmosts, except for Kleombrotos, who was at the head of an army in Phokaia. Some historians think that Kleombrotos had been in Phokis since the treaty of 375, but it would perhaps be more reasonable to assume that, in accordance with the terms of that treaty, the Spartans had recalled Kleombrotos and had then, when things had once again heated up, transported him a second time across the Korinthian gulf to take up a station in Phokis sometime between 373 and 371. Now he sent to the home authorities asking for orders.

Back in Sparta, Prothoos, one of the ephors, spoke in the assembly, saying that it seemed to him that they should disband the army according to the terms of the treaty, and they should ask all the cities to contribute to the building of a temple to Apollo, as much as each city wished to give, and then if anyone didn't allow the cities to be autonomous, they should call back whoever was in favor of autonomy and lead them against those who were against autonomy. This course of action, he thought, would be most pleasing to the gods and least irksome to the cities.

According to Xenophon, the Spartan assembly considered this nonsense, and they ordered Kleombrotos not to disband the army. Plutarch, however, says that Agesilaos would not give up and brought about the war, supposing that all of Hellas was on the side of the Spartans. It was no doubt Agesilaos who influenced the assembly and the ephors.

According to Diodorus, "first they sent out ambassadors to Thebes, commanding the Thebans to allow all the cities in Boiotia to be autonomous and to settle Plataia and Thespiai and to restore the land to those who had owned it before. The Thebans answered that since they did not meddle in the affairs of Lakonika it was not acceptable for the Lakedaimonians to influence the affairs of Boiotia."[168]

The home authorities also sent a message to Kleombrotos: If the Thebans did not comply with the Spartan demands, he should lead the army against them. Plutarch records that they also summoned their allies, who, while not exactly enthusiastic, mobilized nevertheless, reasoning that it would be better to obey the ephors rather than face the business end of Lakedaimonian spears, which is just what would have happened had they refused to join in the fight against Thebes. On the other hand, Diodorus says that Sparta's allies "willingly" went into battle.[169]

When Kleombrotos found out that not only had the Thebans refused to set the Boiotian cities free but that they were now mobilizing against him, he led the army toward Boiotia twenty days after all the rest of the Hellenes had signed the peace treaty at Sparta. Plutarch says that Kleombrotos led ten thousand hoplites and one thousand horse and that the Thebans were faced with a danger the like of which they had never faced before: the immediate dissolution of their state (which is exactly what they had done to the Plataians and Thespians), and that a fear such as never before gripped them.[170] Diodorus adds that they sent their women and children to Athens. The Thebans, however, were more than ready for war; they had had a lot of practice lately and had learned how to fight from the best drill instructors in Hellas - the Spartans, who had forced them to fight by invading their country two or three years in a row. Indeed, Antalkidas, seeing the king returning wounded from his battles with the Thebans, had famously remarked that they had paid him well for their instruction in the art of war. Epameinondas and Pelopidas led the Thebans, and they knew all about Spartan tactics, having fought on the Spartan side against the Arkadians in 385.

Epameinondas was given command of the army, six thousand strong, and six boiotarkhs were sent with him. Diodorus reports that various bad omens were observed as the army left Thebes: first they ran into a blind herald, who, just doing his job, was making a rather formulaic announcement regarding the recovery of slaves, basically, don't "lead out" slaves; "don't hide" them; recover them, and bring them back![171] The older Thebans thought this was a bad omen, and they advised Epameinondas to pay attention to this portent. Epameinondas brushed them off, saying: "One omen is best: to defend the fatherland."[172] As if that were not enough, the "secretary was leading the way, holding a spear with a headband (or pennon) tied to it [this recalls the famous scene in the Iliad where Khryses holds a golden staff around which is wound the garland of Apollo as he begs Agamemnon to accept a ransom for his daughter[173]], and was signifying the orders of the leader [Diodorus must mean Epameinondas]; a breeze arising" ripped the pennon away and deposited it right on top of the tomb of some Lakedaimonians and Peloponnesians who had been killed and buried there during one of Agesilaos' invasions. Once again the elderly people who happened to be there begged Epameinondas not to lead out the army, since clearly the gods did not want him to do so. This time he didn't answer and just continued the advance. Pelopidas' wife had also had been in tears at his departure, but that didn't stop him joining the army.

Epameinondas led his army to Koroneia, which put him in a good position to intercept Kleombrotos marching east into Boiotia on the road that passed through the mountains separating Boiotia from Phokis. Kleombrotos, unwilling to fight in the narrow pass, marched south, took a round-about route along the coast, wiped out the Thebans under a certain Khaireas, who were guarding the southern pass, thus avoiding the main Theban army, passed by Thisbe, and stopped at Kreusis, where he captured twelve Theban triremes. From there he advanced north-eastward to Leuktra where he camped and, according to Pauanias, observed the following "sign come from god." When the Lakedaimonian army took the field they also took with them a flock of sheep to provide sacrifices for the gods and auguries before battle. The leaders of the flock on the march were goats called "sheep-leaders." Wolves attacked, but only killed the "sheep-leaders."[174] Kleombrotos probably should have realized that this portended his own death and that of the other Lakedaimonians, compared to whom, their allies were like sheep.

Epameinondas' scouts must have informed him of Kleombrotos' circumambulation, so he turned back and found the Lakedaimonians encamped near Leuktra. He, in turn, camped on a hill in sight of his enemies and held a council of war. According to Pausanias, no decision could be made until the seventh boiotarkh, Brakhyllides, returned from guarding the pass at Kithairon and voted, along with Epameinondas, for battle. Diodorus repeats this story. Plutarch adds that Pelopidas, although he was not a Boiotarkh, but was in command of the Sacred Band, supported Epameinondas' decision to fight. In the Lakedaimonian camp, Kleombrotos's friends urged him to give battle, and his political enemies pressured him to the same end. He would soon achieve what Agesilaos, in his two invasions of Boiotia, could not: Kleombrotos would bring the Thebans to open combat in the traditional hoplite manner, only Epameinondas would change the rules by inventing the oblique order of battle.

Back across the plain, Epameinondas, no doubt remembering the omens at the gate, manufactured an omen of his own: "some men recently come from Thebes he persuaded to say that the weapons from the innermost shrine of Herakles incredibly disappeared, and the word in Thebes being spread abroad was that ancient heros had taken them and had left to help the Boiotians." He also exhibited another man, who, having consulted the oracle of Trophonius, reported that the god (a manifestation of Zeus), had commanded them, when they won at Leuktra, to institute a contest in honor of Zeus, which they did, and which was still celebrated in Diodorus' time.[175] And some "rustic soothsayers" approached Epameinondas, to whom they related the story of the daughters of Leuktros (after whom the plain of Leuktra was named), and Skedasos, who, raped by the Lakedaimonians, cursed the homeland of their ravishers and then immolated themselves. The curse was, of course, about to be fulfilled, according to the soothsayers. Pausanias and Plutarch also record variants of this story, the latter chronicler producing an especially elaborate version in which Pelopidas dreams that Skedasos, who, in this version, also killed himself, advises him to sacrifice a virgin to his daughters in order to gain victory over the Lakedaimonians. During the resultant big debate about human sacrifice a young female horse wanders by and ends up being the "virgin" sacrifice.

After all this soothsaying Epameinondas called an "assembly" to which was introduced an exiled Spartan who said that there was an old saying among the Spartans that they would lose hegemony when they were defeated at Leuktra by the Thebans.[176] Xenophon mentions the omens and the disappearance of the arms from the temple of Herakles, adding "some say that all these things were the handiwork of the [Theban] leaders."[177] But all this supernatural stuff seems to have encouraged the Thebans, and battle was joined shortly thereafter.

The two armies met on the flat plain near the town of Leuktra in July of 371. Epameinondas knew that the Spartan King would take the position of honor on the right of the Spartan line. There, Kleombrotos would be surrounded by his own band of three hundred chosen warriors called Hoi Hippeis, "the horsemen." Opposite Sparta's best, Epameinondas posted the best of the Thebans - the Sacred Band, as the spearhead of a phalanx fifty shields deep.[178] As noted above, all the omens had pointed to a slaughter of the Spartans, but they didn't seem to care. Xenophon even implies that Kleombrotos and his staff had a little too much of the wine ration at lunch.

Hoplite armies didn't only consist of hoplites. Each man had at least one servant who carried his gear and probably helped him put it on right before a battle. There were also the people who followed the army around selling things. While the Thebans were arming themselves, the merchants and some of the servants who didn't want to fight began to leave the vicinity. The Spartan mercenaries and light troops with some of the allied cavalry pursued them and chased them back to the Theban camp. Then the real battle started.

With his right refused, Epameinondas and the left wing of the Theban phalanx advanced obliquely toward the right wing of the Spartan army. Kleombrotos may have realized that the Thebans facing him were lined up much deeper than his own formation, twelve shields deep. He drew up his cavalry in front of his phalanx, to screen his movements, and he began to extend his own line to his right in order to out-flank the Thebans. He may also have been shifting units from the left rear to deepen his right in response to the augmented Theban left. While this was going on, Epameinondas ordered the Theban cavalry forward, and in the brief skirmish that followed the Spartan horsemen were no match for their opponents.

Kleombrotos had run out of time. Plutarch says that he was trying to "extend his right and lead it around in a circle" to surround Epameinondas. Before he could complete his maneuvers, the Spartan cavalry was in full retreat and getting tangled up in their own hoplites, and Pelopidas at the head of the Sacred Band was running straight at the Spartan king and his three hundred man bodyguard.

It was the usual practice for Hellenic armies to put their best men on the right. The Spartans used this tactic to good effect, usually crushing their enemy's left and then rolling up his line. In response to this, Epameinondas had devised the oblique order of battle. He refused his own right and put all his weight on his left. The Spartan left, made up of allied troops, never engaged the Theban right, but Pelopidas and the deepened Theban left struck the Lakedaimonian line like a juggernaut.

Although they were not completely formed up, at first the Spartan line held. These were men whose only occupation in life was the practice of arms. At home they did nothing but train; abroad they fought. They initially bore the weight of the Theban left, and the phalanxes locked together in the othismos aspidon - "the push of shields." Stabbing with spears, butt-spikes, short swords, hacking with kopides, they stood toe-to-toe, shield-to-shield, face-to-face, and dealt each other savage blows, pushed forward and bolstered from behind by their fellows. The Spartans died where they stood: Kleombrotos the king, according to Diodorus practically cut to pieces; Sphodrias his tent-mate; Kleonymos, the son of Sphodrias, who was knocked down, got up, was knocked down again, got up again and rose to his feet, only to fall a final time, paying in blood his debt to Arkhidamos; "the horsemen," following in the tradition of the three hundred who had died with Leonidas at the Hot Gates defying the awesome might of the Persian empire one hundred and nine years before - all fell, beaten down under the crushing weight of the Theban phalanx, fifty ranks of sharp spears crashing into the Spartans while they were changing formation.

A particularly bloody fight developed around the body of the Spartan King: for the Thebans a trophy, for the Lakedaimonians a last chance to preserve their honor. One can only imagine the lines locked together over the bloody corpse of Kleombrotos, the frantic hacking and screaming as men on both sides died to possess the mangled body of the descendant of Herakles. Finally, the Spartans somehow managed to recover the corpse, and at this point, unable any longer to bear the weight of the Theban phalanx, they began to give ground. Seeing this, Sparta's allies, stationed on the left of the line, who had not been so keen to fight in the first place, immediately began to withdraw. Those Spartans left alive on the right fought their way out of the disaster and carried the body of Kleombrotos back to their camp.

The older men wanted to reform the phalanx and re-engage the enemy, but too many Spartans had died, and the allies, always less bellicose than their Lakedaimonian commanders, were unwilling to renew the conflict. The Spartans sent a herald over to the Thebans to ask for a truce to recover the bodies of the dead, which was the accepted method of admitting defeat. The truce was granted, the Spartans eventually recovered their dead, and the Thebans put up a battlefield trophy.

Epameinondas had refused his right, putting all of his weight on his left, which caused the Spartan right to retreat while sustaining heavy losses. The quick and effective attack of the Theban cavalry calls to mind Pelopidas' similar use of cavalry at Tegyra. The Spartan allies on the left withdrew without fighting at all. Diodorus reports "not less than four thousand" Lakedaimonian dead and "around three hundred Boiotians."[179] Pausanias' figures for the dead at Leuktra: "of the Boiotians, forty-seven men, of the Lakedaimonians themselves more than a thousand."[180] Xenophon says "nearly a thousand" Lakedaimonians were killed.[181]

Back in Sparta they were celebrating the Festival of the Naked Boys. The men's chorus was on stage when the bad news arrived. In true Spartan fashion everybody made believe that they didn't care, and the performance went on as if the worst defeat in Spartan history had not happened. Of course the next day those whose relatives had died walked around town smiling as if they had just won the lottery, while most of the survivors' families didn't dare show themselves, and those who did were "gloomy and downcast."[182] Things got worse.

The ephors mobilized whatever remaining forces were available including their allies the Mantineans, Korinthians, Sikyonians, Phliasians, and Akhaians and put Arkhidamos in charge (his father being in his early seventies and unwell), intending to transport him across the gulf of Korinth in order to reopen hostilities in Boiotia. At the same time, the Thebans sent a messenger to Athens in order to form some kind of alliance against the Lakedaimonians. The Athenians didn't go for it. An all-powerful Thebes just across the mountains was less-than-pleasing to the people of Attika.

The Thebans had also sent a message to Jason of Pherai, who headed south with his mercenaries and his cavalry, where he linked up with the Thebans, who were all for an immediate joint attack on the Spartan camp. Jason wisely and shrewdly pointed out that to attack the Spartans when their backs were to the wall would certainly lead to a wholesale slaughter, and he persuaded the Thebans that such a course of action could negate all that they had gained by their recent victory. Jason, who clearly wanted to preserve a balance of power among the poleis south of Thessaly, just happened to be a Spartan proxenos and was able to negotiate a truce. That night, the Lakedaimonian army packed up and set out on the road to Kreusis. At Aigosthena in Megara they ran into Arkhidamos, who led a withdrawal to Korinth and there disbanded the army, sending the allies to their homes and leading the Lakedamonians to theirs.

Jason marched back to Pherai, sacking a city or two on the way, including Spartan-dominated Herakleia, which guarded the pass of Thermopylai. His growing power alarmed and alienated just about everyone in the Hellenic world, and he was assassinated sometime in 370. Jason was succeeded by his two brothers, one of whom killed the other and was then killed in the summer of 369 by his nephew, Jason's son, Alexandros, but not before he killed Polydamas, who had visited Sparta back in 375 to ask for an alliance, which the Spartans had been forced by circumstances to refuse, but which the Thebans didn't, which is why Jason came south after the battle of Leuktra.

The Thebans kept busy the rest of the summer of 371, advancing on Orkhomenos, intending, according to Diodorus to "reduce the city to utter slavery."[183] Epameinondas convinced them to enroll the Orkhomenians among their allies (Diodorus must mean that they forced them to join the Boiotian League), and they seem also to have made some kind of treaty of friendship with the Phokians, Aitolians, and Lokrians.

Sometime after this, probably in the winter of 371/early 370, the Athenians invited all the cities that wished to adhere to the King's Peace to a conference at Athens. Everybody took an oath to preserve the autonomy of all the cities, except the Eleans, who said that they owned the Marganians, Skilluntians, and Triphylians. As a result of this, the Mantineians, whose city had been dismantled by the Spartans in 385, voted to reconstitute their city and build a wall around it. The Lakedaimonians didn't like this, so they sent Agesilaos, now about seventy-two years old, who, as Xenophon says was a "hereditary friend," since the Mantineians had served his father well in battle against the Messenians, to persuade them to wait awhile.[184] The Mantineians nicely refused, but Agesilaos went away quite angry anyway. No doubt, old as he was, he would have taken the field against them, but then every polis that had sworn to uphold the autonomy of every polis would have had to mobilize and defend the Mantineians. So the Lakedaimonians just had to sit back and take it.

With the Spartans reduced to spectator status, all the cities of the Peloponnesos began to flex their respective muscles. Certain Tegeans wanted to unite the cities of Arkadia (basically the middle of the Peloponnesos), and, of course certain other Tegeans didn't like this idea, so, as was usual in those days when political opponents couldn't agree or compromise, they started killing one another. The Mantineians helped one side; the survivors of the resultant slaughter fled to Sparta. The ephors decided that in accordance with the autonomy clause,

155

which stipulated that if one city tried to dominate another, those cities who had signed the treaty should come to the aid of the injured party, this would be a good time to send out Agesilaos, this time with an army, to punish the Mantineians for their recent defiance. Agesilaos advanced into Tegean territory, plundering the countryside. He waited for the Tegeans and Mantineians to join forces and then drew his army up in line of battle not far from Mantineia. Although it was the middle of winter (early 370), he waited four days for the Mantineians to come out and fight. When they didn't, he led the army back to Sparta.

The Arkadians, Agrives, and Eleans then sent ambassadors to Athens in order to form an alliance against the Spartans. The Athenians refused, and the ambassadors then went to the Thebans, who did not refuse. Unhindered by the Lakedaimonians, the cities of Arkadia joined together in a league and commenced the construction of their capital, which they called Megalopolis, Great City, and the Mantineians began to rebuild their walls, probably in the spring of 370. It was also around this time that, as a result of the loss of Lakedaimonian power and influence throughout the Peloponnesos, Xenophon was evicted from his estate at Skillous by the Eleans and took up residence in Korinth.

INVASION 370

Now allied with the Arkadians, Epameinondas, Pelopidas, and the Theban army wasted no time marching south and arriving at Mantineia. But it was late in the year of 370, and since the fighting seemed to be over, Epameinondas decided go back to Thebes. He and Pelopidas had been elected boiotarkhs for this year, and their term of office was now up, so they indeed should have returned to Thebes and relinquished their commands. However, as Xenophon records, news came of the unrest of the Perioikoi and the quite natural Spartan manpower shortage as a result of Leuktra, and with these things in mind, the Arkadians, Argives, and Eleans were able to persuade Epameinondas to undertake an invasion of Lakonia.[185]

The Thebans marched toward Karyai, a bit to the northeast of the city of Lakedaimon, while the Arkadians slaughtered the Spartan outpost near Oeon, almost due north of Lakedaimon itself, and then marched to join the Thebans. Their combined forces (Plutarch says they were seventy thousand strong[186]), arrived next at Sellasia, which they looted and burned. From there they marched to the Eurotas River.

Across the river stood the un-walled city of the Lakedaimonioi and a hoplite army composed of any who could bear arms, including six thousand helots promised their freedom if they would fight, standing, waiting for the Thebans to cross. The Thebans called on Agesilaos to come out and fight, but Epameinondas didn't press his luck; the river was high, and he knew that the Spartans were desperate. Once across the Eurotas anything could happen.

Leaving Sparta behind and marching south they continued to loot and burn as they went. Xenophon says that "the women of the city could not bear to see the smoke" of the burning houses.[187] They crossed the Eurotas near Amyklai and plundered the land. After a minor skirmish with three hundred Spartan hoplites and some cavalry, they continued south. Joined by some perioikoi, they attacked the Spartan naval base at Gythion, which they don't seem to have taken. They and their allies raided the length and breath of the land and then turned west, toward Messenia.

Pausanias ascribes Epameinondas' liberation of Messenia to a prophetic dream. It's more likely that it was the result of sound political and military thinking on the part of the inventor of the oblique order of battle: freeing the Messenians would leave a hostile state to the west of a Lakedaimon weakened by the loss of a major chunk of territory and probably half of its helots. But, in accordance with the usual practice, Epameinondas ordered some seers to take the auspices, which turned out to be auspicious, so, after a few more sacrifices, building was begun on Messene. Sometime during his invasion of the Peloponnesos, Epameinondas sent a Theban named Pammenes with a force of a thousand picked Thebans to defend the Arkadians if the Lakedaimonians should try to prevent the foundation of Megalopolis.

The Spartans sent ambassadors to their old enemy Athens, asking for military aid against the Thebans. The Athenians, after listening to a bunch of speeches in praise of the Spartans and being reminded of Leonidas' sacrifice at Thermopylai and fearing the increased power of their former ally (which probably had more effect than the speeches), assented, and in accordance with the terms of the King's Peace, reinforced at Athens the winter before, which stipulated that all signatories must come to the aid of any state whose autonomy was threatened, and the Theban invasion of the Peloponnesos did seem to threaten Spartan autonomy, at least to the

Athenians at this point, although at the moment Epameinondas was actually freeing the Messenians, whose autonomy had been violated by the Spartans for the last three hundred years or so, sent out Iphikrates, who led twelve thousand men (his specially armed peltasts?) to Korinth. There, he waited a few days, for what reason the ancient sources do not tell. Urged on by his men, he advanced into Arkadia, where he seems to have assaulted some fortified positions – Xenophon is rather obscure: "and willingly, if he led them against a wall, they attacked."[188]

It now being winter, and with the Arkadians, Argives, and Eleans heading home loaded with plunder, the Thebans also decided to leave the Peloponnesos, where, since they had burned and looted the entire countryside, it was becoming more difficult every day to find food for the men and fodder for the horses. At the same time, Iphikrates returned to Korinth, intending to intercept the Thebans. It's worth reading Xenophon's words on Iphikrates' next movements:

> If indeed now some other thing he did well as a strategos, I find no fault. This time however, I find fault with respect to all the things he did and [I find] these thing uselessly done by him. For while attempting to guard [the road] near Oneion so that the Boiotians would not be able to go home, he left unguarded the best pass by Keykhreion.

It's pretty obvious that by "some other thing he did well as a strategos," Xenophon means his defeat of the Spartan mora near Lekhaion back in 390, but he couldn't actually bring himself to mention it by name. Xenophon continues to censure Iphikrates for sending out his entire cavalry to see if the Thebans had by-passed his position at Oneion, when a few scouts would have sufficed, and for letting his cavalry engage the Thebans when they found them, in which engagement they suffered a loss of about twenty killed. Iphikrates' force was too big for a reconnaissance and too small to fight the Theban army.

"The Thebans departed in such manner as they wished."[189] Pausanias adds an action: "opposite Lekhaion it happened [that the Thebans] were going to pass through the narrow and difficult [parts] of the road; Iphikrates, the son of Timotheos, having peltasts and another force of Athenians, attacked the Thebans." (It might be interesting to note that the word επιχειρει, which I've translated as "attacked," literally means "put hand to.") Pausanias continues: "Epameinondas turned those attacking, then reaching the city of Athens itself," where Iphikrates "prevented" the Athenians going out to fight, so the Thebans just went home.[190] Where were the men of the Sacred Band during all this? Nobody mentions them, but, being the Thebans' best, they were probably in the thick of it.

Upon their return to Thebes, Epameinondas and Pelopidas found themselves in very hot water: on trial for their lives for not laying down command when they should have and for prolonging their term of office for four months, rather illegally. Nepos tells the story: "After he returned, his colleagues were accused of this crime [not laying down command at the appointed time]. He permitted them to transfer the whole case against him." He did this by advising them to say that they had just been following his orders. This got them off the hook, but Epameinondas was still on it, and no one expected him to appear in court. He showed up, denied nothing, confessed his guilt, and was not unwilling to pay the penalty prescribed by the law.

> But one thing he sought from them: that they should inscribe on his tomb: Epameinondas by the Thebans was punished with death, because he forced them at Leuctra to overcome the Lacedaemonians [I'm using "c" here because in Latin these words are spelled that way, and Nepos wrote in Latin] whom before him [as] imperator no Boeotian dared to face in line of battle and because in one battle saved not only Thebes from destruction but even maintained the liberty of all

Greece and so completely conducted the affairs of both to the point that the Thebans attacked Sparta, the Lacedaemonians considered it satisfactory if they were able to be safe, and he didn't stop the war before Messene rebuilt had enclosed their city [Sparta] in a siege.

At this everybody had a good laugh, nobody voted, and Epameinondas was more famous than ever.[191]

Plutarch, in his life of Pelopidas, tells us that Epameinondas took all this quite calmly, even though a certain Menekleidas somehow kept him from being reappointed boiotarkh. Pelopidas, on the other hand, hounded Menekleidas until he was brought to trial and fined so heavily that he was driven to some type of treasonous activity. Plutarch's account of the political fortunes of his hero Pelopidas ends there, and we don't know what happened to Menekleidas after that. It probably wasn't anything good, at least from Menekleidas' viewpoint.

INVASION 369

As the next campaigning season approached, ambassadors from the Lakedaimonians and their allies arrived in Athens, where they finalized a mutual defense pact in which each side would "lead five days at a time."[192] The Athenians sent Khabrias south with an army. Epameinondas, leading the Theban army (Pelopidas was in Thessaly with an army, helping the locals fight Alexandros of Pherai), was already on the march. The Lakedaimonian/Athenian coalition, twenty thousand strong, took up defensive positions at the southern end of the isthmus of Korinth. "From Keykhreion as far as Lekhaion with palisades and deep trenches they cut off the passage [of the isthmus]." This was no doubt the work of Khabrias, who was experienced in matters of fortification.

Xenophon says that the Lakedaimonians and Pelleneans were stationed at the "most easily assailable" spot, which seems to have been a pass on high ground south-east of Korinth.[193] The Thebans and their allies camped about three and half miles away. From there, they set out at night and arrived "when the night watch had already ended," and the Spartans were waking up.[194] Epameinondas and the Sacred Band led the attack. The sleepy Lakedaimonians and their sleepy allies didn't have a chance. Those who weren't killed retreated. Xenophon blames the Lakedaimonian polemarkh for not requesting allied support, which could have come from the forces stationed at Keykhreion further to the south-east. Instead, the polemarkh, un-named by Xenophon, made a truce with Epameinondas, which allowed him to withdraw and the Thebans to march down into the Peloponnesos and join their allies, the Arkadians, Argives, and Eleans in an immediate attack on Sikyon. It was Pammenes who captured the harbor by manning a merchant ship with soldiers disguised as its crew and master. As they left the ship and mingled with the locals, Pammenes led an attack on the city. With the inhabitants' attention focused on attack from without, the merchantman's crew took control of the harbor. It's tempting to think that the merchant ship was manned by men of the Hieros Lokhos, Thebes' best, acting as special-forces.[195] Epameinondas then turned south-east and ravaged Epidauros.

From Epidauros they marched north-west into Korinthian territory. The Korinthians met them outside the gate that faces Phlios. According to Diodorus, the Thebans "defeated them in battle" and pursued them to the walls. The Sacred Band must have been Epameinondas' main striking force, as at Tegyra and Leuktra, since they seem to have been in the forefront of the pursuit, for, as Xenophon tells us, they rushed the gates, which were no doubt open to receive the retreating Korinthians.[196] Within a hundred yards of the city wall they ran into a body of Khabrias' peltasts. The Athenian strategos must have gone to the support of the Korinthian hoplites with his light troops. Unburdened by the hoplites' huge shields and body armor, the peltasts climbed onto the burial monuments that lined the road and rained down sling-stones and javelins. Men in the front ranks of the Sacred Band were struck. Some fell dead in their tracks; others suffered painful wounds caused by the sharp javelins and bullet-like sling-stones. Unable to come to grips with their foes, the Thebans turned in flight. The peltasts climbed down and chased them for about half a mile; they couldn't engage the heavily armed hoplites hand to hand, but they could throw stones and javelins at their retreating backs. Then they returned to the city and hauled away the bloody bodies of their enemies. A truce was agreed upon, and the Thebans took back their dead. The Korinthians put up a battlefield trophy. Pelopidas was in Thessaly, and the leader of the Band on this occasion is not recorded. Diodorus mentions another pitched battle in which Khabrias was victorious, but Xenophon says nothing of this, either because it did not happen (Diodorus often gets confused), or because he didn't think it worth his while to mention it.

While these things were going on, twenty triremes full of two thousand Kelts and Iberians sailed in and disgorged their contents, including fifty horsemen. These were mercenaries sent by Dionysios, the tyrant of Syrakousai, to help the Spartans. On the day after their arrival, the Thebans and their allies drew up in battle order and destroyed anything worth anything between the sea and the hills upon which Korinth stood. The Korinthian and Athenian cavalry made no move to stop them. It's worth recording Xenophon's description of what happened next: "But the horsemen from Dionysios, as few as there were, these men scattered here and there riding alongside and riding up [to the enemy] threw javelins, and when [the enemy] rushed at them they retreated, and turning back, threw javelins."

To the Hellenes these Kelts and Iberians were wild barbaroi who seemed to be playing with the more disciplined Hellenic infantry: every so often they would dismount and nonchalantly take a little rest in sight of their enemies, who quite naturally would seize this opportunity to rush upon them. Probably with some amusement, they would then jump back into the saddle and ride out of range. Any of the Thebans or their allies who pursued them too far, would have to retreat while the Kelts and Iberians "pressed them, and throwing javelins, did terrible things." Xenophon says that they "forced the whole army...to advance and retreat."[197]

A few days of this convinced the Thebans and their allies to go home. When Epameiondas returned to Thebes "enough suspicion arose concerning him for sparing the Lakedaimonians [when he first broke through their lines at Korinth] for the sake of private goodwill... [that] the multitude, angered, removed him from the Boiotarkhia..."[198]

The Kelts and Iberians then invaded the territory of Sikyon, which had gone over to the Thebans. The Sikyonians came out against them, and in what seems to have been a pitched battle, were defeated with a loss of seventy killed. Dionysios' mercenaries then took a place called Deras by storm. Summer was now drawing to a close, so they sailed back to Syrakousai, no doubt loaded with a lot of nice stuff that used to belong to somebody else.

THE BOY PHILLIPOS

While all this was going on, Pelopidas was in Thessaly with an army. He captured Larrissa and forced Alexandros to seek terms. The two didn't get on well, and we can imagine Pelopidas losing his temper. Alexandros departed with his bodyguard. Then Pelopidas was invited to Makedon, where he was to arbitrate in a dispute between the Makedonian King, also named Alexandros, and Ptolemy of Aloros. The details of his involvement are not known, but both Plutarch and Diodorus report that he settled the matter and took as hostage Alexandros' brother Philippos (we'll call him Philip from now on because he is well known by that name as Philip II, the father of Alexander the Great), who was about thirteen at the time.[199] Some historians agree with this date (369) for Philip's trip to Thebes, and some don't.

After his father's death the year before, the new administration (his brother Alexandros II was king, but it seems that his mother was running the show), sent Philip as a hostage to the Illyrians, but that does not mean that he could not have been back at the Makedonian capital, Pella, in time to be sent to Thebes with Pelopidas. Nepos is not much help dating Philip's trip to Thebes. He writes, rather ambiguously, "with Amyntas dead (which means any time after 370), his wife, Eurydice, the mother of Perdiccas and Philip, with these two boys, fled to Iphicrates and by his resources was defended." Aeschines gives us a better timeframe. He says that Alexandros was also dead, killed by Ptolemy, probably with the connivance of his own mother, Eurydike, who "sent for" Iphikrates, who was lurking around Amphipolis with a fleet, who helped her by driving away a certain Pausanias who wanted the throne and had many supporters.[200] That would put Philip's trip to Thebes in 368.

The Athenians had founded the aforementioned city of Amphipolis at the mouth of the Strymon River sometime in the middle of the fifth century but lost it to the Spartan strategos Brasidas in 423 during the Peloponnesian War. The Peace of Nikias, between Sparta and Athens in 421, should have returned Amphipolis to its original owners, but the cities in that region had formed the Khalkidian League and were not about to give up their autonomy. Back in 371 at the peace conference at Lakedaimon, "Amyntas, the father of Philip," through his commissioner, "voted to help take Amphipolis with the Athenians and other Hellenes."[201] Amyntas died a year later, and no attempt was made to retake Amphipolis. But the Athenians never forgot that they had once owned Amphipolis, and they wanted it back, so Iphikrates was sailing around its vicinity, just in case an opportunity should arise.

Whether he went to Thebes in 369 or 368, this Philip would be the future Philip II of Makedon and the father of Alexander III, the Great. It was perhaps while he was under Iphikrates' protection that Philip became acquainted with the military reforms that made his host famous throughout antiquity. Did he see Ipihkratean peltasts in action against Pausanias' forces? It must have been shortly after the Iphikrates episode (whenever it happened), that Philip was sent to Thebes. There, he lived with Pammenes, and no doubt was influenced by the tactics of Epameinondas and Pelopidas. Did he already, young though he was, mentally combine the long spears and small shields of Iphikrates' peltasts with the deep formation of the Thebans? He must have talked to veterans of Tegyra and Leuktra and learned of the oblique order of battle and of the Thebans' effective use of cavalry in both encounters.

EVENTS IN THE PELOPONNESOS AND POINTS NORTH

When spring 368 came around the Arkadians started acting up. According to Xenophon: "they marched against Lakonian Asine" (which on my map is really in Messenia), defeated the garrison and killed the polemarkh, Geranor, and they acted in a high-handed manner with respect to their allies and everybody else. This did not please the Thebans.[202]

While this was going on, a man named Philiskos of Abydos (a town a little to the north-east of ancient Troy, in what we call Asia Minor), sent by the satrap of that region, Ariobarzanes, who was on good terms with Antalkidas, but probably ultimately at the request of Artaxerxes II, arrived in Hellas with, as Xenophon says "a lot of money."[203] He called the Thebans, their allies, and the Lakedaimonians to a peace conference at Delphi. The Lakedaimonians wanted Messenia back, the Thebans wouldn't go for that, and the conference broke up.

Philiskos carefully recruited two thousand mercenaries, paid them, turned them over to the Lakedaimonians, and went home. At the same time, another force of mercenaries sent by Dionysios showed up. The Spartans and their allies, including the Athenians, were probably meeting in Korinth. The Athenians wanted to send the mercenaries to Thessaly against the Thebans, which at the time meant Pelopidas and Ismenias with a mercenary army of their own and Alexandros of Pherai as their target. The Lakedaimonians wanted the mercenaries to stay in the Peloponnesos, and that's what happened: they "sailed around to Lakedaimon," where Arkhidamos added them to his own force and set out on campaign. "And Karyai he took by force, and as many as he took alive, he cut [their] throats. From there, immediately marching to Arkadian Parrhasia with his army, he ravaged the land."[204]

When the Arkadians and the Argives marched against him, he withdrew and encamped on the hills above Melea. At this point, Kissidas, the leader of Dionysios' mercenaries, in a quite mercenary fashion, informed Arkhidamos that his term of employment was up and that he was going home, and immediately left with his troops on the road to Sparta. The Messenians cut him off at "a narrow [part] of the road. There he sent to Arkhidamos and urged him to help. That man indeed helped."[205] Xenophon doesn't go into detail about Arkhidamos' assistance or what happened to the Messenians. In his next sentence the Spartans are at the intersection of the roads to Melea and Eutresis where they run into the Arkadians and Argives who are attempting to block Arkhidamos' return to Sparta.

Arkhidamos then drew up his army in line of battle and gave an inspirational speech. As he finished speaking, lightning and thunder exploded in a clear sky, "and there stood near the right wing [the Greek word is κερας, which really means "horn"] a temenos [in this case a bit of land sacred to a god] and a statue of Herakles, from whom he [Arkhidamos] is said to be descended."[206] These good omens roused the Lakedaimonians so much so that it was difficult for their leaders to restrain them as they surged forward. And when Arkhidamos advanced, most of his opponents did not await his attack. Those who did were killed. The Lakedaimonian horse and the Kelts pursued the rest and killed many of them as they fled.

Arkhidamos put up a trophy and sent the herald Demoteles straight home to tell everybody of the victory and that not one Spartan had died, but many of their enemies had been killed. Hearing the news, everybody, starting with Agesilaos, who must have been very proud of his son, burst into tears of joy. When report of the battle reached the Thebans, they were not displeased to learn that the uppity Arkadians had suffered a reverse, and one can imagine them having a good laugh about it. Many scholars think that this battle was the Arkadian incentive for the foundation of Megalopolis; the ancient sources tell us no more than that it was founded after Leuktra.

At the same time that all this was going on in the Peloponnese, Pelopidas and Ismenias were up in Thessaly from whence they traveled to Makedon where they made a deal with Ptolemy, who had killed the legitimate king, Alexandros, and married his mother, Eurydike. Ptolemy would be regent for Alexandros' younger brother, Perdikkas. It was perhaps at this time that Philip was sent to Thebes as a hostage. Upon returning to Thessaly, Pelopidas and Ismenias ran afoul of the other Alexandros, who took them captive. (If they were detained by Alexandros, who took Philip to Thebes?) While imprisoned by Alexandros, Pelopidas sent his captor a message predicting his escape and revenge. Alexandros marveled at his audacity but did nothing more than restrict his visitation rights; he was already ragged, dirty, and ill-fed. Plutarch says that Alexandros' wife, the daughter of Jason of Pherai, sympathized with her husband's prisoner.

Back in Thebes a certain Diomedon of Kyzikos, sent by Artaxerxes, tried to "corrupt" Epameinondas "with money."[207] First he bribed Epameinondas' eromenos (literally: "man being loved"), Mikythos, to enlist his support. Philosopher that he was, Epameinondas rebuked both of them, made Mikythos give back the five talent (a huge sum of money) bribe, and sent Diomedon packing.

When the Thebans heard about Pelopidas' imprisonment, they sent eight thousand hoplites and six hundred horse marching to Thessaly. Alexandros asked the Athenians for help. They immediately sent out "thirty ships and a thousand soldiers of whom the strategos was Autokles."[208] Arriving in Thessaly, the Thebans, commanded by some one whose name is nowhere recorded in the ancient sources, found the Thessalians uncooperative allies and Alexandros and his numerous cavalry reinforced by the Athenians.

Alexandros must have refused battle. He was on his own soil; no doubt he occupied some strong position. His cavalry scouts probably kept him well informed of the Theban army's movements. He could be easily supplied, while his enemies, who had probably counted on the Thessalian cities for logistical support, soon found out that they could not. Deserted by the Thessalians and running out of food, the Thebans began to withdraw. This must have been what Alexandros was waiting for. As they marched off, his horsemen shadowed their column, killing and wounding those in the rear.

"Epameinondas, being a private at that time, by the citizen-soldiers was appointed strategos."[209] One can imagine the Theban hoplites quickly losing confidence in the un-named boiotarkhs and shouting the name of Epameinondas as the only one who could get them home safely. Taking the light-armed troops, probably archers and slingers, and the horse, Epameinondas fought a rear-guard action. The infantry missile-troops would have been able to keep Alexandros's cavalry at a distance, and Epameinondas probably used his own horse to counterattack at moments most favorable to the Thebans. Alexandros had to give up the pursuit. Upon the army's return to Thebes, the boiotarkhs were fined heavily. Where was the Sacred Band during all this? Who commanded them? The ancient sources are silent.

PELOPIDAS GOES EAST

Pelopidas sat and stewed in Alexandros' prison for the rest of the year, along with Ismenias. But when spring 367 came around, so did Epameinondas, with an army. Plutarch's bio of Epameinondas is lost, and he doesn't go into much detail regarding events in Thessaly in his *Life of Pelopidas*. There seems to have been no decisive battle, just some maneuvering by Epameinondas, which convinced Alexandros to release his prisoners.

Upon learning that a certain Euthykles was representing Lakedaimonian interests at the court of the Great King and mindful of the monetary support given the Spartans by Philiskos the year before, the Thebans sent Pelopidas on a diplomatic mission to Persia to undermine the Spartan position there. The Athenians, hearing of this, wasted no time sending out their own ambassadors, Timagoras and Leon. Artaxerxes was impressed by Pelopidas' military exploits, the fame of which had preceded his physical appearance at the court, though the Persian King seems to have also favored his old friend Antalkidas. However, it was Pelopidas who won the diplomatic contest: the King ratified the autonomy of Messenia, suggested that the Athenians cease their naval activity (they were still sailing around Amphipolis), and put a clause in the treaty to the effect that if they didn't obey, they would be attacked, presumably by those states that would sign the treaty.

The ambassadors then returned home. The Athenians, unhappy with Timagoras' performance and on the pretext that he had accepted too many expensive gifts from the king, had him executed. The Theban attempt to have the treaty ratified by the various poleis failed, and their high-handed attitude further alienated their Arkadian allies.

EPAMEINONDAS GOES SOUTH AGAIN

With the Arkadians slowly drifting away from their former pro-Theban stance, Epameinondas thought that it would be a good idea to make an alliance with the Akhaians, which would sustain his influence in the Peloponnese. So, in the spring of 366 he marched south (it would not be unwise to speculate that he took with him Thebes' best troops – the Sacred Band), and with the support of the Argives, forced the pass at Mt. Oneion and invaded Akhaia. Things went well at first, the various Akhaian aristocratic governments allied themselves with Thebes, and Epameinondas went home. However, upon the complaints of the Arkadians that these aristocratic arraignments actually favored the aristocratic Spartans, the Thebans sent harmostes to the Akhaian poleis; "they with [the help of] the multitude, drove out the best men and established democracies in Akhaia."[210] The Akhaian "best men" banded together and took back their cities one by one, after which they became strong supporters of the Spartans.

While all this was going on in Akhaia, the Phliasians, still staunch allies of the Lakedaimonians, defeated the Sikyonians and their Theban allies in a pitched battle, then turned around, and with the help of the Athenian strategos Khares, defeated the Argives, with whom they had been at war for at least the last two years. Then they turned back again, and with the aid of Khares, caught the Sikyonians cooking dinner at a position that they had fortified inside Phliasian territory. Terrified at the sudden approach of their enemies, the Sikyonians fled. Khares and the Phliasians occupied the position and ate the Sikyonians' dinner.

At the same time, "Themison, tyrant of Eretria, seized Oropos," an important Athenian port on the northern coast of Attika, possibly at the urging of the Thebans, who had probably planned the subsequent scenario: the Athenians recalled Khares and took the field with their entire force. "The Thebans, helping him [Themison], receiving the city entrusted [to them] did not give it back." [211] (Were the Sacred Band among the occupying force?) Athens' allies did not come to her aid, and the possession of Oropos was left to be decided by some kind of lawsuit. And, with Khares out of the way, the Sikyonians were able to recover territory lost to the Phliasians. Khabrias was charged with treason for failing to prevent the defection of Oropos. Defended by the philosopher Plato, he was acquitted.[212]

Unhappy with their allies, the Athenians accepted an offer of alliance from the Arkadians, the sworn enemies of Athens' other ally, Lakedaimon, considering that it would better to have Sparta's enemies allied with Sparta's friends than with Sparta's other enemies, the Thebans, with whom, of course, the Arkadians were still allied anyway. The Athenians now decided that they needed unimpeded access to the Peloponnese, so they planned to seize Korinth, the ally of their ally Sparta. Since they openly debated this in the assembly it's not surprising to note that the Korinthians heard of it, and by the time Khares arrived with a fleet, offering his support for the present government of Korinth, the Korinthians had already nicely asked the Athenian troops on duty to leave the city and its environs.

Then, according to Xenophon, the Korinthians, Phliasians, "and those coming with them" made a separate peace with Thebes, after asking the Lakedaimonians if it would be ok. Diodorus says that five years after Leuktra the "King of the Persians...persuaded the Hellenes to end the wars and to put together a common peace."[213] Xenophon doesn't mention the Persian King, but "those coming with them" could imply a common peace that didn't include the Lakedaimonians, who would never give up their claim to Messenia, whose autonomy was guaranteed by the terms of the King's Peace.

It was now autumn 366, and Ariobarzanes, the satrap of Hellespontine Phrygia, joined what historians call The Satrap's Revolt, which had been going on for sometime now, with Egypt and provinces to the east of Phrygia in open rebellion against Artaxerxes II, the Great King of Persia. The Athenians saw this as an opportunity: Timotheos had been laying low since his political enemies had removed him from command of the fleet around Korkyra and his subsequent trial and acquittal back in 374. Now, with his rivals discredited by the Oropos episode, he was given thirty triremes and eight thousand mercenaries and sent east to liberate the island of Samos from the Persians. Arriving at the island, Timotheos laid siege to the city of the same name.

AGESILAOS GOES EAST

"Around about this time, Dionysios himself having died already before, his son sent aid to the Lakedaimonians, twelve triremes, and leading them, Timokrates."[214] With his help, the Lakedaimonians recovered Sellasia. And then Timokrates went home. We should probably date this to spring or summer of 365, since in his next paragraph, Xenophon writes: "not long after this..." and then goes on to describe fighting between Elis and the Arkadian League, which happened in 365. The Eleans had the worst of it, and the Arkadians occupied Olympia, which caused the Eleans to ally with Lakedaimon.[215] Akhidamos led out the army and engaged the Arkadians. His tactical disposition seems to have been faulty. He seems to have been caught in column of march by the Arkadians in line of battle, or he was trying a column against line attack, perhaps in some type of imitation of Theban tactics. In any case, he was stabbed right through the thigh and lost about thirty men before he was forced to retreat. A truce was agreed. The Arkadians put up a trophy; the Lakedaimonians went home.

In the east, after a ten-month siege, Timotheos took Samos in the summer of 365 and then seems to have acted in concert with Agesilaos, who, according to Xenophon, accomplished the work of a great general while acting as an ambassador, somehow relieving the sieges of Assos, a town south of Ilion, and Sestos, a town on the European side of the Hellespont, opposite Abydos. One is tempted to wonder whether Agesilaos restricted himself to diplomatic duties or perhaps acted as a military advisor to Ariobarzanes. It would not be unreasonable to speculate whether it was Agesilaos who convinced Mausolos, the satrap of Karia, to join the revolt, for he sent Agesilaos back to Sparta with a "magnificent escort" and "money."[216]

Back at Thebes, Epameinondas, concerned with Athenian naval activity, no doubt including their successful capture of Samos, convinced the Thebans to hire a Karthaginian shipwright to build them a fleet of their own. In Makedon, Perdikkas killed Ptolemy and assumed the throne, and probably at this time, Philip returned home, where his brother gave him a political job.

KYNOSKEPHALAI

It was probably spring 364, when Epameinondas set out with the new Theban fleet. He spent the summer sailing around the coast of Asia Minor, doing his best to diplomatically dismantle what scholars call the Second Athenian Confederacy.

We don't exactly know in what month the ancient Olympics took place, whether it was spring or summer, but the Eleans and Arkadians managed to fight a battle in the middle of it, with the spectators watching and cheering them on as if it were part of the games. The Eleans defeated the Arkadians, who were supported by two thousand Argive hoplites and four hundred Athenian horse, but were unable to recover Olympia, which had been heavily fortified by the Arkadians.

Around the same time, the Thessalian cities asked Thebes for military aid against Alexandros of Pherai. The Thebans decided to send Pelopidas and seven thousand men. Before they could set out there was an eclipse of the sun (July 13, 364[217]), which everyone considered a very bad omen, perhaps presaging the fall of a great man. Enthusiasm for the war turned to dread, and Pelopidas' friends advised him not to go. Like the Spartans at Leuktra, Pelopidas ignored the omens and left for Thessaly with three hundred non-Theban volunteer cavalry. He was dying to get his hands on Alexandros, his former tormentor.

Upon arrival at Pharsalos he quickly gathered a force of Thessalians and set out in Alexandros' direction. Alexandros, learning that Pelopidas' army was half the size of his own, confidently marched to meet him. When the disparity in numbers was reported to Pelopidas he characteristically laughed it off, saying: "Better - for we will defeat a greater number." Plutarch mentions "a few Thebans around Pelopidas," and it is tempting to believe that these were all or some of the Sacred Band, following their beloved leader when the rest of the Thebans would not.[218]

The ground west of Pherai is broken and hilly country, and both sides made for the high ridge called Kynoskephalai, Alexandros making his camp east of the ridge by the Thetideion, the Temple of Thetis, on a low eminence where one hundred and sixty odd years later the Romans would camp before their legions smashed the Makedonian phalanx of Philip V on the same ridge of Kynoskephalai. Pelopidas, approaching from the west, ordered his infantry to occupy the ridge, while he personally led the cavalry around the ridge to the south and toward the Thetideion. The Thessalian cavalry were victorious, pursuing Alexandros' horse out into the plain and removing them as a factor in the battle. However, Alexandros was first to reach the heights with his infantry.

For a hoplite to be effective he has to be right in your face; his spear is for thrusting, not throwing, and to maintain formation he can only march so fast; sure, he can run, but carrying a huge body-shield and wearing armor, not too far. It's a particularly bad idea for hoplites to attack up-hill, but this is just what Pelopidas did. He had ordered the Thessalian phalanx forward, up rising ground, toward Alexandros' army drawn up on the crest of the ridge. Advancing against what Plutarch calls "strong and high places," the Thessalian hoplites were met by a storm of missile weapons; those in the front were killed, and the rest "accomplished nothing."

Seeing this, Pelopidas managed to recall his cavalry and ordered it to attack the enemy formation, probably from the south against Alexandros' left, where the ground sloped less steeply, while he kept them pinned down by renewing the frontal assault. In this he foreshadowed a favorite tactic of Alexander the Great, the very man who, twenty-six years later, would put an end to the Sacred Band forever. Pelopidas, having just fought in the cavalry action, led the infantry attack himself, jumping down from his horse and pushing his way into the front line. His presence roused the Thessalians, and they advanced, only to be beaten back. Pelopidas would not give up and attacked again and again. Finally, this unrelenting pressure, and the fact that they could now see the Thessalian cavalry returning, caused Alexandros' men to waver. They began to retreat in good order.

As his enemy backed down the ridge, Pelopidas gained the crest. Looking down he could see all of Alexandros' army. It still maintained formation. But already it was filled with "fear and confusion" at the prospect of being trapped between the relentless hoplites above and the cavalry now advancing on their flank or rear.

Pelopidas stood looking all around, eager for a sight of Alexandros. He found him on his right, out in front of his mercenaries, rallying them and dressing their lines. Plutarch says he was "burned up at the sight" and "could not restrain his anger by his reason." In a mad rage Pelopidas leapt out of formation and ran off straight at Alexandros, yelling at him to come out and fight. Considering the fact that Pelopidas was able to spot his enemy so easily, he must have stationed himself on the left of his own line, across from his enemy's right - just like at the battle of Leuktra. The Thessalian hoplites must have followed, but they were too far away to run and still maintain formation.

Alexandros saw Pelopidas coming at him and ducked back into the ranks of his mercenary body-guard. Some of the mercenaries in the front rank ran out to meet Pelopidas hand to hand. Plutarch doesn't tell us what kind of weapon Pelopidas had at this point; perhaps he still had his spear (the Hellenes, unlike the Romans, who liked to come to close quarters and decide the issue with the points of their short swords, favored the thrusting spear, and would only draw their swords when their spears were lost or broken); perhaps it had been broken in the fighting before. From Plutarch's description it sounds like

Pelopidas was armed only with a sword: "Of the mercenaries, those in the front rank, engaging hand to hand, were beaten back by Pelopidas; some, being struck, died; most, from a distance, striking him with their spears through his armor, covered him with wounds." Nevertheless, he beat back the mercenaries and some of those he struck fell and never rose again. The rest stayed in formation or perhaps surrounded him. It is clear that by this time he had no spear, for he was unable to come to grips with his enemies while they were able to stay out of his reach and strike him with their spears. He was stabbed many times, right through his armor. When the Thessalians saw this they broke into a run, but Pelopidas fell before they could reach him.

With the hoplites running downhill at them and the cavalry charging uphill at them, Alexandros' army disintegrated. The Thessalian horse pursued them for a great distance and filled the country with corpses, cutting down more than three thousand. Pelopidas had used his infantry to fix Alexandros' phalanx in position while his cavalry attacked from rear or flank. Although Pelopidas' horse never came to grips with Alexandros' phalanx, it is clear that they were to be used as shock troops. By these combined arms tactics Pelopidas had defeated a more numerous opponent.

The death of Pelopidas was a heavy blow to the Thebans who were there. They lamented him as father, teacher, and sotera - savior, a title usually reserved for gods. Were the men who regarded Pelopidas in such adoration devoted members of the Sacred Band? Plutarch only identifies them as Thebans. The Thessalians were equally upset; Pelopidas had led them to victory and preserved their freedom and the freedom of their wives and children. They crowded around the body, still in their armor, sweating and bleeding. They cut their hair and their horses' manes; too distraught to eat, they went to bed hungry. The body of Pelopidas was brought home to Thebes for burial.

As the summer of 364 waned, the Thebans, perhaps a little jumpy after the death of Pelopidas, perhaps suspecting a revolt by Orkhomenos (which had been forced by the Thebans to join their Boiotian League), destroyed that ancient city, killing all the men and selling the women and children into slavery. Epameinondas didn't like it, but he was off with the fleet, and by the time he got the news there was nothing he could do about it.

The Arkadians in possession of Olympia soon started dipping into the temple treasuries in order to pay their troops. The Mantineians didn't like this and led the rest of the Arkadian League in passing a resolution to end this practice. The Arkadians, fearing that they might be audited (and if their accounts didn't tally they'd have to make up the balance with their lives), called in the Thebans for help. The rest of the Arkadian League didn't want the Thebans around, and so the Mantineians, Eleans, and Akhaians asked the Spartans and Athenians to help them keep the Thebans out of the Peloponnesos.

MANTINEIA

In summer 362 Epameinondas came south leading the Thebans, the rest of the Boiotians, the Euboians, and some Thessalians. Once in the Peloponnesos, he took up a position at Nemea, intending to attack the Athenians as they marched south. When he heard that they were sailing directly to Sparta, he moved to Tegea where he was joined by the Argives, Messenians, Tegeans, Megalopolitans, Aseans, and other smaller states that didn't really have a choice. His opponents gathered at Mantineia, to the north. When he heard that Agesilaos was on the march toward Mantineia, he immediately led his own army toward the now undefended capital of the Lakedaimonians. "Divine fate" in the guise of a Kretan, warned the Spartan King of Epameinondas' movements, and Agesilaos quickly returned home.[219]

Xenophon points out that when Epameinondas arrived he wisely decided to avoid house-to-house fighting on level ground. He could probably see the teenagers and old men posted by Agesilaos on the rooftops, no doubt armed with missile weapons, and the other troops draw up here and there guarding all accessible points. Undaunted, he seems to have scouted out the best approach and attacked from the rising ground to the north of the un-walled city. According to Xenophon, Akhidamos, with less than a hundred men, counter-attacked uphill, and the Thebans did not "receive those around Akhidamos, but fled."[220] The Lakedaimonians pursued them a bit too far and began to take casualties. The Thebans must have regrouped at a distance from the city. The Spartan pursuit ended. A truce was agreed; the Thebans took up their dead, and Arhkidamos put up a trophy.

Diodorus tells how Epameinondas' men, unable to breach the fortifications of Sparta and losing many of their own number in the process, "were recalled by the war trumpet." Then, "going forward, to the city, they called out the Spartans to a pitched battle or, they said, to admit [that they were] weaker than their enemies, the Spartans answering that [at] a convenient opportunity they would contend for everything." Unable to make any headway, and worried that the Arkadians would show up to reinforce the Lakedaimonians, Epameinondas withdrew to Tegea.[221]

Plutarch mentions Isidas, the incredibly handsome son of Phoibidas, who fought without armor, shield, or cloak, which ordinarily would mean that he was wearing a khiton, but who, according to the Boiotian biographer, had "richly anointed his body with oil" and was "gymnos," "naked," when he went into battle.[222] One can, perhaps, be forgiven for wondering why Isidas was naked and oiled up when he knew that the Thebans were coming and that anyone else who could lift a weapon was at a post assigned by Agesilaos. Plutarch continues: "holding in one hand a spear and in the other a sword, he charged out of [his] house, and, pushing his way through the middle of those fighting..." but then Plutarch's Greek gets obscure; it seems that in his striving for literary quality he likes to use unusual words. For example, while Xenophon invariably calls a spear "doru," Plutarch has to use the word "λογχην,"which properly means "spear point." (Substituting "spear point" for "spear" is a nice use of metonymy, but not very accurate.) But the sense of Plutarch's story about Isidas is this: Isidas throws himself on the enemy, strikes and kills anyone he encounters, doesn't get a scratch on him, is later crowned by the ephors for bravery and then fined a thousand drakhmas for fighting without armor.

Maybe they really fined him for being late to Agesilaos' muster. Maybe, being a young, good-looking guy, he had stayed up a little too late the night before, partying, and had overslept, missing Agesilaos' return and muster. Getting up with a hangover, oiling up, and then realizing that the Thebans were in the city, he charged out of his house and did what Spartans did best.

On reaching Tegea, Epameinondas halted his infantry but sent his cavalry on ahead in an effort to catch the Mantineians gathering in the harvest and with "all their cattle and all their people most likely outside Mantineia."[223] The Athenian cavalry, exhausted and hungry, reached Mantineia just before the Theban and Thessalian horse. As Epameinondas had guessed, the people and cattle were outside the walls. Tired as the Athenians and their horses were, outnumbered, and having suffered some kind of "misfortune at Korinth," they nevertheless took the field upon the appearance of their hostile counterparts. Xenophon tells how, "as soon as they saw the enemy, they dashed together." The desperate attack of the Athenians saved the Mantineians, but "of them good men died."[224] At this point one cannot help admiring Xenophon despite all of his pro-Spartan bias and selective reporting, for one of those "good men" was his son Gryllos. Philosopher and warrior that he was, Xenophon must have considered it unseemly to mention his private grief. He laconically reports that the Athenians gave back the enemy dead under a truce. It is noticeable that he does not mention the Athenians putting up a trophy, which would have been standard practice if they had been completely victorious.

Epameinondas now decided to risk all in a pitched battle.[225] He led his whole force against Mantineia. The road north from Tegea, where Epaminondas had his base, to Mantineia, passes at one point between two steep hills. In this space, about a mile wide, the Mantineians waited. With them were their allies the Athenians and the Spartans, all under the command of the Spartan King Agesilaos, who was now about eighty-two years old. When Epameinondas came in sight of the enemy he left the road and drew up his army in line of battle. Both sides looked at each other. There were close to sixty thousand men under arms, and the biggest battle ever fought between Hellenes was about to happen.

Epameinondas' army just marched off and halted at the foot of a mountain to the west of the road. His enemies believed that he was not going to fight and was about to make camp. Some of the Mantineians started to do likewise, and their allies began to relax. Epameinondas' army, while still in line, was subtly changing formation as units from the right rear crossed behind the army to the left, to deepen that flank for a decisive blow.

When this maneuver was complete, Epameinondas advanced his left obliquely against his enemies. Xenophon compares his formation to a trireme advancing with the "prow forwards," the prow, in this case, formed of the Sacred Band of Thebes. Xenophon seems to be describing the Theban left advancing in column, intending to blitzkrieg their way through the Spartan line.

When they saw this, the Mantineians and their allies rushed to rearm and reform. In front of his hoplites Epameinondas had stationed his cavalry, reinforced by hamippoi (literally "men as fast as horses"), light infantry who would add weight to their attack. In a tight formation they slammed into the hastily drawn up line of enemy cavalry. As they had at Leuktra, they forced the opposing cavalry back into their own hoplites, this time charging through the gaps in the line with them. Epameinondas and fifty ranks of Thebans and Boiotians were right behind them. On his right the cavalry of both armies was also engaged, while his right wing of hoplites advanced slowly. On the far right, on some rising ground, Epameinondas had stationed some cavalry and infantry to threaten the left flank of the Athenians while he struck the Spartans and the Mantineians with the deepened column of his own left wing. The shock of so many men colliding together was enormous. As Diodorus wrote, "striking one another with their spears, they ruined most of them, at which point they continued the contest with their swords." Epameinondas was in the front rank, as Diodorus says, leading his "best men [the Sacred Band] in close order. He threw himself into the midst of the enemy."

The Spartans could not endure the pressure of the Boiotians' reinforced left wing. They began to give way. As they fell back, the Thebans and Epameinondas pressed them closely. Just as the Spartan line gave way, and the Thebans leapt forward in pursuit, a Spartan named Antikrates stepped into the path of the charging Epameinondas and thrust his spear through the Theban leader's breastplate. (Alternate versions have Antikrates using a sword, which doesn't sound right.) The force of their meeting broke the shaft and left the metal point in Epameinondas' body. "He fell down on the spot, overcome by the blow." A brief but bloody struggle ensued above the mortally wounded Epameinondas, but the Spartans were soon in full flight. The Thebans pursued them, but not very far; the fall of Epameinondas had taken the heart out of them. The cavalry also returned, leaving the fleeing Spartans unmolested.

Diodorus tells what happened next:

Epameinondas, still living, was carried to the camp. The healers, being summoned, declared flatly that should the spear be taken out of his chest, death would soon follow. With the greatest courage Epameinondas performed the last act of his life. First he called his shield-bearer and asked him if he had saved his shield. The shield-bearer answered yes and placed the shield where Epameinondas could see it. Then he asked which side had won. When the young man said that the Boiotians were the victors, Epameinondas said 'ορα εστι τελευταν' – 'it is time for the end,' and he ordered them to draw out the spear-point. His friends who were there cried out, and one of them said, 'you die childless, Epameinondas,' and burst into tears. 'No, by God,' said Epameinondas, 'I

leave my two daughters - Leuktra and Mantineia.'
And when the spear-point was taken out he
calmly breathed his last breath.[226]

The Spartans asked for a truce so that they could recover their dead. The Thebans granted it, and claiming victory, put up a battlefield trophy. On the other side of the field the Athenians had slaughtered the cavalry, peltasts, and hamippoi who had been trying to outflank them, and, giving back their bodies under a flag of truce, declared themselves victorious and put up their own trophy. With Epameinondas dead the Thebans didn't know what to do, and since neither side wanted to renew hostilities a peace treaty was signed confirming the status quo - except by the Spartans who would not recognize the independence of Messenia. Everybody else got to keep what they already had, and the biggest battle ever fought between Hellenes, a battle that should have changed everything, changed nothing and ended in a stalemate. At this point Xenophon ended his *Hellenika* (he probably just couldn't bring himself to write anymore), and around the same time Ariobarzanes ended his life when his son betrayed him and he was crucified.

KING PHILIP

Shortly after this, perhaps in Autumn 362 or spring 361, at the request of the Egyptian King, still in revolt against the Persian King, Agesilaos took a thousand men to Egypt, where he met Khabrias in command of the Egyptian fleet. After successfully and profitably helping the locals slaughter each other, in what turned into a civil war, the Lakedaimonian King sailed for home in mid-winter 361/360 loaded with money, which he no doubt intended to spend on the re-conquest of Messenia. On the way, he stopped at Kyrene in Libya, where, eighty-four years old and having been wounded in every part of his body by every weapon known to man, Agesilaos died of old age. When the body was stripped (it was about to be covered with wax for the trip back to Sparta), it was found to be a mass of scar tissue. Arkhidamos succeeded to the throne. (Kleomenes II, the brother of Agesipolis, was the other Spartan King, but you don't really hear much about him in the ancient sources.)

A year after the death of his old friend, Xenophon followed him to the Elysian Fields. Artaxerxes II joined them, and Perdikkas, the king of Makedon, was defeated and killed fighting the Illyrians. Philip became regent for his nephew Amyntas. He did such a good job as regent that the Makedonian army (in truly Homeric fashion, but in accordance with custom), elected him king. Philip's dream was to expand and Hellenize his kingdom. He set about accomplishing the second of these objectives by inviting Philosophers and artists and such from all over the Hellenic world to his capital, Pella. His imperialistic ambitions would be realized by a combination of diplomacy and warfare. But first he had to spend some money bribing the Paionians and Thrakians to leave him alone while he defeated another claimant to the throne named Argaios, who was backed by the Athenians.

In the following year (358), Alexandros of Pherai woke in the middle of the night to see his wife standing over him. With her were her three brothers, one holding his feet, another pulling his head back by the hair, and a third stabbing him with a sword. The people of Pherai used his body as a trampoline. He had not been a popular ruler.

While the people of Pherai were busy stomping their former tyrannos into the ground, Philip II of Makedon was busy paying back the Illyrians. According to Diodorus:

> so the armies approached one another; with a great shout they dashed together in battle, Philip commanding the right wing, with the best of the Makedonians fighting with [him]; he ordered the horsemen to ride past and attack the barbarian flanks; he himself, attacking the front of the enemy, joined in a sharp battle. The Illyrians, drawing themselves up in a powerful square, joined in battle. At first, for a long time the battle was equally balanced...then the horsemen pressing the flanks and rear [of the Illyrians], and Philip with [his] best [men] fighting heroically, the mass of Illyrians were compelled at the same time to rush to flight.[227]

Diodorus seems to place Philip with his infantry, on the right, where he orders his cavalry to advance. One would think that Philip would have been leading his aristocratic household cavalry, the Hetairoi (Companions) himself. Did the Makedonian king station himself with his infantry in order to inspire them by his presence while ordering one of his very competent senior officers to take command of the horse and lead them against the flanks and rear of the Illyrians? And did

Diodorus make a mistake when he wrote that the Illryians were in a square formation? Here we must bear in mind that Diodorus is not the most reliable source; he often makes mistakes, and he invariably embellishes for literary effect; the ellipsis in the passage above represents such an embellishment. Was it really the Makedonian infantry, not the Illyrians, who were in a square formation? Is this the first literary reference to the soon-to-be famous Makedonian phalanx, and were Philip's "best" his newly organized pezhetairoi, foot companions? (On the other hand, Diodorus could be correct, and the Illyrians could have been drawn up in an enormous column or compact mass, akin to the cuneus formation reported by the Romans with respect to their Germanic enemies. Even if this is so, it does not mean that Philip's men were not formed into the Makedonian phalanx.) At this point he has been king or regent of Makedon for a year, long enough for him to have armed his foot soldiers with the Iphikratean panoply, and long enough for him to have taught them how to fight in the deep Theban formation. Did Philip indeed fix his enemy in position with a frontal attack by his phalanx, while his horsemen, the knightly class of Makedon, delivered the death blow from the flanks and rear? According to Diodorus, Philip had six hundred horse to the Ilryians' five hundred. Had he already armed the Hetairoi with the sarrisa; did it give them the edge in this battle, allowing them to drive the Illyrian horse from the field?

Frontinus (ca. 35–103 CE), the Roman author, himself a Consul with military experience, agrees that Philip was on the right with his best troops and mentions a flank attack on the Illyrian left.

> Philip, the King of Macedon, waging war against the Illyrians, as he noticed the front of the enemy packed with men chosen from the whole army, the sides (or flanks) however, weaker, with the strongest of his own men stationed on the right, attacked the left side (or flank) of the enemy, and

with the whole line thrown into disorder he won a victory.[228]

This account seems to support Diodorus, although it also sounds a bit like a description of the oblique order of battle. And one wonders how Philip knew that "the front of the enemy [was] packed with men chosen from the whole army," unless he had learned this from spies or deserters.

Diodorus' description recalls Pelopidas' use of cavalry at Kynoskephalai and the flank attacks of Alexander the Great. It would not be unreasonable to imagine Philip leading his pezhetaroi on foot (like Henry V at Agincourt), fighting on the right in the position of honor, fixing the Illyrians in place with a violent frontal assault by the new style phalanx, and, since he slightly outnumbered the Illyrians in cavalry, ordering his left wing horse to fight a holding action, while his no doubt reinforced right wing cavalry drove their opposite numbers from the field and then struck the Illyrians in the flank, executing, on different flanks, the same cavalry tactics that his son would use at Issus.

By 357, Athens' allies were tired of playing second fiddle to the Athenians, and sought to break away from what we call The Second Athenian Confederacy, by fighting what we call The Social War (Socii being the Latin word for allies). Khabrias was sent to persuade them to reconsider. His first target was the island of Khios. Sailing into the harbor, he outdistanced his own fleet and was soon surrounded by the triremes of his enemies. Nepos records his death: "his ship, struck by a ram, began to sink. Although he would have been able to flee, if he had thrown himself into the sea...he preferred to die." The rest of his crew jumped overboard and swam to safety. "But Khabrias, thinking that a noble death is preferable to a dishonorable life, was killed, fighting hand to hand, by the weapons of the enemy."[229]

At the same time, the Athenians led by Timotheos fought the Thebans in Euboia, and when both sides had done enough damage, the Thebans went home. And while they were thus occupied, Philip captured Amphipolis. The Athenians declared war, but they were too busy fighting their own allies, so Philip continued to expand his territory eastwards. In the year after he captured Amphipolis, the inhabitants of Krenides, a town to the east of the gold mines of Mt. Pangaios, asked him for help against the Thrakians. Philip wasted no time: he drove off the Thrakians and took possession of Krenides, which he then named after himself: Philippi, thus inaugurating the Hellenistic custom, practiced profusely by his prominent progeny, of naming cities after oneself.

Turning his attention westwards, to secure his boundaries he married Olympias, the daughter of Neoptolemos, king of Epeiros, who would later give birth to Alexander the Great. The Athenians allied themselves with the Thrakians, Paionians, and Illyrians, who were promptly defeated by Philip. In Asia Minor Artabazos revolted against the Persian King, and the Thebans sent Pammenes with five thousand men (including the Sacred Band?) to help him. "And Pammenes, helping Artabazos, and defeating the Satraps in two great battles, gained a great reputation for himself and the Boiotians." Both Frontinus and Polyainos mention a battle in which Pammenes directed his left to withdraw, while he attacked the Persians with his best troops (the Sacred Band among them perhaps), and all of his cavalry on his right. Did Pammenes fix the Persian line with his infantry and flank them with his cavalry used as shock troops, or is this a description of Pammenes using the oblique order of battle in conjunction with a cavalry attack in a replay of Leuktra and Mantineia, or somehow a combination of both tactics? [230]

By 355 the Athenians had lost the Social War, and the Second Athenian Confederacy was all but done. In this year Philip received an arrow in the left eye at the siege of Methone (a town on the Thermaic Gulf). The ancient sources tell us that the arrow was signed by a man names Aster, who, when Philip took the city, was crucified by the Makedonian King. While all this was going on, the Hellenes had once again divided themselves into two hostile camps - the Phokaians, Athenians, Spartans, and Akhaians against the Thebans, Boiotians, Lokrians, and Thessalians, fighting for control of sacred Delphi in what scholars call The Third Sacred War.

THE AMPHIKTIONIC COUNCIL

The Delphic Amphiktiony was a religious body charged with maintaining things at Delphi and keeping an eye out for sacrilegious behavior, which it was empowered to punish. It had no real authority, but like the Pope in the middle ages or the Emperor of Japan, it had a great influence on political affairs. So, when the Thebans manipulated the Amphiktionic council and heavy fines were levied upon the Phokaians and Spartans, all Hellas was once again divided into two armed camps.

Philip managed to get himself involved when the Thessalian cities asked him to help them against Lykophron and Peitholaos, two of the three brothers who had killed Alexandros (the third had recently died), and who were now ruling Pherai backed by the Phokaians. They proved themselves to be no better than Alexandros, and were pursuing his old policy of neighborly aggression. Philip beat the Phokaians and drove Lykophron and Peitholaos out of Pherai, which he characteristically kept for himself. He then marched south, toward Thermopylai, the pass into Hellas. The Athenians, Spartans, Akhaians, Phokaians, with Lykophron and Peitholaos and their two thousand mercenaries held the pass against him. Philip turned back into Thessaly where he was elected archon for life.

With Philip gone, the rest of the Hellenes went back to fighting among themselves. The Thebans and the Spartans were at it again in the Peloponnesos: some of the Megalapolitans wanted to go back to their former towns; those who opposed this idea called on the Thebans for help. Pammenes led three thousand hoplites and three hundred horse into the Peloponnesos and, by threats and destruction of property, preserved the integrity of Megalopolis. No doubt the Band was in the thick of things.

The Makedonian King meanwhile was off on the eastern fringes of his kingdom, punishing recalcitrant erstwhile adherents and establishing friendly relations with Byzantion, which happened to sit right at the mouth of the Bosphoros and controlled the grain route into the Black Sea. This didn't go over well with the Athenians who had lost the Peloponnesian War some fifty years before when the Spartans cut off their grain supply. For the last five years they had been fighting a cold war with Philip in this region. In 351 the Athenian Demosthenes delivered his First Philippic, denouncing Philip and his policies. For rest of his life he would wage a war of words against Philip and his son Alexander.

In the next few years Philip was able to outmaneuver the Athenians in Thrake and stir up trouble for them in Euboia. People in Athens began to think about making friends with Philip. Then the Boiotians, who were still fighting the Sacred War with the Phokaians, called upon Philip to help them punish their enemies, who were sacrilegiously selling off the temple treasures to pay their mercenaries. The Phokaians in turn appealed to Athens. This seemed like the opportunity to confront Philip, but then the Phokaians changed their leaders and their minds. The Athenians quickly signed the Peace of Philokrates with Philip based on the status quo. Philip marched south to Themopylai and accepted the surrender of the Phokaian leader, who was allowed to depart with his men. The Sacred War was over, and though some of the victorious states called for harsh penalties to be inflicted on the Phokaians, they got off pretty lightly, having to pay a large fine and dismantle their cities and live in villages. They also lost their two votes on the Amphiktionic Council, which were given to Philip. It was the Theban-dominated Amphiktionic Council which had started the war with Phokis, ostensibly for religious, but really for political reasons. Now Philip had two votes on a Hellenic council whose actions were sanctioned by the ultimate authorities - the gods themselves.

For the next two years Philip was busy in Makedon and was again fighting the Illyrians. Then he came south and reorganized Thessaly. He sent ambassadors to the Athenians, who were complaining about the terms of the Peace of Philokrates. This prompted Demosthenes' Second Philippic. In 343 Philip put his wife's brother on the throne of Epeiros, further strengthening his western boundaries. While Philip was engaged in king-making, Demosthenes was touring the Peloponnessos gathering allies. Argos, Arkadia, and Messenia managed to ally themselves with both Athens and Makedon. In the same year, Artaxerxes III personally led his army, including about twenty thousand Hellenic mercenaries, of whom one thousand were from Thebes, in the re-conquest of Egypt.

The year 342 was a busy one for Philip. He made peace overtures, which the Athenians rejected, and embarked on a final conquest of Thrake. Athens sent Diopeithes to Thrake, where he began to raid Makedonian territory. At the same time, Philip and Athens were fighting a cold war in Euboia, Philip backing the tyrants and the Athenians restoring the democracies. The next year Demosthenes delivered his Third Philippic. He was by now the leading statesman in Athens and managed to form alliances with Byzantion and Perinthos. Philip promptly laid siege to both cities and captured the Athenian grain convoy. The Athenians smashed the stone stele upon which was inscribed the Peace of Philokrates and declared war. By 339 Philip had tired of besieging Byzantion and Perinthos and went back to Pella. But luck was with him.

The Amphiktionic council voted fines against the Amphissans; they refused to pay. The council appointed Philip as general against them. Philip took the western route down into Hellas, bypassing Themopylai. Demosthenes hurried to

Thebes to form an alliance against Philip. Philip sent envoys to Thebes to form an alliance against Athens. The Thebans, fearing that Philip would become too powerful if he beat Athens, threw in their lot with the Athenians. In the spring of 339 Philip destroyed the Amphissans' ten thousand mercenaries and took Delphi and Naupaktos. He sent envoys to Athens and Thebes seeking a peaceful solution. Demosthenes persuaded them to fight.

KHAIRONEIA

After the long cold war between Philip and Athens, the fate of Hellas was decided on August 4th, 338 BCE, when the Makedonians under Philip and Alexander met the Athenians and Thebans led by Khares and Lysikles near the town of Khaironeia. Philip, on the right, advanced against the Athenians, whose left was protected by the high ground around Khaironeia. On the left of the Makedonian line his eighteen-year-old son Alexander faced the Thebans, whose flank was anchored on the river Kephisos. It was now that Philip, who had spent three years as a hostage in Thebes, turned the Thebans' own tactics against them. As Epameinondas had done at Leuktra and Mantineia, he refused his right and attacked the Thebans on his left. The two phalanxes crashed together, neither side giving ground. By all accounts the fighting between the Makedonians and the Thebans was fierce and not over quickly.[231]

With his left engaged, Philip, adding further sophistication to the oblique order of Epameinondas, actually seems to have withdrawn his right. This difficult maneuver enticed the Athenians to leave their defensive position and, perhaps confident of victory, to pursue Philip in a rather disorderly fashion. Alexander had been waiting for this. Stationed with the Companion Cavalry, the Hetairoi, behind his infantry phalanx (or posted on the left, intending to ride behind his own phalanx), he expected his father to lure out the Athenians by a feigned withdrawal and to create a flank where there was no flank, an opening that he knew would be there, and through which he could lead the Hetairoi in order to completely envelope the Thebans; it was a master plan, devised by Philip, which worked perfectly. As he was to do many times in the future, Alexander personally led the Hetairoi through the gap created by the Athenians' hasty and ill-considered advance and attacked the Thebans in the rear. Under pressure from the Makedonian phalanx in front and the Companions in the rear the Theban line disintegrated. The Sacred Band alone stood firm.[232]

The hoplite spear (doru) was six to eight feet long; the sarissa of the Makedonians was, at this time, probably twelve feet long and used by both Hetairoi and infantry. A cavalry attack in real life is not like the movie version: there is no wild charge of disorganized horsemen into an equally disorganized enemy. The Hetairoi did not gallop into battle. In a deep, close order formation they moved, perhaps at a slow trot, against the rear of the Sacred Band, stabbing downward with their longer spears. One can only imagine the outnumbered and out-flanked Theban hoplites turning their rear ranks about face and desperately stabbing back with their shorter weapons or hacking with swords at their enemies' spear shafts, perhaps finally grappling with blood-slippery bare hands as they were slowly squeezed between the infantry in their front and the horsemen in their rear. With no hope of escape they maintained formation and fought until they were struck down, until the only men standing in that part of the field were blood-soaked Makedonians who knew they'd been in a fight. While this was going on, Philip returned to the offensive and easily put the disordered Athenian phalanx to flight.

There is no mention of Athenian or Theban cavalry in the ancient sources. Some scholars, following the account of Diodorus, believe that the battle on the left, between Alexander's troops and the Thebans was wholly an infantry affair, and that the longer spears used by the Makedonians enabled them to kill more of their enemies before they themselves could be struck, and thus wear down the opposition by simple attrition. However, Philip's tactic of creating a flank where there was no flank (recorded by Polyainos, writing in the 2nd century CE[233]), was so perfectly imitated by Alexander at Gaugamela that one has to wonder whether Alexander, facing Darius, improvised his movement to the right, or had learned it from his father years before.

The use of cavalry as shock troops, or at least as a determining factor in battle, had been demonstrated by Pelopidas, probably at Tegyra, and certainly at Kynoskephalai, where the phalanx of Alexandros of Pherai had been forced to withdraw (and eventually dissolved), under the pressure of hoplites to its front and cavalry to its rear. Pammenes seemed to have used his cavalry as shock troops against the Persians, and Philip seems to have done the same against the Illyrians.

At Khaironeia Philip not only withheld his right, he performed a difficult withdrawal in the face of his enemy. This feigned retreat caused the Athenians to leave their position and open a gap between themselves and the Thebans, which was exploited by Alexander and the Companion Cavalry. While Alexander's infantry fixed the Theban phalanx in place, his cavalry attacked from the rear and demolished it. At the same time, Philip advanced against the Athenians, who had broken formation in order to pursue what they assumed to be the retreating Makedonians. Unable to reform to meet Philip's advance, the Athenians withdrew in disorder. Philip's use (and refinement) of the oblique order of battle, the deepened phalanx, and his employment of cavalry as shock troops enabled him to emerge victorious from this epoch-ending battle.

When the fighting at Khaironeia was over, Philip toured the battlefield. Stepping over the gory corpses of his late enemies, he came upon the remains of the Sacred Band. Plutarch says he was amazed as he looked on them lying there amid the broken weapons, still in formation, having died where they stood, their bodies entwined in a final, bloody embrace. When he learned their identity, tears rolled out of his good eye and down his cheek. A brave man himself, he was awed and impressed by the fatal courage of these men who preferred death to dishonorable flight. He cursed: "Anyone who thinks that these men did or suffered anything shameful should die a painful death!"[234]

Today a stone lion stands on the battlefield of Khaironeia. Buried beneath it, in seven rows, are the remains of two hundred and fifty-four men. Their identity is disputed, but some scholars believe that Philip, in admiration of the Sacred Band and their extreme sacrifice, perhaps in gratitude to these men whose tactical innovations were the basis of his military organization, raised a monument to their courage and laid them to rest in the very ground that they would not yield. Twenty-three hundred years later they are still at their post.

EPILOGOS

Two years later Philip was dead, killed by a man named Pausanias, either a jealous lover or an agent of Olympias. As Alexander assumed the throne, the Thebans revolted. The new king of Makedon wasted no time; he crushed the Thebans and ordered his men to sack the town. While this order was being carried out, a group of his Thessalian allies brought to him a woman. She had been raped by their leader, who then forced her to show him her most valuable belongings. These, she said, were hidden down a well, and as he bent over to take a look, she pushed him in. Thereupon she dropped stones on him until he died. To Alexander she freely admitted the truth of the story and proudly declared that she was the sister of Theagenes, the last leader of the Sacred Band, who had died fighting for freedom. Alexander let her go. Perhaps he felt a certain kinship with those men who had met death at his hands. Before the attack on Thebes he had sacrificed at the Tomb of Iolaos, where the members of the Band had taken their vows of love, and though he was later married twice, his longest lasting relationship was with a man named Hephaistion. When Hephaistion took sick and died, Alexander, heartbroken, executed his doctor. Not long after the death of Hephaistion, worn out from his labors and his many wounds, Alexander himself died.

Appendix One: Barbarians

The ancient Hellenes were a bit ethnocentric; they laughed at foreigners who could not speak their language, saying that their speech sounded like bar, bar, bar, bar, bar. So they called them barbaroi (βαβαροι). Today the word 'barbarian' is used to describe uncivilized behavior or aspect; however, to the ancient Hellenes, the range of barbarism extended from the wild Skythians of the wintry north through the decadent, bejeweled Persians to the east, to the northern shores of Africa and the incredibly old and mysterious country of the Egyptians, and to the head-hunting Keltoi on the fringes of Hellenic awareness.

Appendix Two: Politics

The Hellenes' political systems were not unlike our own. Although they did not have organized political parties, most Hellenic states were divided along economic lines, with the mass of the people, the demos, opposed to an aristocratic elite. Barbarians and states on the fringes of the Hellenic world, like Makedon, still had hereditary kingships. Some places, like Syrakousai, were ruled by Tyrants. A tyrannos, like Dionysios of Syrakousai, was someone who had seized power by unconstitutional means. The Spartans, of course, had to be different. They had two kings, a senate, and a board of magistrates. The Spartan kings each had their own political supporters. It is not entirely farfetched to think of Hellenic politics (aside from kings and tyrants), as Democrats vs. Republicans, except in the case of the Spartans where it was probably more like Republicans vs. Republicans.

Appendix Three: Προκαλεω

Προκαλεω (prokaleo) is the Greek word I've translated as "call forth." That is actually what it means. The word καλεω means call; the προ is the part that means "forth." It can also mean "offer," "invite," "challenge," and is used as a legal term by Demosthenes, and, I'm sure, by other orators.

In the Iliad προκαλεω means a verbal challenge. Somebody is always προκαλεωing somebody else to single combat or advising someone to προκαλεω someone else to single combat. So if we're translating the Iliad and we come across the word προκαλεω we can safely translate is as "challenge," or "call out," just like in a TV western when the bad guy says to the good guy, "I'm callin' you out."

Diodorus also uses προκαλεω to mean "invite," and in one passage (16.55.4) it can be translated as "lured," i.e., "Many, lured [lit. "called forth"] by hopes of these benefices, outstripped one another [in] giving themselves and their fatherlands into Phillip's hands." Elsewhere (16.73.3) he metaphorically writes, "The rewards [strictly speaking the word επαθλα, which I've translated as "rewards," means the "prizes rewarded for victory in an athletic contest"- see how confusing this translating stuff can be!] of victory called forth the manly virtue of those fighting."

He also uses προκαλεω just like Homer: as a challenge to single combat, as when (17.100.2) "stimulated by drink he [a Makedonian named Koragos] challenged to single combat Dioxippos the Athenian," or when (15.61.2) "Polydoros... died from poison, having been challenged to a drink[ing match]."

In these cases a specific person is challenged, but Diodorus also uses προκαλεω to mean a more general challenge: "When Artaxerxes was king, fighting against the Kadousians, and one of the Kadousians, known for [his] strength and manliness, challenging him who wished of the Persians to fight, and no one dared to answer, but Dareios alone undertaking the risk, killed the challenger and was honored by the king with great gifts." (17.6.1)

And again (19.99.3) when Alexander, attacking a town in India, having mounted to the top of the enemy's battlements, found himself alone, the ladders carrying his Makedonian comrades having broken under the weight of the armored men swarming upon them, jumped down into the city and "many blows he took on his helmet, not a few he received on his pelta. Finally, struck by an arrow under the breast, he fell to one knee overpowered by the blow." One of the defenders ran up immediately, expecting to easily finish off the wounded king. As he brought down his weapon Alexander stabbed him in the side under the ribs. "The wound being in a vital place, the barbarian fell, and the king took hold of the young tree that was near and standing firm challenged those of the Indians wishing to fight." One might think that Alexander's presence alone, since he was attacking their city, would have been enough of a challenge, but since Diodorus actually uses the word διαγωνίζομαι, "to fight," it really sounds to me like Alexander, who was kind of a hot-head anyway, and was totally fearless, and who read the Iliad every day, and who now stood over the dead or dying body of his latest victim, and was wounded and bleeding himself, in pain, and with adrenaline rushing through his system, did actually yell something like "come on and fight!"

Diodoros also records how the στρατεγος Satibarzanes, taking off his helmet and showing who he was, challenged whoever was willing of the [opposing] στρατεγοι to single combat. (17.83.5)

The above accounts are clearly unambiguous invitations to single combat. But what about the question that started all this? Did Agesilaos issue a verbal challenge to Gorgidas' Thebans and Khabrias' Athenians to come down and fight? Herodotus tells (3.13.1) how, at the battle of Plataia in 379, the Persian commander, Mardonios, sent a herald to the Spartans complaining because the Spartans, who were supposed to be so tough, hadn't sent a herald to him, "challenging and wishing to fight with the Persians alone." Since the Spartans sent no challenge, Mardonios sent his own, "Why not then, with you before all the Hellenes thought to be the best and before all the Barbarians we, with equal numbers let us fight… whichever of us two wins, wins for the whole army." The Persian herald must have stood before the Spartan phalanx and yelled out his speech, for when no one answered him he returned to Mardonios, and the Persian attack began. Here we see a formal challenge brought by heralds. But the heralds in this case are βαρβαροι.

Heralds were, of course, employed throughout the Hellenic world and beyond. They were professional announcers just like the announcers we have today on TV and radio; the job was passed from father to son in Sparta (Herodotus 6.60.1); they were sent on diplomatic missions (Thucydides, 2.5.5., 2.6.2., 2.6.3., 2.12.2; Pau. 3.8.3, etc., et al.); they called soldiers to assembly, as in the fifth book of Xenophon's *Anabasis*, just like their ancestors did in the third book of *The Iliad*, and after a battle they were sent by the losers to ask the winners for permission to pick up their dead (Plutarch, *Lysander*, 29.2; *Nikias*, 6.5; *Lysias*, 2.7; Thuc.,3.24.3, 4.38.4; Diod., 13.111.1, 16.17.5, 16.25.2; Xen., *Hell.* 4.3.21, 6.4.15; Pausanias, 9.13.11; etc.). In book fourteen of Diodorus' history, Dionysios, the tyrant of Syrakousai, draws his army up in battle order in front of the walls of Leontini and through a herald demands the surrender of the city. In book six of Herodotus' history, Miltiades' herald orders the Parians to hand over one hundred talents or be attacked. Heralds are also sent to offer peace terms (Thuc., 3.52.3, 4.30.4, 4.114.1, 7.3.1). But were they used by the Hellenes to issue formal challenges to battle?

It seems to have been the practice then, as it is now, (only now we don't use heralds, and the Hellenes did), to issue a formal declaration of war to one's enemies (Polyainos, 5.5.6, Thuc., 1.29.10) though this custom was sometimes abused as when, "Demetrios sent a herald to the Boiotians to announce war. The herald at Orkhomenos gave the letter of war to the boiotarkhs. Demetrios encamped at Khaironeia the next day. The Boiotians were terrified at war being announced and being near at the same time" (Polyainos, 4.7.11). There were also surprise attacks, the Thebans attacking Plataia (Thuc. 2.2) without any advance warning, and "the Λακεδαιμονιοι neither sending a herald to declare war on the Messenians nor renouncing [their] friendship...swore an oath" that nothing would stop them before "the land of Messenia was taken by the spear" (Paus. 4.5.8). This does not seem to have been an extraordinary procedure for the Spartans, if we can believe the words of Pyrrhos to the Spartans, as reported by Polyainos (6.6.2), "you are not accustomed to announce beforehand [when] you are intending to make war."

So we see that the Hellenes, when they felt like it, sent a herald with a formal declaration of war, and when they didn't feel like it, didn't. Unlike Mardonios at Plataia, they don't seem to have been in the habit of sending heralds out to challenge each other to a pitched battle. So we can probably rule out the possibility that Agesilaos sent a herald to ask the Thebans and Athenians to come down from the high ground and fight it out in the plain. But what about an informal, verbal challenge?

Diodorus (15.65.4) tells how Epameinondas' men, unable to breach the fortifications of Sparta, and losing many of their own number in the process, "were recalled by the war trumpet." Then, "going forward, to the city, they called out the Spartans to a pitched battle or, they said, to admit [that they were] weaker than their enemies." In other words either fight or admit defeat. This is clearly an informal verbal challenge issued by one side to another. That there were many on the Theban side calling out is shown by Diodorus' use of the third person plurals: προσελθοντες (they going forward) and προεκαλουντο (they calling out).

Προκαλεω is also used in rather an ambiguous way. Epameinondas, in front of some Lakedaimonian fortifications, "challenged the enemy to fight" (Diod.15.68.4). When no one came out from the walls, "he took the fight to the enemy."
"Alkibiades... before the city, having drawn up his army in battle order, challenged the Kymaians to a battle" (Diod.13.73.5). "Imilkos led out the whole army, and before the

walls, formed line of battle, challenging the Syrakousians to a battle" (Diod.14.62.4).

Sometimes προκαλεω is used with διαγωνιζομαι, "to fight." "Agis...formed his army in line of battle and challenged those in the city to fight over the trophy" (Diod. 13.73.1). Nektanebos...came to Takho and challenged [him] to fight for the kingdom (Diod.15.93.2). Sitting with your army in battle order in front of someone's city wall would seem to have been enough of a challenge without any further provocation. In the case of Nektanebos and Takho it sounds like it could have been a verbal challenge.

Regarding Agesilaos and the stratagem of Khabrias, Diodorus writes, "[Agesilaos], understanding from [his] attempt [i.e., the attack of his light infantry] that they [the Thebans and Athenians] would dare, [if] forced, to fight for the victory, in the plain he challenged [them]." Προκαλεω here is used with a third person singular ending, so it would have to have been just one person (according to Diodorus' grammar), and since the person being written about is Agesilaos, it would have had to have been Agesilaos himself verbally calling out his enemies, and I just can't picture the sixty-six-year-old king yelling at the Thebans and Athenians to come down and fight, nor can we expect that the highly disciplined Spartan warriors standing in line of battle would have been yelling out informal challenges, the example (for us, not for them, since it hadn't happened yet), of Epameinondas' men at Sparta notwithstanding. They would have waited in silence, like good Spartans, to see what their enemies were going to do. And, since we know that in some instances just lining up in battle order in front of one's enemies constitutes a challenge, it seems pretty clear that in this case the challenge was non verbal.

List of Personal Names

Agesilaos - King of Sparta, 399-360 BCE

Agesipolis - King of Sparta, 395-380 BCE

Alexander - King of Makedonia, 336-323 BCE, conqueror of the Persian Empire; also the name of the tyrant of Pherai, who imprisoned Pelopidas; also the famous Alexander's dead uncle

Alkaios - Lyric poet of the late seventh - early sixth century BCE

Androkleidas - Theban democrat bribed by Artaxerxes II to incite Sparta's rivals to take up arms against her

Antalkidas - Spartan strategos who gave his name to the Persian-brokered peace of 387 BCE

Antimenidas - Brother of the poet Alkaios, served as a mercenary with the Babylonians in the early sixth century BCE

Ares - The Hellenic God of War

Ariobarzanes – satrap (=Persian governor) of Hellespontine Phrygia after Pharnabazos

Arkhidamos - Son of Agesilaos and king of Sparta, 360-338 BCE, killed fighting in Sicily in the same year that Philip defeated the Hellenes at Khaironeia

Arrian - Hellenic historian (96-c.180 CE), who wrote a history of Alexander

Artaxerxes (II) - king of Persia, 405-358 BCE; and Artaxerxes III, King of Persia, 359-337

Demosthenes - (384-322 BCE), Athenian orator, vehemently opposed to Philip

Diodorus - first century BCE Sicilian historian

Dionysios - Tyrant of Syrakousai, 430-367 BCE

Epameinondas - Theban magistrate and military commander who devised the oblique order of battle

Ephorus - writer of history, used by Diodorus; his books are lost to us.

Euagoras - King of Kypros, 410-374 BCE

Gorgidas - Theban who first organized the Sacred Band

Herakles - Son of Zeus and Alkmene, a mortal woman; famous throughout the Hellenic world, still well known today as a figure of popular culture

Iolaos - younger eromenos of Herakles

Iphikrates – Athenian strategos, whose military innovations were in part the basis of the Makedonian phalanx

Ismenias - Theban democrat bribed by Artaxerxes II to incite war against Sparta in 394 BCE; ambassador sent with Pelopidas to Thessaly and Makedon, possibly the son of the aforementioned

Jason of Pherai – attempted to unite Thessaly

Kallias – Spartan proxenos at Athens, strategos

Kallistratos - Athenian statesman

Kallisthenes - nephew of Aristotle and historian of the fourth century BCE

Khabrias - Athenian strategos, whose record of long and distinguished service to his polis is described in Nepos' *On The Great Generals of Foreign Nations*

Kleombrotos - Spartan King, 380-371 BCE, killed at Leuktra

Kleonymos - son of Sphodrias, boyfriend of Arkhidamos, killed at Leuktra

Kyros - (430-401 BCE), Brother of the Persian King Artaxerxes II

Leontiades - Theban tyrant, killed by Pelopidas during the liberation of Thebes in 379

Lykourgos - Legendary or semi-legendary Spartan Lawgiver

Lysander - Spartan strategos who defeated the Athenians in 404 BCE and ended the Peloponnesian war

Nepos, Cornelius (c.99-24 BCE) Roman historian and biographer

Olympias - wife of Philip, mother of Alexander

Pausanias - king of Sparta, 408-395 BCE; also the name of the second century CE author of *A Description of Greece*

Pelopidas – one of the liberators of Thebes, second leader of the Sacred Band

Perdikkas – brother of Phillip II, killed fighting the Illyrians

Pharnabazos – Satrap (=Persian governor) of Hellespontine Phrygia

Pheidon - Tyrant of Argos and perhaps the man who developed the hoplite phalanx in mid-seventh century BCE

Philip II - king of Makedonia, 359-336 BCE

Philokrates - Athenian statesman who proposed peace with Philip

Phoibidas - Spartan who seized the Kadmeia and was later killed in battle with the Thebans

Plato - (429-347 BCE), Philosopher and writer

Plutarch - (c.50-c.120 CE), born in Khaironeia, a writer of many diverse works, the source of much material used in this book

Polybius - (c. 200-118 BCE), Hellenic historian

Sphodrias - Spartan who attempted to capture the Peiraieus, the port of Athens, killed at Leuktra, 371 BCE

Timotheos – son of Konon

Thucydides - Athenian strategos who took part in and wrote a history of the Peloponnesian War (431-404 BCE)

Tiribazos - Persian who negotiated the Treaty of Antalkidas

Xenophon - (c.428-c.354 BCE), Athenian aristocrat, friend of Agesilaos, our only primary source for much of the fourth century BCE

Xerxes I - king of Persia, 486-465 BCE, defeated by the Greeks at Salamis, 480 BCE

List of Place Names

Aigina - island rival of Athens, located between the southwest coast of Attika and the northeast coast of the Peloponnese

Akhaia – northern coast of the Peloponnese, bordering on the Gulf of Korinth

Akarnania – region in west-central Hellas

Amphissa - polis northwest of Delphi

Amyklai – polis south of Lakedaimon

Argos - located in the eastern part of the Peloponnese, ancient rival of Sparta

Arkadia - the north-central Peloponnese

Asia - In the period covered by this treatise Asia and Asia Minor refer to modern Turkey.

Athens - since her defeat of the Persian fleet at the battle of Salamis, 480 BCE, the leading naval power in Hellas

Attika - the territory of Athens

Boiotia - region in central Hellas

Bosphoros - the strait that connects the Black Sea with the Propontis

Byzantion - Polis situated on the southeastern shore of the Bosphoros, present day Istanbul

Delion - town on the eastern border of Attika and Boiotia, scene of an Athenian defeat by the Thebans in 424 BCE

Delphi - according to the Hellenes, the center of the world, their most holy place

Eleutherai - Boiotian town, ten or so miles south of Thebes

Elis - Polis in the northeast of the Peloponnese

Egypt - at the time of the events chronicled in this treatise, a province of the Persian King

Erythrai - polis in Boiotia, east of Plataia

Euboia - large island, north of Attika and Boiotia

Eurotas - river upon the west bank of which lies the un-walled city of Lakedaimon

Haliartos - polis ten miles or so northwest of Thebes

Hellespont – Hellenic name for the strait between Asia and Europe that joins the Mediterranean Sea with the Propontis

Illyria - Makedon's western neighbor

Imbros - island north of the Mediterranean mouth of the Hellespont

Kadmeia - the akropolis of Thebes

Karia - Southeast Asia Minor

Karthage - maritime city in Africa

Karyai – polis northeast of Lakedaimon

Khaironeia - Northwest of Thebes, the site of Philip's victory over the Hellenic poleis in 338 BCE

Khios - Island off the coast of Asia Minor, north of Samos, south of Lesbos

Kithairon - mountain on the southern border of Boiotia

Klitor - Polis thirty miles or so east of Elis, in the Peloponnese

Korinth - located in the northeast Peloponnese at the southern end of the Isthmus of Korinth

Koroneia - town, ten miles west of Haliartos, gives its name to the battle of Koroneia, 394 BCE, in which Agesilaos, returning from Asia, defeated the Argives and Thebans

Kreusis – Boiotian polis on the northern shore of the Gulf of Korinth, southwest of Leuktra

Kynoskephalai - Thessalian site of Pelopidas' last battle; also a place in Boiotia

Kypros - large island in the northeast corner of the Mediterranean Sea

Lakedaimon - the Spartans' name for their capital city; consequently they called themselves Lakedaimonioi.

Lakonia - the southwestern corner of the Peloponnese, territory of the Spartans

Larrisa – a city in Thrake

Lekhaion - port of Korinth on the Korinthian Gulf

Lemnos - island opposite the Mediterranean mouth of the
    Hellespont

Lokris - political entity northwest of Thebes

Leuktra - ten miles or so southwest of Thebes, site of the battle
    in which Epameinondas, Pelopidas, and the Sacred Band
    of Thebes ended Spartan hegemony forever, 371 BCE

Makedon - north of Hellas proper, struggling kingdom, finally
    united by Philip II

Mantineia - located in the central Peloponnesos, site of
    Epameinondas' last battle, 362 BCE

Megalopolis - capital of the Arkadian League

Megara - located on the southern shore of the isthmus of
    Korinth, about twenty-five miles south of Thebes

Mesopotamia - the Hellenic name, 'between rivers,' for the
    ancient lands of Akkad and Sumer, what is now Iraq

Messenia - the southwestern part of the Peloponnesos, finally
    conquered by the Spartans in the seventh century BCE
    after a series of wars, liberated from Sparta by
    Epameinondas

Mykenai - north of Argos in the Peloponnesos, the site of a
    Bronze Age kingdom

Mytilene - Polis on the island of Lesbos

Naupaktos - polis on the northern shore of the gulf of Korinth

Nemea - district southwest of Korinth, site of a Spartan victory over the Thebans, Athenians, Korinthians, and Argives, in July, 394 BCE, sometimes referred to as the battle of Korinth

Olympia - Peloponnesian site of the Olympic Games

Orkhomenos - polis twenty or so miles northwest of Thebes; also the name of a polis in the Peloponnese

Pella - Philip's capital

Peloponnessos - the southern half of Hellas, separated from the north by the Gulf of Korinth, connected by the Isthmus of Korinth

Perinthos - polis on the northern shore of the Propontis, southwest of Byzantion

Persia - modern Iran; the first Persian Empire existed from the mid sixth century BCE until it's destruction by Alexander the Great in the last quarter of the fouth century BCE.

Pharsalos - polis in Thessaly, west of Pagasai

Pherai - Thessalian polis, west of Pagasai, east of Pharsalos

Phokis- political entity northwest of Boiotia

Phrygia - Region in Asia Minor, bordering the Propontis

Plataia - Boiotian town about ten or twelve miles southwest of Thebes

Propontis - the body of water between the Bosporos and the Hellespont

Rhodes - recognized as a naval power throughout antiquity, an island off the southwest corner of Asia Minor

Sellasia – polis almost directly north of Sparta

Sikyon – polis a little northwest of Korinth

Skillous – near Olympia, Xenophon's estate, while the Spartan hegemony lasted

Skolos - Boiotian polis, northeast of Erythrai

Skyros - Aegean island, east of Euboia

Sparta - mostly used as the literary alternate of Lakedaimon

Syrakousai - the most powerful Hellenic city in Sicily, modern day Syracuse

Tanagra - Boiotian polis, northeast of Thebes

Tegea – Arkadian polis

Tegyra - north of Lake Kopais in Boiotia, where the Sacred Band defeated a larger number of Spartans

Thebes - most powerful city of Boiotia

Thermopylai - pass leading from Thessaly into Hellas

Thespiai - Boiotian polis, west of Thebes

Thessaly - northwest region of Hellas, south of Makedon

Glossary

Amphiktionic Council - religious council, possessing no temporal power but whose sanction could legitimize the actions of states; to oppose the Amphiktionic Council was sacrilegious.

Aspis – the round, concave hoplite shield

Baldric - strap worn over the shoulder that supports a sword or shield

Boiotarkhes - magistrate of the Boiotian league

Boiotian League - Theban dominated political administration of Boiotia

Daric - Persian gold coin featuring an archer on the obverse

Doru – the Greek word for a thrusting spear

Ephors - the five chief magistrates of Sparta

Gerousia - ruling council of Sparta

Greaves - armor for the lower leg

Harmostes - Governor

Helots - various peoples conquered by the Spartans and reduced to serfdom

Hieros Lokhos - The Sacred Band

Hoplite - Hellenic heavy infantryman

Hoplon - the Hellenic word for 'tool' or 'weapon,' applied to the round, concave shield; probably the plural form, hopla, gave the hoplite his name.

Javelin - a missile weapon, larger than an arrow, smaller than a Hellenic spear

Kopis (plural = Kopides), curved sword shaped somewhat like a modern Kukri or 'Gurka' knife, sharpened on the concave edge, used to cut with a downward blow

Line of Battle - a formation composed of rank and file, with a wide frontage but less depth; in the case of the typical Hellenic phalanx, eight ranks deep

Mora - Division of the Spartan army, variously reported as five hundred, seven hundred, or nine hundred men

Panoply - the complete set of armor for a hoplite, consisting of helmet, breast and back plates, shield, and greaves, including sword and spear

Peloponnesian League - league of cites dominated by Sparta

Peloponnesian War - war between Sparta and Athens, 431-404 BCE, and most of the Hellenic states backing one side or the other

Peltast – light troops, un-armored, armed with javelins; named from the half-moon shaped shield, the pelte.

Perioikoi - communities around Sparta dominated by the Spartans

Phalanx - the Hellenic phalanx usually consisted of eight man files lined up side by side to form a line of battle eight ranks deep.

Polemarkh – literally "war-leader"

Polis - used of a Hellenic city or state

Proxenos - the native resident of a state who represented the interests of a foreign state; see footnote 136 and Liddell and Scott under προξενος.

Rapier - long stabbing sword

Shield-wall - a front of overlapping shields, over which offensive thrusts are made

Skiritai - The men of Skiritis formed a special unit in the Spartan army.

Strategos - the Greek word for a military commander, whether on sea or land

Tyrannos - one who has seized power by unconstitutional means; there were good and bad tyrannoi.

Time-line

Circa 1200 - the end of many Bronze Age kingdoms in Hellas and throughout the eastern Mediterranean

Circa 650 - introduction of hoplite tactics in Hellas

Circa 600 - final conquest of Messenia by Sparta

490 - Athenians and Plataians defeated the Persians at Marathon.

480 - Battle of Salamis, Greek navies defeated the Persian navy.

479 - Battle of Plataia, mostly Spartan victory over Persians

431-404 - Peloponnesian War, between Athens and her allies and Sparta and her allies; the Spartans, with financial aid from the Persians, were victorious.

401 - After the death of Kyros at the Battle of Kounaxa, Xenophon helped lead the ten thousand Hellenic mercenaries out of Mesopotamia.

399 - Agesilaos became King of Sparta.

396 - Agesilaos crossed to Asia.

394 - Recall of Agesilaos, battles of Nemea and Koroneia

391 - Democratic revolt in Korinth

390 - The Athenians, in alliance with Persia's enemies, extended their influence in the eastern Mediterranean.

386 - The Peace of Antalkidas

385 - Spartan division of Mantineia

382 - Spartan seizure of the Kadmeia

379 - Liberation of Thebes

378 - Spartan invasion of Boiotia

377 - Another Spartan invasion of Boiotia

375 - Battle of Tegyra

371 - Battle of Leuktra and death of Kleombrotos

364 - Battle of Kynoskephalai and death of Pelopidas

362 - Battle of Mantinea and death of Epameinondas

360 - Death of Agesilaos

359 - Philip elected king by acclamation of the Makedonian army.

338 - Battle of Khaironeia

334 - Destruction of Thebes by Alexander

323 - Death of Alexander

Bibliography
Primary Sources

Aeschines. *On the Embassy*. Trans. Charles Darwin Adams, Ph.D. Cambridge, MA: Harvard University Press, 1919.

Aristophanes. *Aristophanes*. 3 vols. Trans. Benjamin Bickley Rodgers. Cambridge: Harvard University Press, 1960.

Aristotle. *Politics*. Trans. H. Rackham. Cambridge: Harvard University Press, 1959.

Campbell, David, A., comp. *Greek Lyric Poetry*. Bedminster, Bristol: Bristol Classical Press, 1982.

Herodotus. *Herodotus*. 4 vols. Trans. A. D. Godley. Cambridge: Harvard University Press, 1963.

Hesiod. *Hesiod: The Homeric Hymns and Homerica*, Trans. Hugh G. Evelyn-White. Cambridge: Harvard University Press, 1982.

Homer. *The Iliad*. 2 vols. Trans. A. T. Murray. Cambridge: Harvard University Press, 1988.

Thucydides. *History of The Peloponnesian War*. 4 vols. Trans. Charles Forster Smith. Cambridge: Harvard University Press, 1959.

Plato. *The Symposium of Plato*. Edited by R. G. Bury. Cambridge: W. Heffer and Sons Ltd., 1932.

Plutarch. *Moralia*. Dialogue on Love. Translated by W. C. Helmbold. Cambridge: Harvard University Press, 1961.

Xenophon. *Hellenica*. Trans. C. L. Brownson. Cambridge: Harvard University Press, 1961.

Xenophon. *The Persian Expedition*. Trans. Rex Warner, Baltimore: Penguin Books, 1967.

Xenophon. *Memorabilia and Oeconomicus,* Trans. E. C. Marchant, Cambridge: Harvard University Press, 1965.

Xenophon. *Scripta Minora.* Trans. E. C. Marchant. Cambridge: Harvard University Press, 1962. [This contains *The Lacedaimonians* and *Agesliaos*.]

Xenophon. *Symposium and Apologia.* Trans. O. J. Todd. Cambridge: Harvard University Press, 1923.

Secondary Sources

Adcock. F. E. *The Greek and Macedonian Art of War*. Berkeley: University of California Press, 1957.

Arrian. *Anabasis of Alexander*. Trans. by E. Iliff Robson. Cambridge: Harvard University Press, 1961.

Barber, G.L. *The Historian Ephorus*. New York: AMS Press, 1979.

Boardman. John, Jasper Griffin, and Oswyn Murray, ed. *The Oxford History of the Classical World*. Oxford: Oxford University Press, 1986.

Bradford, Ernle. *Themopylae: The Battle for The West*. New York: Da Capo Press, 1993.

Buck, Robert, J. *Boiotia and the Boiotian League, 423-371 B. C.* Alberta: University of Alberta Press, 1994.

Buckler, John. *The Theban Hegemony: 371-362.* Cambridge: Harvard University Press, 1980.

Connolly, Peter *Greece and Rome at War.* London: Macdonald & Co (Publishers) Ltd, 1988.

Connolly, Peter and Hazel Doge, *The Ancient City.* Oxford: Oxford University Press, 1998.

Cook, J.M. *The Persian Empire.* New York: Schocken Books, 1983.

Davidson, James *Courtesans and Fishcakes.* New York: HarperCollins, 1997.

Delbruck, *History of the Art of War.* 4 vols. Trans. Walter J. Renfroe, Jr., Lincoln: University of Nebraska Press, 1975.

Diodorus. *Library of History.* Trans. by C. H. Oldfather. Cambridge: Harvard University Press, 1954.

Dover, K. J. *Greek Homosexuality.* Cambridge: Harvard University Press, 1989.

Drews, Robert. *The End of The Bronze Age.* Princeton: Princeton University Press, 1993.

Fine, John V. A. *The Ancient Greeks.* Cambridge: Harvard University Press, 1983.

Fitzhardinge, L. F. *The Spartans.* London: Thames and Hudson Ltd., 1980.

Fontenrose, Joseph. *The Delphi Oracle.* Berkeley: University of California Press, 1978.

Frontinus. *Stratagems. Aqueducts of Rome.* Trans. C. E. Bennett, Mary B. McElwain Loeb Classical Library, 1925.

Garland, Robert. *The Greek Way of Death.* Ithaca: Cornell University Press, 1985.

Hackett, General Sir John, ed. *Warfare in The Ancient World.* New York: Facts on File, Inc., 1989.

Hanson, Victor Davis. *The Western Way of War.* New York: Alfred A. Knopf, 1989.

Hopper, R. J. *The Early Greeks.* New York: Harper & Row, 1977.

Laërtius, Diogenes. *The Lives and Opinions of Eminent Philosophers.* Trans. By CD Yonge. London: George Bell & Sons, 1895.

Munn, Mark H. *The Defense of Attica: The Dema Wall and the Boiotian War of 378-375 B.C.* Berkeley: University of California Press, 1993. http://ark.cdlib.org/ark:/13030/ft0q2n99ng/

Nepos, Cornelius. *On The Great Generals of Foreign Nations,* Cambridge: Harvard University Press, 1960.

Pausanias. *Description of Greece.* 4 vols. Trans. W. H. S. Jones. Cambridge: Harvard University Press, 1961.

Plutarch. *Plutarch's Lives.* 11 vols. Trans. Bernadotte Perrin. Cambridge: Harvard University Press, 1959.

Poyanenus. *Stratagems of War.* 2 vols. Trans. Peter Krentz and Everett L. Wheeler. Chicago: Ares Publishers, Inc., 1994.

Smith, John Sharwood. *Greece and The Persians*. Bedminster, Bristol: Bristol Classical Press, 1990.

Snodgrass, A.M. *Arms and Armor of The Greeks*. London: Thames and Hudson, 1967.

Strabo. *The Geography of Strabo*. 8 Vols. Trans. Horace Leonard Jones. Cambridge: Harvard University Press, 1961.]

Warry, John. *Warfare in the Classical World*. London: Salamander Books Ltd., 1980.

Wilcken, Ulrich. *Alexander the Great*. Trans. G. C. Richards. New York: W. W. Norton & Company, Inc., 1967.

Yeomans, Donald K. Jet Propulsion Laboratory/California Institute of Technology: Great Comets in History [online]; Accessed Aug. 2, 2010; available from http://ssd.jpl.nasa.gov/?great_comets

Journals

Cook, Brad L. "The Essential Philip of Macedon: A Byzantine Epitome of His Life," *Greek, Roman, and Byzantine Studies* 45 (2005) 189–211.

Rahe, Paul A. "The Annihilation of the Sacred Band at Chaeronea," *American Journal of Archaeology* 85 (1981): 84-87.

Storch, Rudolph H. "The Archaic Greek Phalanx, 750 - 650 BC." *The Ancient History Bulletin* 12.1-2 (1998): 1-7.

Reference Works

Liddell, Henry George and Robert Scott, comps., *A Greek-English Lexicon*, 9th ed. Oxford: The Clarendon Press, 1968.

Hellas

The Peloponnese

Korinth and its environs

Attika

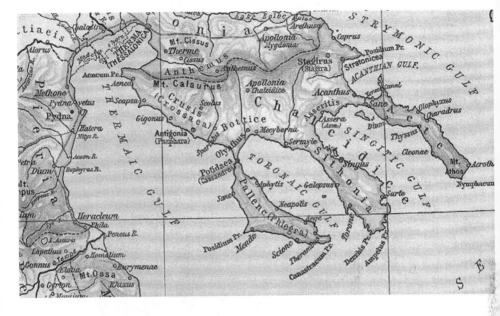

Khalkidike and its environs

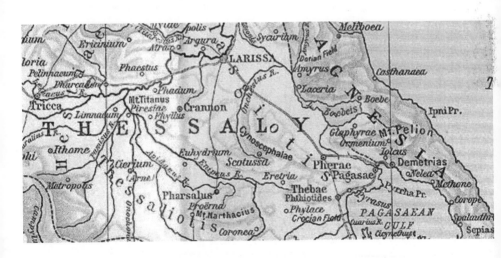

Pherai and Kynoskephalai

235

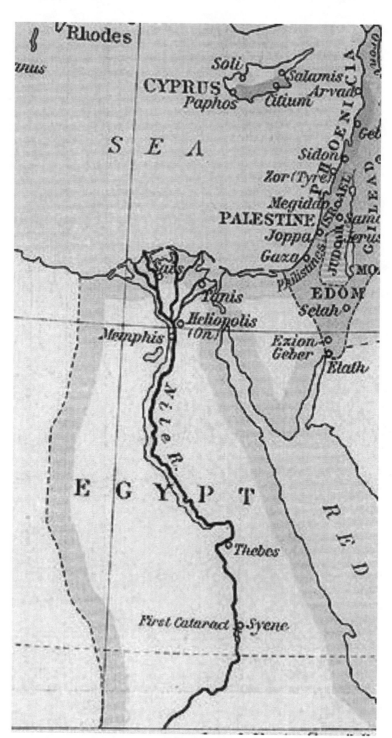

EGYPT

236

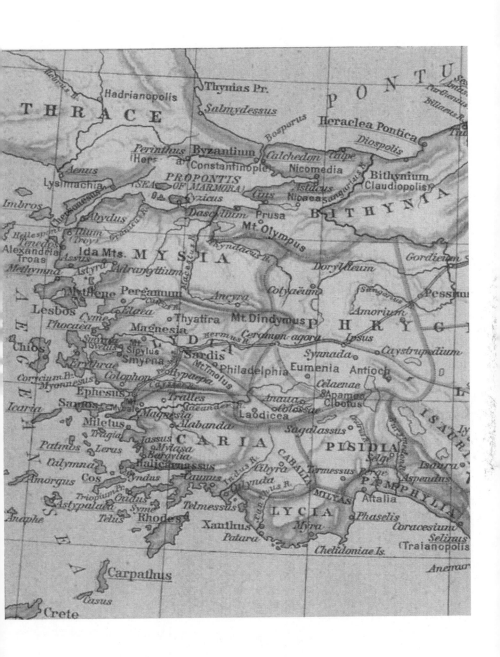

THE COAST OF ASIA

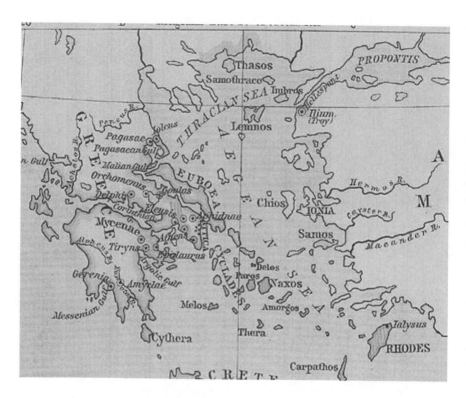

THE AEGEAN SEA

BOIOTIA

NOTES

[1]Victor Davis Hanson, *The Western Way of War* (New York: Alfred A, Knopf, 1989), 98-102, for the well-known fear of the Spartans.

[2] Peter Connolly, *Greece and Rome at War* (London: Macdonald & Co. Ltd, 1988), illustration 5, p. 100, and 7, p. 107; Aristophanes, *The Archanians*, trans. Benjamin Bickley Rogers (Cambridge: Harvard University Press, 1960), 279. "ασπις εν τω φεψαλω κρεμησεται. "And the shield among the sparks will hang," i.e., over the fire place.

[3] Plutarch, *The Parallel Lives*, trans. Bernadotte Perrin, (Cambridge: Harvard University Press, 1957), vol. V. *Pelopidas*, XVIII.1. "επιλεκτων τριακοσιων, οις η πολις ασκησιν και διαιταν, "three hundred chosen men, to whom the city provided training and a living;" Thucydides, *History of The Peloponnesian War* trans. Charles Forster Smith, (Cambridge: Harvard University Press, 1959), Vol. III.V.67. "Αργειων οι χιλιοι λογαδες, οις η πολις πολλου ασκησιν των ες τον πολεμον δεμοσια παριεχε." "one thousand picked men of the Argives to whom the city provided much training in regard to war at the public expense."

[4] Xenophon, *The Lacedaemonians*, trans. E. C. Marchant, (Cambridge: Harvard University Press, 1962), VII.2. "εν δε τη Σπαρτη ο Λυκουργος τοις ελευθεροις των μεν αμφι χρηματιον απειπε μηδενος απτεσθαι... " "but in Sparta Lykourgos forbid all free men to engage in business."

5 Horace Leonard Jones, trans. *The Geography of Strabo* Vol. IV. (Cambridge: Harvard University Press, 1961), 8.5.4.

6 Plutarch, *Lycurgus*, X, XII, XVI.4 - XVIII; Xenophon, *The Lacedaemonians*, II.V.

7 Plutarch, *Moralia.* trans. W. C. Helmbold, (Cambridge: Harvard University Press, 1961), 237.11-12.

[8] *Moralia* 750.C.

[9] Xenophon, *The Lacedaemonians,* II. 13.

[10] Plutarch, *Lycurgus*, XV. 7.

[11] Plutarch, *Moralia*, Sayings of Spartan Women, Gyrtias, 1,2.

12 Plutarch, *Moralia*, Sayings of Spartan Women, Other Spartan Women To Fame Unknown, 5.

13 Plutarch, *Moralia*, Sayings of Spartan Women, Other Spartan Women To Fame Unknown, 10.

[14] Plutarch, *Moralia*, Sayings of Spartan Women, Gorgous, 3,5.

[15] Plutarch, *Lycurgus*, XXII.1-2.

[16] For the kings of Sparta: Herodotus, *The Histories*, trans. A. D. Godly, (Cambridge: Harvard University Press, 1963), VII.204, VIII.131, VI.56; Aristotle, *Politics*, trans. H Rackham, (Cambridge: Harvard University Press, 1959), III.IX. 2. for the Gerousia and assembly: Plutarch, *Lycurgus* V.6, VII.1.; for citizenship: Aristotle *Politics* IV.III.14. "φανερον οτι το γε οπλιτικον αναγκαιον εστι μοριον τησ πολεωs," "it is evident that the hoplites by necessity are part of the state," see also VII.V.7. and VII.VIII.5., for those not considered citizens; for the helots: Thucydides, *History of The Peloponnesian War*, V.LXVII.1; Xenophon, *Hellenica*, trans. C.L. Brownson, (Cambridge: Harvard University Press, 1921), III.iv.2. Helots emancipated for military reasons were called "νεοδαμωδεις," lit. "new people."

17 Xenophon, *The Lacedaemonians* VI.1. "Εναντια ... τοις πλειστοις," "Opposite ... to most."

[18] Xenophon, *The Lacedaemonians* XI.5-10; F. E. Adcock, *The Greek and Macedonian Art of War*, (Berkeley: University of California Press, 1957), 8; Herodotus, *The Histories* IX.61- 65.
"μουνωθεντες Λακεδαιμονιων και Τεγεηται.," "left alone, the Lakedaimonians and the Tegeans..." and
"Εν δε Πλαταιησι οι Περσαι ωs ετραποντο υπο των Λακεδαιμονιων..." "at Plataia the Persians were thus put to flight at the hands of the Lakedaimonians...;" Xenophon, *Hellenica* II for the surrender of Athens, III and IV for Agesilaos' victories in Asia and Greece.

[19] Snodgrass, *Arms and Armor of the Greeks* (London: Thames and Hudson, 1967), 14 - 27, though his belief that the "terrain [in Greece] is ...too rough" for chariots is probably incorrect; hoplites do not operate well on rough ground, yet for 300 years hoplites dominated the battlefields of Greece; Robert Drews, *The End of The Bronze Age* (Princeton: Princeton University Press, 1993), 104 - 134.

[20] Drews, *The End of The Bronze Age*, passim. Throughout the eastern Mediterranean there were mass movements of peoples and mass destruction

of many urban centers around the year 1200 B.C. Snodgrass, *Arms and Armor of the Greeks*, 35-47; John Warry, *Warfare in the Classical World* (London: Salamander Books Ltd., 1980), 13-16; Drews, *The End of The Bronze Age*, 192-208; Homer, *The Iliad* , trans. A. T. Murray, 2 vols. (Cambridge: Harvard University Press, 1988), VI. 119 - 231, and XXI.149 - 199, for examples of challenges to single combat, and II.362 for units composed of tribes ("φυλα"), and clans ("φρητρας"). Naturally Homer is not an historian and the *Iliad* is not an historical document, nevertheless, the archaeological remains bear witness to his descriptive accuracy and the widespread, both chronologically and geographically speaking, and historically documented, practice among warrior aristocrats of verbal challenges to single combat would seem to argue for Homer's accuracy in this respect also.

[21] Rudolph H. Storch, "The Archaic Greek Phalanx, 750 - 650 BC," *The Ancient History Bulletin* 12.1-2 (1998): 1 – 7; David A. Campbell, trans., *Greek Lyric Poetry*, Tyrtaeus (8) (Bedminster Bristol: Bristol Classical Press, 1982), lines 35-38.

[22] Pheidon may have been the king, or tyrant of Argos when the Argives defeated the Spartans at the battle of Hysiai, around 669 B.C., presumably because his army was organized as a hoplite phalanx, and the Spartans weren't. See R. J. Hopper, *The Early Greeks* (New York: Harper & Row, 1977), 128-130, 167.

[23] See Snodgrass, 49-77, "The hoplite shield…is frequently mentioned in ancient sources as the 'Argive' shield," (because it first made its appearance in Argos, at the battle of Hysiai?); The Greeks' usual word for the hoplite shield is 'aspis,' but see Henry George Liddell and Robert Scott, comps., *A Greek-English Lexicon*, 9th ed. (Oxford: The Clarendon Press, 1968), s.v. "'οπλον…2. in Att., 'οπλον was *the large shield*, from which the men-at-arms took their name of 'οπλιται." Used in the plural "'οπλα" means "weapons," so the hoplites could just as well have taken their name from the plural of hoplon, which would have mean something like "fully-armed;" Connolly, 51-63.

[24] For Assyrian shields see: James B. Pritchard, ed., *The Ancient Near East: Volume I An Anthology of Texts and Pictures* (Princeton: Princeton University Press, 1973), Figs. 54 and 101; for Middle Eastern phalanx formation see: General Sir John Hackett, ed., *Warfare in the Ancient World* (New York: Facts on File, Inc., 1989), 20, 25. "…Sumerian phalanx illustrated on the Vulture Stele…;" for the Karians see: Herodotus, *The Histories* I.171; Hackett, *Warfare in the Ancient World*, 57; for Antimenidas see: David A. Campbell, *Greek Lyric Poetry* (Bedminster, Bristol: Bristol

Classical Press, 1982), 61, (Alcaeus 350), and Strabo, *The Geography of Strabo*, XIII.II.3.

[25] For more about hoplites: Hackett, *Warfare in the Ancient World*, 58-59; Connolly, *Greece and Rome at War*, 48; Hanson, *The Western Way of War*, 160-184; Adcock, F. E., *The Greek and Macedonian Art of War*, 4.

[26] For the stuff about the shield: Thucydides, *History of The Peloponnesian War* V.LXXI.1; For the Spartan ability to maneuver: Xenophon, *The Lacedaemonians* XI.5-10.

[27] Plutarch, *Agesilaus*, II.2.

[28] Plutarch, *Agesilaus*, VI.5-6.

[29] Xenophon, *Anabasis*, trans. Carleton Brownson, (Cambridge: Harvard University Press, 1998), I.viii.21-29.

[30] Xenophon, *Agesilaus*, V.4-6; Plutarch, *Agesilaus*, XI.4-7; *Moralia*, Sayings of Spartans, 209.15.

[31] Homer, *The Iliad*, XXIII. 71-74.

[32] Diodorus, *Library of History*, trans. C. H. Oldfather, (Cambridge: Harvard University Press, 1954), XIII. 101.

[33] Plutarch, *Lycurgus*, XXII.5.

[34] Plutarch, *Agesilaus*, XVII.2.; and see Xenophon, *Hellenica,* VI.iii.10.

[35] Xenophon, *Hellenica,* VI.iii.14.

[36] Plato, *The Symposium of Plato*, Edited by R. G. Bury, (Cambridge: W. Heffer and Sons Ltd., 1932), XXX.212 D-212 E.

[37] The battle is described in: Xenophon, *Hellenica*, IV.iii.10-21; *Agesilaus*, 2.6-2.16; Plutarch, *Agesilaus*, XVIII. 1-3; Spartan cloaks are described in: Plutarch, *Moralia*, Ancient Customs of the Spartans, 24; and see: Xenophon, *The Lacedaemonians,* X.3.

[38] Prof. Cliff Rogers, email to author, June 11, 1999; see also: Hans Delbruck, *History of the Art of War* trans. Walter J. Renfroe, Jr., 4 vols. (Lincoln: University of Nebraska Press, 1975) 4:176. "When the foot troops were engaged in such a close and heavy combat, one would have expected that one side would give way and break formation, but this did not

happen, for both sides, as if in agreed alternation withdrew a few paces, had their units take a firm position the ground, and continued to fire at one another into the night, an action so unusual that it could hardly be believed if there had not been so many witnesses present." A description of two pike regiments engaged at the battle of Edgehill in 1642.)

[39] Poyanenus. *Stratagems of War*. 2 vols. Trans. Peter Krentz and Everett L. Wheeler. (Chicago: Ares Publishers, Inc., 1994.) 2.1.19. Here's the whole text from Polyainos:
"Αγησιλαος θηβαιοις παρετασσετο. οι δε την Λακωνικην φαλαγγα 'ρηχαι βουλονενοι και διεφξελθειν καρτερως ηγωνιζοντοκαι φονος αμφοτερων πολυς. Αγησιλαος παρηγγειλε, 'παυσαμενοι της θυμομαχιας διαστωμεν.' οι μεν διεστησαν, θηβαιοι δε διαδραμοντες εφευγον. Αγησιλαος κατα την ουραγιαν αυτοις επεκειτο, και ουκετι φονος ην αμφοτερων, αλλα μον ων των φευγοντων." And here's a very literal translation: "Agesilaos was drawn up in battle order in front of the Thebans. They, wishing to break the Lakonian phalanx and pass through, fought (or "were fighting") strongly (or "mightily," etc.), and there was much slaughter of both sides. Agesilaos ordered: 'stopping the desperate fight, let us separate (or retire).' So they separated (διεστησαν, the same word Plutarch uses, which I translated as "retired," but which seems to have a different meaning here), and the Thebans, running through, fled. Agesilaos pressed on their rear, and no longer was there a slaughter of both sides, but of those fleeing only".

[40] Xenophon, *Agesilaus*, II.13; and see: Plutarch, *Agesilaus*, XIX.1.

[41] Xenophon, *Agesilaus*, II.14-15.

[42] Plutarch, *Agesilaus*, XIX.2; Xenophon, *Agesilaus*, II.15-16.

[43] Hesiod, *Hesiod: The Homeric Hymns and Homerica*, Theogony, Trans. Hugh G. Evelyn-White. (Cambridge: Harvard University Press, 1982.), 453-465.

44 Hesiod, Theogony, 478-500.

[45] Hesiod, The Homeric Hymns, III. To Pythian Apollo, 363.

[46] Diodorus, XVI. 26-27.

[47] For the real story of the Pythia and her oracular responses see: Joseph Fontenrose. *The Delphic Oracle* (Berkeley: University of California Press, 1978), 196-23.9, and Plutarch, *Moralia*. The Oracles at Delphi; For instances of bribery: Herodotus V.63.1, 66.1, VI.66.1-3, 75.3; and

Thucydides V.16.2; and for a brief history of Delphi: John V. A. Fine. *The Ancient Greeks*. (Cambridge: Harvard University Press, 1983), 115-118, 297-298.

[48] Xenophon, *Anabasis*, V.3; Diogenes Laertius, II.6.52.

[49] Xenophon, *Hellenica*, IV.v.1-18, for Agesilaos' capture of Peiraion, and the victory of Iphikrates.

50 Pausanias, *Description of Greece*, trans. W. H. S. Jones, (Cambridge: Harvard University Press, 1961), vol. IV. *Boiotia*, XIII.1.

51 Plutarch, *Pelopidas*, III – IV.

52 Xenophon, *Hellenica* V.ii.27. It was accepted practice in the ancient world for an author to compose speeches for his subjects based on what they, according to each one's particular character and the prevailing circumstances, would have said. Therefore, while the exact words used by Leontiades are probably not accurately recorded by Xenophon, it is tempting to suggest that perhaps he heard the story from someone who heard it from Phoibidas.

53 Xenophon, *Hellenica* V.ii.28. "Φοιβιδας...ου μεντοι λογιστικος γε ουδε πανυ φρονιμος εδοκει ειναι."

54 Plutarch, *Pelopidas* VI.1. A *drakhma* was the average day's wages.

55 Diodorus, *Library of History* XV.20.2-3.

56 Plutarch, *Pelopidas* V.1-2; *Agesilaos* XXIV.1.

57 Xenophon, *Hellenica* V.III.5-8.

58 Xenophon, *Hellenica* V.iii.19.

59 Diod. 15.23.2.

60 Diod. 15.23.3-4.

61 Xen. Hell. 5.3.27.

62 Xen. Hell. 5.4.1.

63 Plut. Pel. 6.3.

64 Plut. Pel. 6.2.

65 Plut. Pel. 7.1.

66 Plut. Pel. 7.3.

67 Xen. Hell. 5.4.4.

68 Xen. Hell. 5.4.3.

69 Plut. Pel. 8.3 – 5.

70 Plut. Pel. 9.4.

71 Plut. Pel. 9.4.

72 Plut. Pel. 9.5 – 7.

73 Plut. Pel. 10.1- 2.

74 Plut. Pel. 10.4.

75 Plut. Pel. 11.2

76 Plut. Pel. 11.3 – 6.

77 Plut. Pel. 12.2.

78 Plut. Pel. 12.4.

79 Plut. Pel. 13.2.

80 Diod. 15.25 - 15.27.

81 Xen. Hell. 5.4.12.

82 Plut. Pel. 13.2; Xen. Hell. 5.4.13; Diod. 15.27.3.

83 Diod. 15.29.

84 Xen. Hell. 5.4.25.

85 Xen. Hell. 5.4.27.

86 Xen. Hell. 5.4.31.

87   Xen. Hell. 5.4.32 – 33.

88   Plut. Pel. 18.1.

89   Xenophon, Symposium VIII. 32.
      "...στρατευμα αλκιμωτατον αν γενοιτο εκ παιδικων τε και ερασtων."

90   Plato, *The Symposium of Plato* (Cambridge, 1932), 178. C.
      "...η στρατοπεδον εραστον..."

91   Diodorus, *Library of History* XII.70.1.
      "προεμαχοντο δε παντων οι παρ' εκεινοις ηνιοχοι και παραβαται καλουμενοι, ανδρες επιλεκτοι τριακοσιοι."

92   Xenophon, *The Lacedaemonians* II.12

93   Plutarch, *Pelopidas* XVIII.2.

94   Xenophon, *Hellenica*, V.IV.39.

95   Xenophon, *Hellenica*, V.iv.40. A *mora* is a division of the Spartan army.

96   Xenophon, *Hellenica*, V.iv.40. τα δόρατα seems a strange word to use here, since dopu is usually used of a thrusting spear and not a javelin and the accompanying verb, ἐξακοντίζειν, usually means "to throw." Perhaps, as Gerald of Wales writes, the Spartan horsemen, like the Welsh of Gwynedd, would sometimes throw their spears a short distance with deadly effect. See *The Journey Through Wales*, book II, chapter 5.

97   Xenophon, *Hellenica*, V.IV.41. A harmost is a Spartan military governor.

98   Diodorus, *Library of History*, XV.32.3.

99   Diodorus, *Library of History* XV.32.3; and for the career of Khabrias, see: Diodorus, *Library of History* XV.29.2-4, and Nepos, *On The Great Generals of Foreign Nations*, XII.

100   Diodorus, *Library of History*, XV.32.4-5.

101 Diodorus, *Library of History*, XV.32.6.

" 'ο Αγησιλαος θαυμασας..."

102 Diod. 15.32.6. "προεκαλεῖτο"

103 Diodorus, *Library of History*, XV.32.6; Xenophon, *Hellenica*, V.IV.41.

104 For Khabrias' stratagem, see: Nepos, *On The Great Generals of Foreign Nations, XII.1;* Diodorus, *Library of History* XV32.3-6; and for Agis at Mantinea, see: Thucydides, *History of The Peloponnesian War,* V.65.1-74.1.

105 Plutarch, *Agesilaos,* XXVI.2-3.

106 Xen. Hell. 5.4.42.

107 Xen. Hell. 5.4.42.

108 Xen. Hell. 5.4.43.

109 Xen. Hell. 5.4.44 – 45.

110 Diod. 15.33.6.

111 Xen. Hell. 5.4.45.

112 Polyaenus, *Strategems of War,* trans. Peter Krentz and Everett L. Wheeler, (Chicago: Ares Publishers, Inc., 1994), II.5.

113 Xen. Hell. 5.4.46.

114 For the campaign of 377 see: Xenophon, *Hellenica,* V.iv.47-55; Diodorus, *Library of History,* XV.34.1-2.

115 Xenophon, *Hellenica,* V.iv.49-50; Diodorus, *Library of History,* XV.34.2.

116 Xen. Hell. 5.4.52. Once again Xenophon writes "τα δόρατα ἐξηκόντιζον."

117 Xenophon, *Hellenica,* V.iv.53. "θαττον η βαδην." The men of Skiritis formed a special unit of the Spartan army, see: Diodorus, *Library of*

History, XV.32.1; Thucydides, *History of The Peloponnesian War,* V.67.1; Xenophon, *The Lacedaemonians,* XII.3, XIII.

118 Xenophon, *Hellenica,* V.iv.54. "μαλα πολλους"

119 Xenophon, *Hellenica,* V.iv.58.

120 Xen. Hell. V. iv. 56 - 57.

121 Xen. Hell. IV.2.16.

122 Xen. *The Lacedaemonians.* XIII.3.

123 Xen. *The Lacedaemonians.* XIII.2.

124 Xen. Hell. V. iv. 59.

125 Xen. Hell. V. iv. 64 – 65.

126 Plu. Pel.XV.5.

127 Plutarch, *Pelopidas,* XVII.

128 Plutarch, *Pelopidas,* XVI.1-2; Diodorus, *Library of History,* XV.37.1-2. Diodorus writes that Pelopidas set out "επιλεκτοις ανδρασι πεντακοσιος" i.e., "with five hundred chosen men." So, Plutarch's "των ιππεων ου πολλους" i.e., "of the horsemen not many " would number his cavalry force at two hundred.

129 Xen. Hell. 6.1.2- 3.

130 Xenophon, *Hellenica,* VI.ii.1. Xenophon must be referring to the Athenian naval activity directed against the Spartans and the coasts of the Peloponnese.

131 Diodorus, *Library of History,* XV.38.1-3. Αρετη is variously translated as: "goodness, excellence...manhood, valour, prowess," etc. See Liddell & Scott's *Greek-English Lexicon.*

132 Diodorus, *Library of History,* XV.40.1-5.

133 Dio. 15.42.1.

134 Dio. 15.42.3.

135 Dio.15.42.5.

136 Dio.15.43.1.

137 Dio.15.43.2.

138 Dio.15.43.3.

139 Dio. 15.43.6.

140 Dio. 15.44.2.

141 Dio. 15.44.4.

142 Cornelius Nepos, *On The Great Generals of Foreign Nations*, Trans. J. C. Rolfe (Cambridge: Harvard University Press, 1960), Iph. 1.4

143 Hackett, *Warfare in the Ancient World*, 100.

144 Herodotus, VII.69-70.

145 Nepos, Iph. 3.

146 Pausanias, *Description of Greece,* 9.1.3.

147 Diodorus, *Library of History,* XV.46.4.

148 Pausanias, *Description of Greece.* 9.1.1; Diodorus, *Library of History,* XV.46.6.

149 Dio. 15.46.6.

150 Dio. 15.50.2.

151 Arist. Meteor. 343b 19; Dio. 15.50.2. calls it a "torch"; Donald K. Yeomans, Jet Propulsion Laboratory/California Institute of Technology: Great Comets in History [online]; Accessed Aug. 2, 2010; available from http://ssd.jpl.nasa.gov/?great_comets.

152 Dio. 15.50.3.

153 Dio. 15.48.2-3.

154 Plu. Agesilaos. XXVII.3.

155 Dio. 15.50.4.

156 Xen. Hell. 6.3.1 - 6.3.2.

157 Xen. Hell. 6.3.3.

158 Xen. Hell. 6.3.4 - 6.3.5.

159 Xen. Hell. 6.3.6.

160 Xen. Hell. 6.3.7-9.

161 Xen. Hell. 6.3.10-17.

162 Xenophon, *Hellenica*, VI.iii.19-20. "Δεκατευθηναι," which I have colloquialized as "pay the piper," really means to "be made to pay the tithe." See Liddell and Scott's Lexicon.

163 Plutarch, *Agesilaos*, XXVII.3-XXVIII.2.

164 Diodorus, *Library of History*, XV.50.4.

165 Pausanias, *Description of Greece*. 9.1-2.

166 Pausanias, *Description of Greece*. 9.1-2.

167 Xen. Hell. 6.4.1.

168 Dio. 15.51.3-4.

169 Diod. 15.51.4; "προθύμως."

170 Plu.Pel. XX. 1.

171 Diod. 15.52.3.

172 Diod. 15.52.4; "εἷς οἰωνος ἄριστος ἀμύνεσθαι περὶ πάτρης."

173 Homer, *The Iliad*, I.14-15.

174 Paus. 9.13.4.

175 Diod. 15.53.4.

176 Diod. 15.54.1-4.

177 Xen. Hell. 6.4.7

178 Xenophon's account of the battle of Leuktra is found in: *Hellenica*,
     VI.iv.4-15. " Οι ιππεις" are mentioned in VI.iv.10; see also: Plutarch,
     Agesilaos, XXVIII.3-6, and *Pelopidas*, XX.-XXIII.4; Diodorus,
     Library of History, XV.52-56; Pausanias, *Description of Greece*,
     9.13.3-12.

179 Diod. 15.56.4.

180 Paus. 9.13.12.

181 Xen. Hell. 6.4.15.

182 Xen. Hell. 6.4.16.

183 Diod. 15.57.1.

184 Xen. Hell. 6.5.4: "πατρικος φιλos."

185 Xen. Hell. 6.5.23.

186 Plut. Pel. 24.2. and Plut. Ages. 31.1.

187 Xen. Hell. 6.5.28.

188 Xen. Hell. 6.5.49.

189 Xen. Hell. 6.5.51.

190 Paus. 9.14.6-7.

191 Nepos E. VIII.1.

192 Xen. Hell. 7.1.14.

193 Xen. Hell. 7.1.15; Diod. 15.68.3.

194 Xen. Hell. 7.1.16.

195 Polyaen. V.XVI.3 ; Frontinus, Str.3.2.10.

196 Diod. 15.69.1; Xen. Hell. 7.1.18-19.

197 Xen. Hell. 7.1.21.

198 Diod. 15.72.2.

199 Plut. Pel. 26.4; Diod. 15.67.4.

200 Aeschines 2.27-29; Nepos, XI.3.2.

201 Aeschin. 2.32.

202 Xen. Hell. 7.1.25.

203 Xen. Hell. 7.1.27; Diod. 15.70.2.

204 Xen. Hell. 7.1.28.

205 Xen. Hell. 7.1.29.

206 Xen. Hell. 7.1.31.

207 Nep. Ep. 4.

208 Diod. 15.71.3.

209 Diod. 15.71.6.

210 Xen. Hell. 7.1.43.

211 Diod. 15.76.1; Fine, 586; Xen. Hell. 7.4.1.

212 Diogenes Laërtius, *The Lives and Opinions of Eminent Philosophers*, trans. CD Yonge (London: George Bell & Sons, 1895), Life of Plato, XVIII.

213 Diod. 15.76.3; Xen. Hell. 7.4.6-10.

214 Xen. Hell. 7.4.12.

215 Xen. Hell. 7.4.13.

216 Xen. Ages. 2.26-27.

217 Fine. 592.

218 Plutarch, *Pelopidas,* XXXI-XXXIII, for an account of the battle.

219 Xen. Hell. 7.5.10.

220 Xen. Hell. 7.5.12.

221 Diodorus. 15.65.4.

222 Plut. Ages. 34.7.

223 Xen. Hell. 7.5.14.

224 Xen. Hell. 7.5.17.

225 Accounts of the campaign and battle of Mantinea are found in: Diodorus, *Library of History*, XV.82-88; Plutarch, *Agesilaos*, XXXV.1-2; Xenophon, *Hellenica*, VII.v.1-25.

226 Dio, XV.85-87.6.

227 Dio. XVI.4.5-6.

228 Frontinus. *Stratagems. Aqueducts of Rome.* trans. C. E. Bennett, Mary B. McElwain (Loeb Classical Library, 1925), II.3: Philippus, Macedonum rex, adversus Hyllios gerens bellum, ut animadvertit frontem hostium stipatam electis de toto exercitu viris, latera autem infirmiora, fortissimis suorum in dextro cornu collocatis, sinistrum latus hostium invasit turbataque tota acie victoriam profligavit.

229 Nepos, 12.4; Diodorus, XVI.7.3.

230 Diod. 16.34; Polyaenus, 5.16; Frontinus, II.3.3.

231 For Khaironea see: Diodorus, XVI.85.5-6; Paul A. Rahe, "The Annihilation of the Sacred Band at Chaeronea," *American Journal of Archaeology* 85 (1981) : 84-87; Plutarch, *Alexander*, IX.2;.and for the influence of Epameinondas and Iphikrates on Philip's military organization, see: Ulrich Wilcken, *Alexander the Great*, trans. G.C. Richards (New York: W.W. Norton & Company, Inc., 1967), 30-33.

232 James G. DeVoto, "The Theban Sacred Band," *The Ancient World; Warfare in Antiquity* Vol. XXIII No.2. (1992)

233 Polyaenus. *Stratagems of War*. Trans. Peter Krentz and Everett L. Wheeler (Chicago: Ares Publishers, Inc., 1994), IV.2.2.

234 Plutarch, *Pelopidas*, XVIII.5

INDEX

Alkibiades 23, 36, 209
Alkidas 127
Alypetos 106
Amphipolis 166, 167, 172, 193
Amphissans 197, 198
Amyklai, Amyklaioi 58, 109, 158
Amyntas III 66, 166, 167
Amyntas, son of Perdikkas 189
Anabasis 207
Anaxibios 61
Androkleidas 30, 68, 74, 75
Antalkidas (and the Peace of) 54, 55, 62, 66, 75, 100, 101, 129, 135, 143, 148, 168, 172
Antikrates 187
Aphrodite 27, 29, 75, 78, 107
Aphytis 70
Apothetai 13
Apollo 43, 46, 47-40, 51, 52, 58, 146, 148
Apollonia 66
Ares 11
Argaios, pretender to the throne of Makedon 190
Arginousai 32, 111
Argive shield (ασπις, aspis) 20-22, 43, 58, 125
Argives, Argos 20, 30, 33, 37, 55, 56, 61, 62, 72, 99, 156, 159, 163, 169, 178, 183, 197
Ariobarzanes 175, 177, 188
Aristagoras 17
Aristodemus 33
Aristokrates 127
Aristotle 68, 133
Arkadia, Arkadians 65, 99, 155, 159, 168-170, 173, 174, 176, 178, 197
Arkadian League 156, 176, 182
Arkhias 75, 76, 78-81
Arkhias (the hierophantes) 80
Arkhidamos 88-90, 154, 169, 176, 183, 184, 189

Artabazos 193

Artagerses 26

Artapates 26

Artaxerxes II 25-27, 30, 33, 35, 54-56, 62, 66-68, 119-120, 122, 135, 138, 140, 143, 168, 170, 172, 189

Artaxerxes III 193, 197, 205

Artemis (see also Ephesian Artemis) 49, 52, 53

Aseans 183

Asia 18, 21, 24, 25, 27, 30, 33, 36, 52-56, 62, 105, 122, 168, 178, 193

Asine, 168

Assos 176

Assyrians 21

Aster 189

Athena 42, 110

Athens, Athenians 9, 10, 18, 23, 24, 30-33, 35, 36, 47, 51, 54-59, 61, 62, 67, 72, 74, 75, 77, 83-88, 92, 94, 97-100, 110, 111, 118-120, 124, 125, 127-130, 132, 135-137, 139, 140, 141, 147, 154-156, 158, 160, 163, 164, 167, 168, 172-175, 178, 182, 184, 186, 188, 192-201, 205

Attika 86, 98, 111, 154

Aulis 24, 31, 59, 69

Autokles 138, 170

Babylon, Babylonians 21, 133

Black Sea 27, 61, 196

Boiotia, Boiotians 9, 24, 32, 33, 35, 55, 56, 59, 60, 61, 84, 97, 104, 120, 129-131, 135, 139, 141-147, 183, 193, 194, 207, 208

Boiotian League 24, 62, 66, 99, 100, 120, 129, 137, 139, 155, 182

Boiotarkhoi 24, 74, 83, 86, 100, 130, 148, 149, 157, 156, 161, 164, 171, 208

Bosphoros 62, 196

Boura 134

Brakhyllides 149

Brasidas 167

Bronze Age 19, 31, 110

Byzantion 61, 94, 196, 197

Cavalry 9, 10, 37, 38, 42, 43, 51, 58-60, 68-70, 83, 84, 94, 95, 101-104, 106, 113-116, 130, 131, 147, 151, 158, 159, 164, 169, 170, 171, 178-186, 188, 190-193, 196, 200, 201
Chariots 19, 20
Dactylic hexameter 49, 50
Darius II 24, 25, 54
Darius III 201, 205
Dark Age 19
Delian League 94
Delion 91
Delphi, Delphoi, Delphians 43, 44, 46-49, 51, 52, 164, 194, 198
Delphic Amphiktiony 195-197
Demetrios 207, 208
Demetra 44
Demosthenes 10, 196-198, 205
Demoteles 169
Deras 165
Diodorus the Sicilian 32, 47-49, 55, 66, 68, 71, 82, 83, 85, 67, 91, 92, 97-99, 103, 107, 111, 113, 120, 122-125, 130, 131, 133, 134, 147-152, 153, 163, 164, 174, 184, 186, 187, 190-192, 201, 205-209
Diodoros (son of Xenophon) 51
Diomedon of Kyzikos 170
Dionysios, tyrant of Syrakusa 62, 72, 132, 164, 165, 169, 176, 204, 207
Dionysos, temple of 71
Diopeithes 195
Dorians 12, 46
Dioxippos 205
Earth-Mother: see Gaia
Egypt, Egyptians 19, 56, 62, 66, 97, 119, 120, 122-125, 128, 189, 197, 204
Ekhekrates 49
Eleutherai 85
Elis, Eleans 155-157, 159, 176, 182
Ennosigaion 44

Helike 134
Helikon, Mt. 37-40, 42,
Hellenika 188
Hellespont 27, 62, 176
Hellespontines 38
Hellespontine Phrygia 175
Helots 11-13, 18, 25, 109, 110, 157
Hephaistion 203
Heraion 59, 60
Herakleia 154
Herakles 12, 17, 91, 137, 150, 152, 169
Here 44, 46
Herippidas 29, 38
Herodotus 21, 125, 207
Hesiod 44, 46
Hetairai 78, 81
Hetairoi 190, 191, 200
Hieros Lokhos see Sacred Band of Thebes
Hippoklos 64
Hipposthenidas 76
Histiea 44
Hittites 19
Homer 24, 32, 205
Homotrapezoi 26
Hoplites 9, 11, 18, 20-22, 33, 37-40, 51, 58, 59, 67, 69, 70, 84, 92, 94,
95, 97, 102, 103, 109, 114, 116, 125, 147, 151, 157, 158, 163, 170,
179, 180, 186, 196, 200
Hyakinthia 58
Hymn to Castor 37
Hypaspistes 58, 61
Hypates 82
Iberians 164
Iliad 32, 49, 148, 189, 205
Ilion (Troy) 176
Illyrians 166, 190-193, 197
Imbros 55, 62

Imilkos 209

India 209

Iolaos 91, 203

Ionians 38

Iphikrates 57-61, 62, 121-126, 128, 132, 136, 146, 159, 160, 167, 167, 191

Isidas, son of Phoibidas 184

Isocrates 68

Isthmian Games 56

Ismenias 30, 68,

Ismenias (son of the above?) 170, 172

Italy 128

Itonian Athena 42

Jason of Pherai 117, 118, 154, 170

Kadmeia 66, 67, 73, 77, 83, 84, 91, 130, 138, 139

Kadousians 205

Kallias 58, 88, 136, 142

Kallisthenes 68, 114

Kallistratos 120, 136, 139-141

Karia, Karians 21, 105

Karyai 157, 169

Kastor 37, 82

Kedon 111

Kelts 164, 169, 204

Kephisodoros 82

Kephisos River 37, 199

Keykhreion 162

Khabrias 85, 97-100, 106, 107, 111, 120, 162-164, 189, 192, 209

Khaireas 149

Khaironeia 9, 11, 36, 199-202

Khaldians 133

Khalkidike 66, 67

Khalkidian League 65, 67, 167

Khares 173, 174, 199

Kharon 77-80, 83, 101

Khios 94, 192

Khlidon 77
Khryses 148
Kissidas 169
Kithairon, Mt. 85, 94, 105, 110
Klearkhos 25, 51
Kleombrotos 71, 85-87, 90, 94, 110, 146, 147, 149, 151-153
Kleomenes II 189
Kleonymos 88-90, 152
Kleopatra VII 8
Kleroukhia 72
Klitor 94
Knidos 35, 111
Konon 24, 35, 36, 47, 54, 55, 111, 124
Koragos 205
Korinth, Korinthians 30, 33, 35, 55-58, 60, 61, 67, 72, 153, 154,
162-164, 168, 174
Korinthian gulf 44, 61, 104, 112, 146, 154
Korkyra 112, 127, 128, 132,
Koroneia 36, 37, 51, 52, 115, 149,
Kounaxa 25
Krenides 193
Krete 45
Kreusis 149, 154
Kronos 44-46
Ktesias 26
Ktesikles 128, 132
Kymaians 209
Kynoskephalai (in Boiotia) 85
Kynoskephalai (in Thessaly) 116, 178, 179, 192, 201
Kypros 36, 55, 97
Kyrene 189
Kyros 25-27, 35, 36, 38, 51, 53
Lakedaimon, Lakedaimonians: passim
Lakonia 12, 54, 142, 157
Larrissa 166
Lekhaion 56, 58-60, 160, 162

Lemnos 55, 62
Leon 172
Leonidas 17, 35, 152, 158
Leontiades 66, 74-76, 81, 82, 84
Leontini 207
Leotykhidas 23
Leuktra 63, 74, 101, 115, 131, 149, 150, 153, 154, 157, 160, 163, 174, 178, 180, 188, 193, 199
Leuktros 150
Libya 189
Lokrians, Lokris 30, 113, 114, 155, 194
Long Walls 54
Lykophron 195
Lykourgos 12-15, 17, 92
Lysander 23-25, 27, 31, 32, 47, 54
Lysikles 199
Lysis 64
Lykton 45
Makedonians, Makedon 9, 10, 166, 167, 189-191, 193, 196, 197, 199-201, 204, 205
Mantineia, Mantineians 62, 63, 99, 153, 155-157, 183, 185-187
Marathon 129
Marcellus 74
Mardonios 129, 206, 207
Marganians 155
Mausolos 177
Megabates 27-29
Megabyzos 51-52
Megalopolis, Megalopolitans 156, 158, 170, 183, 196
Megara 85, 96, 107, 154
Melea 169
Melon (or Melos) 75-77, 83, 101
Memphis 124
Menekleidas 161
Menon 109
Mesopotamia 25

Paionians 190, 193
Pammenes 158, 163, 167, 193, 196, 201
Pangaios, Mt. 193
Panthoidas 113
Parians 207
Parnassos, Mt. 44-46
Parrhasia 169
Patroklos 31
Pausanias (assassin of Philip II) 203
Pausanias (Spartan King) 31-33
Pausanias (the writer) 64, 129, 130, 131, 143, 144, 149, 150, 153, 158, 160
Pausanias, pretender to the throne of Makedon 167
Peiraieus 54, 87
Peiraion 56, 57
Peisander 35, 36
Peitholaos 195
Pella 166, 189, 197
Pellene, Pelleneans 66, 67
Pelopidas 64-66, 74-83, 86, 93, 94, 100, 101, 106, 113-116, 149-153, 157, 160-163, 166, 167, 170, 172, 178-182, 192, 201
Peloponnesians, Peloponnesos 12, 18, 23, 25, 30, 32, 56, 85, 118, 120-129, 133, 148, 155, 156, 158, 159, 170, 173, 174, 182, 183, 196
Peloponnesian League 13, 32, 66
Peloponnesian War 23, 30, 32, 35, 51, 55, 75, 94, 129, 135, 167
Pelta (πελτα) 125, 206
Peltasts 37, 38, 58, 59, 61, 69, 70, 85, 95, 98, 102, 103, 106, 110, 132, 159, 160, 163, 167, 188
Perdikkas 166, 170, 177, 189
Perinthos 197
Perioikoi 12, 18, 95, 109, 157, 158
Persia, Persians 17, 18, 24-27, 30, 32, 33, 35, 36, 51, 54-56, 62, 97, 105, 111, 121-125, 128, 129, 135, 175, 205-207
Pharakos 59
Pharnabazos 27, 35, 54, 111, 122-124
Pharsalos 116, 178

Teleutias 68, 69

Ten Thousand, The 25-28, 38, 51, 53

Tegea, Tegeans 155, 156, 183-185

Tegyra 113, 114, 117, 129, 131, 143, 153, 163, 167, 201

Theagenes 203

Thebes, Thebans 9, 10, 24, 30-33, 35-43, 47, 55, 62-69, 72-77, 83-86, 88, 91-110, 112-116, 118-120, 128-131, 135, 136, 138-145, 147-154, 156-163, 166-174, 177-179, 181-188, 192-203

Theban Sacred Band: see Sacred Band of Thebes.

Themison, tyrant of Eretria 174

Thermopylai 17, 35, 152, 154, 158, 154, 195, 197

Theogony 44

Theopompos 114, 116

Thesmophoria 67

Thespiai, Thespians 85, 87, 94, 96, 99, 102-105, 110, 113, 131, 134, 136, 137, 140, 147

Thessalians, Thessaly 33, 117, 118, 154, 162, 166, 168, 170-172, 178-181, 183, 194, 195, 197, 203

Thetideion 179

Thibron 55

Thisbe 149

Thrake, Thrakians 132, 190, 193, 196, 197

Thucydides 22, 23, 207

Timagoras 172

Timokrates (of Rhodes) 30

Timokrates (of Syrakousai) 177

Timotheos 112, 118, 120, 127, 132, 175, 176, 192

Tiribazos 54, 55

Tlemonidas 69

Torone 70

Triphylians 155

Triptolemos 137

Trojan War 24

Trophonius (oracle) 150

Trophy 33, 34, 43, 60, 96, 102, 103, 106, 107, 116, 153, 163, 169, 176, 188

I hope you liked this book. Even though I proof-read it countless times, I bet there are spelling errors and all kinds of stuff that could be corrected. You can email me if you want: sb3.geo@yahoo.com - CH

Thanks to my wife, Kris.